A Portrait of the Young
in the New Multilingual Spain

Child Language and Child Development: Multilingual–Multicultural Perspectives
Series Editor: Professor Li Wei, *University of London, UK*
Editorial Advisors:
Professor Gina Conti-Ramsden, *University of Manchester, UK*
Professor Kevin Durkin, *The University of Western Australia*
Professor Susan Ervin-Tripp, *University of California, Berkeley, USA*
Professor Jean Berko Gleason, *Boston University, USA*
Professor Brian MacWhinney, *Carnegie Mellon University, USA*

Children are brought up in diverse yet specific cultural environments; they are engaged from birth in socially meaningful and appropriate activities; their development is affected by an array of social forces. This book series is a response to the need for a comprehensive and interdisciplinary documentation of up-to-date research on child language and child development from a multilingual and multicultural perspective. Publications from the series will cover language development of bilingual and multilingual children, acquisition of languages other than English, cultural variations in child rearing practices, cognitive development of children in multicultural environments, speech and language disorders in bilingual children and children speaking languages other than English, and education and healthcare for children speaking non-standard or non-native varieties of English. The series will be of particular interest to linguists, psychologists, speech and language therapists, and teachers, as well as to other practitioners and professionals working with children of multilingual and multicultural backgrounds.

Recent Books in the Series
Culture-Specific Language Styles: The Development of Oral Narrative and Literacy
   Masahiko Minami
Language and Literacy in Bilingual Children
   D. Kimbrough Oller and Rebecca E. Eilers (eds)
Phonological Development in Specific Contexts: Studies of Chinese-Speaking Children
   Zhu Hua
Bilingual Children's Language and Literacy Development
   Roger Barnard and Ted Glynn (eds)
Developing in Two Languages: Korean Children in America
   Sarah J. Shin
Three is a Crowd? Acquiring Portuguese in a Trilingual Environment
   Madalena Cruz-Ferreira
Childhood Bilingualism: Research on Infancy through School Age
   Peggy McCardle and Erika Hoff (eds)
Phonological Development and Disorders in Children: A Multilingual Perspective
   Zhu Hua and Barbara Dodd (eds)

Other Books of Interest
Foundations of Bilingual Education and Bilingualism
   Colin Baker
Language Acquisition: The Age Factor (2nd edn)
   David Singleton and Lisa Ryan
Third or Additional Language Acquisition
   Gessica De Angelis

For more details of these or any other of our publications, please contact:
Multilingual Matters, Frankfurt Lodge, Clevedon Hall,
Victoria Road, Clevedon, BS21 7HH, England
http://www.multilingual-matters.com

CHILD LANGUAGE AND CHILD DEVELOPMENT 9
Series Editor: Li Wei, University of London

A Portrait of the Young in the New Multilingual Spain

Edited by
Carmen Pérez-Vidal, Maria Juan-Garau and Aurora Bel

MULTILINGUAL MATTERS LTD
Clevedon • Buffalo • Toronto

Library of Congress Cataloging in Publication Data
A Portrait of the Young in the New Multilingual Spain / Edited by Carmen Perez-Vidal, Maria Juan-Garau, and Aurora Bel.
Child Language and Child Development: 9
Includes bibliographical references and index.
1. Bilingualism in children–Spain. 2. Mulilingualism in children–Spain. 3. Language acquisition. I. Pérez Vidal, Carmen. II. Juan-Garau, Maria. III. Bel Gaya, Aurora.
P115.2.P67 2007
418.0071–dc22   2007029795

British Library Cataloguing in Publication Data
A catalogue entry for this book is available from the British Library.

ISBN-13: 978-1-84769-023-4 (hbk)
ISBN-13: 978-1-84769-022-7 (pbk)

Multilingual Matters Ltd
UK: Frankfurt Lodge, Clevedon Hall, Victoria Road, Clevedon BS21 7HH.
USA: UTP, 2250 Military Road, Tonawanda, NY 14150, USA.
Canada: UTP, 5201 Dufferin Street, North York, Ontario M3H 5T8, Canada.

Copyright © 2008 Carmen Pérez-Vidal, Maria Juan-Garau, Aurora Bel and the authors of individual chapters.

All rights reserved. No part of this work may be reproduced in any form or by any means without permission in writing from the publisher.

Typeset by Techset Composition Ltd.
Printed and bound in Great Britain by the Cromwell Press Ltd.

*To Caterina and Andreu, Gabriel and Josep, Júlia and Enric,
our multilingual children*

Contents

The Contributors ix
Acknowledgements xv
Introduction xvi
Prologue by Miquel Siguan 1

1 Issues in the Acquisition of Two or More
   Languages in Multilingual Environments
   Carmen Pérez-Vidal, Maria Juan-Garau and Aurora Bel 18

**Part 1: The Early Acquisition of Two or More Languages
Within the Family Context**

2 Early Galician/Spanish Bilingualism: Contrasts with
   Monolingualism
   Miguel Pérez-Pereira 39
3 Early Trilingualism: The Development of Communicative
   Competence in English Alongside Basque and Spanish
   Julia Barnes 63
4 Influence of the Linguistic Environment on the Development
   of the Lexicon and Grammar of Basque Bilingual Children
   Andoni Barreña, Mª José Ezeizabarrena and Iñaki García 86
5 Null and Overt Subjects in the Developing Grammars
   (L1 English/L1 Spanish) of Two Bilingual Twins
   *Juana M. Liceras, Raquel Fernández Fuertes and
   Rocío Pérez-Tattam* 111
6 Contributions from Bilingual Specific Language Impairment
   in Catalan and Spanish to the Understanding of Typical and
   Pathological Language Acquisition
   Mònica Sanz-Torrent, Iris Badia and Miquel Serra 135

7 The Simultaneous Development of Narratives in
  English and Spanish
  Esther Álvarez 159

**Part 2: Bilingual and Multilingual Acquisition at Later
Ages and in Instructional Settings**

8 Classroom Bilingualism at an Early Age: Towards a More
  Natural EFL Context
  Ana Llinares García 185
9 First Language Influence on Second Language Acquisition:
  The Case of Immigrant L1 Soninke, Tagalog and Chinese
  Children Learning Catalan
  Elisabet Serrat, Lluïsa Gràcia and Laia Perpiñá 200
10 Predicting Enhanced L3 Learning in Bilingual Contexts:
   The Role of Biliteracy
   Cristina Sanz 220
11 Learning Context Effects on the Acquisition of a
   Second Language Phonology
   Joan C. Mora 241
12 Non-Adult Long-Distance wh- Questions in the
   Non-Native Acquisition of English
   Junkal Gutierrez Mangado and María del Pilar García Mayo 264

Index 287

The Contributors

Esther Álvarez is currently Lecturer at the University of Barcelona, Spain, where she teaches subjects in the field of Linguistics and Applied Linguistics. Her research interests cover the area of bilingual first language acquisition and also multilingual acquisition. More specifically, she has conducted research into the acquisition of English and Spanish from birth in both family and school contexts, as well as the acquisition of English as a third language by Spanish/Catalan bilingual students at school. Her most recent publications have focused on the acquisition of the linguistic and discourse abilities necessary in oral narrative in child bilingual acquisition and in child EFL.

Iris Badia has earned her MA at the University of Barcelona and she is currently enrolled in the Cognitive Science and Language PhD programme of this University. She is member of the Psycholinguistics and Language Pathology Laboratory of the University of Barcelona, whose areas of interest are cognitive processes, typical and pathological language processing and the acquisition of Catalan and Spanish. She also teaches Basic Psychology at the University of Girona as a Teacher Assistant.

Julia Barnes obtained a BA in Spanish and Linguistics from the University of Exeter in the United Kingdom. After moving to Spain she received a degree in English Philology from the University of Alicante and worked for the British Council and the University of the Basque Country. She researched her PhD in the field of childhood multilingualism, which continues to be her main interest along with minority languages and language teaching methodology. She currently lectures and trains language teachers at the Faculty of Humanities and Education of the University of Mondragon.

Andoni Barreña holds a PhD in Basque Philology (University of The Basque Country) and is Senior Lecturer in the Department of Spanish

Language at the University of Salamanca. His main research areas concern First Language Acquisition, Early Bilingual Acquisition and Ethnolinguistics. He is author and co-author of some 50 articles edited in Basque, Spanish and English, and published in Spain, France, The United States, Mexico, and Germany, among others. He is co-author of the book *Words and Worlds. World Languages Review* (Multilingual Matters). He is also a member of a research project for the adaptation to Basque of the MacArthur–Bates CDI.

Aurora Bel is Associate Professor at the Universitat Pompeu Fabra (Barcelona, Spain). She currently teaches Language Acquisition and Psycholinguistics. Her interests comprise the acquisition of Spanish and Catalan as first and second languages in multilingual environments, particularly the acquisition of morphosyntax and semantics. Her latest publications include the acquisition of agreement and the study of the knowledge and factors that explain the use of grammatical subjects by different populations of learners (L1, L2). Currently, she is also focusing on the abnormal development of language and the language of translators.

Maria-José Ezeizabarrena holds a PhD in Linguistics (University of Hamburg, Germany). She is Senior Lecturer in the Department of Linguistics and Basque Studies of the University of The Basque Country (Vitoria-Gasteiz, Spain), where she has also been Academic Secretary since 2005. Her main research areas concern the acquisition of Spanish and Basque as a First Language and Bilingualism. She is a member of several research projects on early language acquisition, including the KGNZ Project for the adaptation to Basque of the MacArthur–Bates CDI.

Raquel Fernández Fuertes is Lecturer in the Department of English at the University of Valladolid (Spain). She specialises in Linguistic Theory, English/Spanish comparative grammar and Bilingual Acquisition, which are all part of her academic activities. She is presently working on the analysis of bilingual data within the framework of generative linguistics. More specifically, her research deals with how linguistic theory can account for the syntactic phenomena that emerge in language contact situations such as code-switching, natural translation and word-order issues (subject/verb, compounds, among others).

Inaki García holds a doctorate in Psychology from the University of the Basque Country. He has researched in the field of Psycholinguistics and

Language Acquisition. He teaches Statistics and General Didactics at the Faculty of Humanities and Education of the University of Mondragon. He is a member of the KGNZ Research Project for the adaptation to Basque of the MacArthur–Bates CDI.

María del Pilar García Mayo is Full Professor of English Language and Linguistics at the University of the Basque Country (Spain). She holds a BA in English Philology from the Universidad de Santiago de Compostela (Spain) and an MA and a PhD in Linguistics from the University of Iowa (USA). Her research interests include Second Language Acquisition both from a generative and an interactionist perspective. Her work has been published in numerous scholarly journals and has also appeared in different edited collections (Georgetown University Press, John Benjamins, Mouton de Gruyter and Multilingual Matters).

Lluïsa Gràcia earned her doctoral degree in Catalan Philology from the Universitat Autònoma de Barcelona in 1986. She is Senior Lecturer of General Linguistics at the University of Girona (Girona, Spain). She has worked on syntax and lexical morphology and the comparison between immigrant languages and Catalan and Spanish. She directs the Group of Lexicon and Grammar and the Office for Linguistic Advice to Immigrants at the University of Girona. She is series editor of the collection Language, Immigration and the teaching of Catalan published by the Departament of Social welfare and the Family and the Departament of Education of the Catalan Generalitat.

Junkal Gutierrez Mangado is currently Assistant Professor in the Department of Linguistics and Basque Studies at the University of the Basque Country. Following her PhD thesis on the acquisition of long distance wh- questions in 2005, her research interests include the acquisition of different aspects of syntax both in L1 (Basque and Spanish) and L2 (English). Within syntax she has worked on the acquisition of different structures involving wh- phrases such as questions and relatives.

Maria Juan-Garau is Associate Professor in English and Vicedean of the Faculty of Philosophy and Arts at the Universitat de les Illes Balears (Spain), where she currently teaches courses in Applied Linguistics and Language Acquisition research methods. She has also taught EFL at secondary and tertiary level and has been involved in language teacher education. Her research interests and publications include bilingual first language acquisition, with a focus on the pragmatic aspects of mixing, the linguistic analysis of specialised language corpora, and the influence of learning context in foreign language acquisition, with special attention to the effects of study abroad.

Juana M. Liceras is Full Professor in the Department of Modern Languages and the Department of Linguistics of the University of Ottawa (Canada) and a member of the Academic Board of the PhD Program in Linguistic Theory of the Instituto Universitario de Investigación Ortega y Gasset of the Universidad Complutense of Madrid (Spain). She is the director of the Language Acquisition Laboratory of the University of Ottawa. Her research interests and publications deal with the relationship between linguistic theory and language acquisition, bilingualism and language contact.

Ana Llinares García is Lecturer in the English Department at the Universidad Autónoma (Madrid). She teaches English language, Pragmatics, Second Language Acquisition, and Bilingualism at postgraduate level. She specialises in second language acquisition and interlanguage pragmatics. Her research focuses on young learners' oral production in bilingual classroom contexts. She currently coordinates a research project on secondary school learners' oral and written production in CLIL classrooms. She has also published articles in prestigious journals including *Intercultural Pragmatics* and *International Journal of Corpus Linguistics*.

Joan C. Mora obtained his PhD in English Linguistics from the University of Barcelona where he is Lecturer in English Phonetics and Phonology in the Department of English Philology. His current research interests are second language (L2) phonetic learning and L2 oral fluency, including speech learning in simultaneous bilingualism, the effect of amount and quality of L2 input on learners' accuracy in L2 speech sound production in formal instructional settings, and the development of L2 oral fluency in stay-abroad learning contexts.

Miguel Pérez Pereira is Full Professor in the Department of Developmental and Educational Psychology of the University of Santiago de Compostela (Spain). His present research interests deal with the acquisition of language in monolingual and bilingual children and language development in blind children. He has published over 35 books and book chapters and over 50 papers in peer-reviewed journals, such as *Journal of Child Language, First Language, British Journal of Developmental*

Psychology, Journal of Psycholinguistic Research, Infancia y Aprendizaje, Journal of Visual Impairment and Blindness and *Archives de Psychologie*. He is the president of AEAL (Asociación para el Estudio de la Adquisición del Lenguaje).

Rocío Pérez-Tattam is a graduate student in the Department of Modern Languages and Literatures of the University of Ottawa. She is currently in the process of completing her doctoral dissertation on native and non-native acquisition of non-finite verbal complements in Spanish by Spanish/English bilingual children and adult native speakers of English. She is also a member of the Language Acquisition Lab at the Department of Modern Languages of the University of Ottawa.

Carmen Pérez-Vidal received her MA in Applied Linguistics from the University of Reading, UK, and her PhD in English linguistics from the University of Barcelona, Spain. She is Associate Professor in English Linguistics and Language Acquisition at Pompeu Fabra University (Barcelona, Spain), where she is Vicerector of Languages and coordinator of the ALLENCAM and SALA projects. Her research interests and recent publications deal with bilingual, second and foreign language acquisition in different contexts of learning: natural, formal, immersion and stay abroad. She has specialised in writing and the age factor, content and language integrated learning and input effects.

Laia Perpiñá earned her MA at the University of Girona in 2005. She is interested in the study of first language influence in second language acquisition. She currently works as a teacher of Catalan for immigrant children and adults, and she is a member of the Office for the Linguistic Advice of Immigrants at the University of Girona.

Cristina Sanz (PhD, University of Illinois, 1994) is Associate Professor at Georgetown University where she co-directs the Center for the Brain Basis of Cognition and directs the Doctoral Program and the Spanish Intensive Language Program. She has established the Catalan Lectureship (1999) and the Georgetown-at-Barcelona Summer Program at UPF (2007). An expert on bilingualism and SLA, her volume *Mind and Context in Adult Second Language Acquisition* received the 2006 MLA's Mildenberger Prize. Dr Sanz co-edited *Spanish Applied Linguistics at the End of the Millennium* (2000) and edited the special volume of *Spanish Applied Linguistics – Cognition & Spanish Bilinguals* (2001).

Mònica Sanz-Torrent earned her PhD in Psychology from the Universitat de Barcelona and is Lecturer in the Basic Psychology Department at this university. She has taught Cognitive Processes and the Psychology of Language and Thought in different Catalan universities. She conducts her research in the Psycholinguistics and Language Pathology Laboratory, whose areas of interest are cognitive processes, typical and pathological language processing and the acquisition of Catalan and Spanish. She currently coordinates a project on ocular movements applied to the study of child language processing.

Miquel Serra is Full Professor of Psychology at the Department of Basic (Cognitive) Psychology of the University of Barcelona. He is the Director of the External Service of Language Pathology and the Laboratory of Psycholinguistics and Language Pathology. He has published and edited 'La adquisición del Lenguaje' (Barcelona: Ariel) with Serrat, Sole, Bel and Aparici. He has also published different tools for profiling language both in research and clinical work. His main research interest and publications deal with language impairment and related topics.

Elisabet Serrat is Associate Professor of Psychology of Language and Thought at the University of Girona (Girona, Spain). She earned her PhD in Psychology from the University of Girona in 1997. She investigates the underlying mechanisms that determine the course of early grammatical development. Her recent research includes the study of second language acquisition by immigrant children and adults. She is a member of the Office for Linguistic Advice to Immigrants at the University of Girona.

Miquel Siguan is Emeritus Professor at the University of Barcelona and Honorary Dean of the Psychology Faculty, where he continues to direct the 'Anuario de Psicología' (Psychology Yearbook), which he founded in 1969. He is also Scientific Director of the UNESCO's LINGUAPAX Project, a Member of the European Academy, and Honorary Doctor of the University of Geneva, among other. His research and publications include books and numerous papers on multilingualism in general and the development of child bilingualism, both at home and at school. Over three decades, he has periodically organised the Catalan Seminar on Languages and Education.

Acknowledgements

This book would not have been possible without the commitment of its contributing authors, who willingly accepted to join in the project enthusiastically and unfailingly. In the process of editing we have received encouragement and support from friends and colleagues across the world. Special mention should be made of our research team in the Stay Abroad and Language Acquisition Project (SALA), and the Language Acquisition in Multilingual Catalonia Research Group (ALLENCAM). Robert DeKeyser and Gabriele Kasper have offered valuable insights through the process of writing. Paul Ambrose and Elisa Barquin have assisted us with the correction and final editing of the chapters; we are particularly grateful for their inspiring comments.

Li Wei, the series editor, offered truly insightful advice, and, most centrally, he believed in this project from the beginning, and gave it all of his support. Tommi and Marjukka Grover at Multilingual Matters have been exceptionally understanding and patient. Most sincere thanks and appreciation to all of them.

We would also like to acknowledge the financial support provided to the ALLENCAM Research Group with the research grant given by the Department of Research of the Catalan Autonomous Government (N.01086).

Finally, we would like to thank all children and learners studied in this book, and their families; they were the real source of inspiration.

Introduction

In bilingual language acquisition research it is currently accepted that when a speaker, either during infancy or later in life, acquires more than one language, this results in one multicompetent linguistic capacity, conceived as a whole. Within this whole, each of the speaker's linguistic systems develops independently, yet in an interrelated way. This multilinguistic system is also seen as dynamic, not static, in the sense that each language may develop, stabilise, or even regress, mainly as a result of frequency of use and the degree of competence attained. Moreover, this view assumes that the conception of a bilingual speaker as the sum of two monolinguals (or a trilingual as the sum of three) is a myth, rather than a reality, with very few exceptions.

This view in itself represents a departure from earlier research, which has focused mainly on contrasting bilinguals with monolinguals, and today variability among bilinguals is of major concern. A related issue is that of how competent bilinguals are in each of their languages, that is, whether they are balanced or unbalanced bilinguals. This relative balance may result mainly from two circumstances. On the one hand, there is the age of onset of L2 learning (AOL) – whether exposure started at birth or later on in life – also referred to as simultaneous bilingualism as opposed to successive, or even second language acquisition. On the other hand, there is the proportion in which the language is spoken in the environment. Furthermore, studies of bilingual acquisition have by and large revealed that the development of two or more languages in childhood, after a relatively slower initial stage, proceeds as 'easily' and productively as monolingual development, and sometimes even more so, including the case of children with language impairment, such as specific language impairment (SLI). These views have been reflected in recent European research and institutional briefs. Finally, psycholinguistic evidence has been accumulating, from Canada and the United States, through Germany, to the Basque country and Catalonia, among many others, showing that bilingualism has a positive effect on a number of cognitive variables, such as mental plasticity, metalinguistic awareness, and processing capacity. Most importantly, research suggests that multilinguals learn new languages better than monolinguals.

These developments in the field of second language acquisition and the study of multilingualism have coincided with several recent phenomena in Spain that have provided a unique opportunity for the development of a large number of language acquisition research teams. First, Spain's rich linguistic heritage has been given renewed importance following the relatively recent return to democracy, and minority languages have been given co-official status in their regions, creating bilingual communities with language combinations such as Catalan and Spanish, Basque and Spanish, or Galician and Spanish. In this new terrain, many of the nation's young are now growing up in bilingual, trilingual or multilingual environments, exposed to different languages at home, in school, or elsewhere in the community (see the Preface for further details). Second, the Spanish society is becoming increasingly cosmopolitan. In the last 10 years a wave of immigration has brought an array of new languages; in Catalonia alone, an estimated 300 languages are spoken today. Third, for the first time in Spain's history, a political infrastructure has been set up to finance and support university research teams and projects. Consequently, researchers have been able to observe, analyse, and foster the complex new multilingual realities in Spain's different communities, sometimes in collaboration with North American, Canadian or European researchers.

From such momentous changes sprang the objective of this book: to try to draw a map of this new multilingual situation, dealing with unique language combinations in different speech communities. The groundwork had already been laid for such an endeavour; the projects under way have already yielded a number of seminal studies, theses, and articles, which very naturally cover different facets of the new sociolinguistic terrain. And thus the present work, *A Portrait of the Young in the New Multilingual Spain*, has been designed as a matrix to host a representative sample of the recently funded research that reflects our changing society, while providing a backdrop from which to approach the many other studies for which there is no space left in this book. The value of the book, then, lies in the fact that it deals with bi/multilingual language phenomena through the lens of language acquisition research, while also treating these phenomena as cases in point. The larger sociolinguistic map is delineated, thus obtaining both individual and societal perspectives. In sum, the sociolinguistic puzzle of contemporary Spain allows for language acquisition research from a rich, multilayered perspective, involving our own official languages – Catalan, Basque, Galician, Spanish – as well as English, Soninke, Tagalog, Mandarin, Portuguese, and French.

Each chapter deals with a particular language combination on the multilingual map. Because our aim is to offer an overview of languages and studies, the different chapters analyse empirical data from a variety of theoretical perspectives – from functionalist and descriptivist to formal generativist – and analyse both natural and formal acquisition settings (the latter include both conventional language learning programmes and also bilingual immersion programmes). A selection is offered of the main issues of interest in language acquisition in general, and bilingual development in particular, and findings are presented from the growing field of trilingual development using both longitudinal and cross-sectional case studies. The choice of studies was also influenced by a desire to include different methods of analysis, but they all aim at contributing to an understanding of the effects of growing up with multiple languages and in multilingual communities, focusing on diverse areas such as lexis, syntax and morphology, phonology, discourse, pragmatics, and literacy. Finally, all of the studies included combine three major components of language acquisition research: (1) a concern for context variables; (2) an interest in describing the languages analysed; and (3) an analytical focus on cognitive factors. In sum, we aim to offer the reader a multifaceted *portrait of the young in multilingual Spain*.

Returning our focus to the recent trends that have transformed Spanish society, we would like to highlight three major effects that these trends have had on our sociolinguistic makeup. First, they have led to a substantial number of children becoming bilingual in two of the official languages of the Spanish state – specifically, Catalan/Spanish, Basque/Spanish, or Galician/Spanish. Furthermore, these same children begin learning a third, foreign, language at school by the age of 6 or even earlier, and some take on an optional fourth foreign language around the age of 12. Second, the societal trends have led to an increased number of multilingual families where two or three languages, including a foreign language, are used in the home. In the case of middle- and upper-class families, this generally involves European languages such as English, French, or German, which are, incidentally, the same foreign languages taught in the school system or in international schools. In contrast, in the mostly lower-class families comprised of recent immigrants from northern Africa, eastern Europe and Asia, foreign languages are also spoken in the home, but these are generally not the same languages that are taught in the school system and are less known in society at large. Third, accompanying the trends previously mentioned, there is a growing concern among parents, and society in general, to see the standards of foreign language competence improve, particularly with regard to English. Indeed, international schools and multilingual programmes of a Content and Language Integrated (CLIL) nature are in high demand, as are private language schools focused on teaching foreign languages to the young as an extracurricular activity, including evening classes and Stay Abroad programmes, which provide immersion contexts.

Part 1 in this volume analyses evidence from young children acquiring different combinations of languages spoken in the environment as their first languages, thus in natural family settings and dealing exclusively with oral data. The studies in this section tackle areas such as lexical acquisition, syntax and morphology, code mixing, and the role of parental language choices on children's degrees of bilingual competence. Some deal with issues that have seldom been reported in studies of early bilingual development in natural contexts, such as bilinguals' acquisition of communicative competence and pragmatics, language development in bilingual twins, the development of bilinguals with SLI development, or the rather unusual data of subjects from lower socioeconomic (SES) backgrounds.

Part 2 focuses on bi/multilingual language acquisition in formal settings throughout the educational system, from nursery school to university, thus dealing with later ages of acquisition, and including written data. In contrast with the preceding section, here all chapters take the perspective of foreign language classroom research. Some deal with well-established issues, such as the role of the L1 and transfer, the acquisition of lexis, syntax and morphology in subsequent languages, the development of the ability to narrate, and the hypothesis of an age factor for language acquisition; others explore areas that have only recently been on the research agenda, such as the discourse functions present in the nursery school classroom, the role of bilingual literacy in developing competence in English as an L3, or the effect of Stay Abroad experiences on the acquisition of English phonology.

In Chapter 1, 'Issues in the acquisition of two or more languages in multilingual environments', Carmen Pérez-Vidal, Maria Juan-Garau and Aurora Bel provide an updated overview of the main issues in the field of language acquisition, bilingualism and multilingualism to be explored in the subsequent chapters. They establish a continuum between monolingual acquisition research at one end, and multilingual research at the other, with bi- and trilingualism lying in the middle as a frame of reference for the whole book, reviewing the concepts of language separation in early acquisition, transfer, and the role of the context, while placing the linguistic phenomena and the methodological strategies in perspective.

Next, in Chapter 2, 'Early Galician/Spanish bilingualism: Contrasts with monolingualism', Miguel Pérez Pereira analyses the communicative and linguistic speech development of 706 children, observing different points in which bilinguals surpass monolinguals, and suggesting that there is an effect of bilinguals' total conceptual vocabularies on the acquisition of grammar, when their two languages are similar.

In Chapter 3, 'Early trilingualism: The development of communicative competence in English alongside Basque and Spanish', Julia Barnes, similarly to the previous chapter, finds a more sophisticated level of English oral communication in her trilingual subject between 1;11 and 3;5 than in monolinguals of the same age, specifically with regards to question formation and pragmatic competence.

Chapter 4, 'Influence of the linguistic environment on the development of the lexicon and grammar of Basque bilingual children', by Andoni Barreña, M. José Ezeizabarrena and Iñaki García, uses data from six longitudinal participants and 972 cross-sectional ones to provide empirical evidence indicating that the degree to which Basque is present in the input, both quantitatively and qualitatively, has a clear influence on lexical and grammatical development after a certain moment, when the critical mass of vocabulary is being consolidated.

In Chapter 5, 'Null and overt subjects in the developing grammars (L1 English/L1 Spanish) of two bilingual twins', Juana M. Liceras, Raquel Fernández Fuertes and Rocío Pérez-Tattam report on the oral production of two Spanish-English bilingual twins and analyse subject representation. They argue that no transfer is found in this specific area of the grammar, which implies that the two systems are kept separate from the early stages.

In Chapter 6, 'Contributions from bilingual specific language impairment in Catalan and Spanish to the understanding of typical and pathological language acquisition', Mònica Sanz-Torrent, Iris Badia and Miquel Serra consider the cases of six (SLI) Catalan/Spanish bilinguals and provide evidence that learning two languages is not challenged by the language impairment.

In Chapter 7, 'The simultaneous development of narratives in English and Spanish', Esther Alvarez presents a longitudinal case study of a Spanish-English bilingual child growing up bilingual within the family and also attending an international school programme, to demonstrate the different levels of proficiency in the young learner's languages while focusing on temporal, spatial and deictic reference in narratives.

Moving on to the chapters on multilingual language acquisition in formal settings, hence to later ages of acquisition, the first two deal with primary school data, the following three with secondary school data, and the last one with university-level data.

In Chapter 8, 'Classroom bilingualism at an early age: Towards a more natural EFL context', using data collected in kindergarten classrooms in the Madrid area, Ana Llinares García analyses five-year-old children's functional use of English as a foreign language in a high-immersion 'bilingual' school. She identifies the task that proves the most successful in promoting learners' discourse initiation episodes, those typically associated with natural L1 acquisition.

In Chapter 9, 'First language influence on second language acquisition: The case of immigrant L1 Soninke, Tagalog and Chinese children learning Catalan', Elisabet Serrat, Lluïsa Gràcia and Laia Perpiñá investigate cross-linguistic morphological transfer and its degree of impact. The authors show that their subjects in the Catalan immersion programme make errors that affect communication in the classroom in an important way and have enduring effects.

In Chapter 10, entitled 'Predicting enhanced L3 learning in bilingual contexts: the role of biliteracy', Cristina Sanz uses questionnaires and written data from a total of 120 high-school learners in a mainstream educational immersion program in Catalonia to identify the overpowering effect of motivation and exposure, followed by language attitudes and balanced written skills, as independent variables predicting bilinguals' successful acquisition of a third language (L3).

In Chapter 11, 'Learning context effects on the acquisition of a second language phonology', Joan C. Mora tackles a new area: the effects of Stay Abroad contexts, with massive exposure to input in English, on the productive and perceptive phonological development of advanced learners, using data from bilingual Spanish-Catalan university students learning English as an L3. The author finds a surprising contrast between the benefits of formal instruction at home as compared to the stay abroad in terms of production.

Finally, in Chapter 12 'Non-adult long-distance wh- questions in the non-native acquisition of English', Junkal Gutierrez Mangado and María del Pilar García Mayo present the findings of a cross-sectional study on the acquisition of English focusing on access-to-UG and a Critical Period in L2 acquisition, with 260 participants of ages ranging from 8 to 18. These seem to follow the developmental path characteristic of these LD questions, producing structures absent not only in their own languages but also in the target language.

This book is specifically directed to professionals interested in language learning in general and bilingualism and multilingualism in particular, researchers and graduate students interested in the issues, the data and the languages of the studies presented. We hope that it will also be of interest to parents, language teachers, language planners, and anyone dedicated to understanding how languages are acquired and can be better learnt in the educational system. We also aim to interest those from countries that may be experiencing the type of transformation that we have experienced in Spain with regards to multilingualism. Finally, this book aims to contribute to the dissemination of a new vision of multilingual linguistic competence.

Prologue

MIQUEL SIGUAN

Introduction

From today's vantage point, it is surprising to remember that little more than a century ago, pedagogues and psychologists spoke out against bilingual education, considering that early exposure to a second language could endanger a child's intellectual development and even impair the development of a solid and balanced personality. Since the end of the last world war, the situation has undergone rapid change: in an increasingly globalised world, knowledge of multiple languages is increasingly common; at the same time, many school systems have moved towards the early introduction of second languages, or even completely bilingual or multilingual education.

Naturally, these changes have been accompanied by a change in attitudes. Now, early contact with foreign languages is considered both desirable and necessary, and it is believed that this contact may stimulate intellectual development and foster a more open and understanding personality. The current debate is not over whether bilingual education is good or bad in and of itself; instead the focus is on what is the most appropriate form of bilingual education for each concrete situation. Most importantly, this change in attitudes has led to a great interest in the phenomenon of bilingualism in all its aspects, both on the individual and societal levels, and has inspired study of this phenomenon from diverse theoretical perspectives: from computational linguistics to sociolinguistics, and from genetic to cultural psychology.

The majority of studies thus far use data from concrete situations to extrapolate more or less general conclusions, and only a few actually obtain and analyse data from a variety of situations, which gives more weight to potential generalisations. The study at hand is of the latter variety; its data and results have come from both familial contexts and bilingual education contexts, from different communities in Spain where languages other than Spanish are spoken. Naturally, to fully understand the phenomena observed and the results obtained, it will be useful to first examine some data that provide a background to the linguistic situation in Spain as a whole, and specifically in those regions where other languages are spoken alongside Spanish.

The Languages of Spain

Historical antecedents

After the Roman occupation of the Iberian peninsula in the 2nd century AD the inhabitants of this region progressively abandoned their languages and adopted Latin, with the exception of the Basques, isolated in the valleys of the Pyrenees mountain range, who maintained the use of their original language. (The Basque language does not belong to any of the Indo-European language families, and pre-dates the arrival of these languages to Europe – in fact it is difficult to classify Basque as belonging to any of the existing linguistic families.) As a result of the decline of the Roman Empire in the centuries of the old Middle Age, the Latin spoken throughout Western Europe diverged and evolved, eventually resulting in new languages, the so-called Romance Languages. In the case of the Iberian Peninsula this phenomenon had a unique progression: after the 9th century, the Muslims occupied the largest part of the peninsula, excluding the mountainous strip in the North, and the new linguistic nuclei that developed in that region eventually evolved into new languages.

The region essentially gave birth to five new linguistic nuclei – Galician, Asturian, Castilian, Aragonese, and Catalan – in addition to fostering the surviving Basque language. With time, and relative to the progressive recapturing of territory, these languages extended to the south: the Castilian language blocked the expansion of Asturian and Aragonese and became the predominant language in the centre of the peninsula, and Catalan became the language of the Aragonese kingdom, extending to Valencia and the Balearic Islands. As for Galician, Galicia's lack of independent political institutions impeded its expansion to the South, contemporary Portugal, and the derivation of Latin produced there, although very close to Galician, underwent an independent development. So, by the 13th and 14th centuries, the eve of the Renaissance, the peninsula had at least three different languages with magnificent literatures, Castilian, Catalan, and Gallo-Portuguese, with different strains in Galicia and Portugal.

At the end of the 15th century, after the union of Castile and Aragon and the final recapture of the peninsula from the Muslims, the Spanish kingdom was born, and, with the separation of Portugal, the Iberian Peninsula became divided into two independent states. The Castilian language became the principal language of the Spanish state and, after the discovery of America, began its expansion into new continents.

In the 18th century, under the monarchy of a French dynasty, Spain adopted a French model of nascent Statehood based on strong centralisation and linguistic order. The Academy of the Language was founded, beginning a policy of linguistic unification that was strengthened in the 19th century with the development of public education. The success was less overwhelming, however, than that of France, and in the mid-19th century people continued speaking different languages in many areas in the north of the peninsula. Despite the fact that Castilian, or Spanish, was the official language and the language commonly used for writing, these Northern populations habitually used their first languages, the regional languages, for oral communication.

In the 19th century, following movements begun in continental Europe, romanticism produced literary renaissances in these regional languages – primarily in Catalan, but also in Galician and Basque – which incited political movements laying claim to the autonomous identities of these cultures. These movements achieved their first victories when the Spanish Republic, established in 1931, conceded Statutes of Autonomy first to Catalonia, and then to the Basque Country and Galicia. The end of the Civil War, and the ensuing regime of General Francisco Franco, however, meant a revocation of the autonomy that had been granted and an effort to impose national unity, which included the prohibition of public use of languages other than Spanish. Over time, however, this imposition led to the opposite of its objective, and resulted in a vindication of democracy accompanied by demands of respect for linguistic and cultural diversity.

The new situation

The Spanish Constitution of 1978 states the following:

(1) Castilian is the Spanish language, official language of the Spanish State. All Spaniards have the obligation to know, and the right to use, this language.
(2) The other languages of Spain will be official in their respective Autonomous Communities, in accordance with their Statutes.
(3) The richness of different linguistic forms in Spain is a cultural heritage that will be the object of special respect and protection.

In accordance with this same Constitution, the Spanish State is organised into 17 Autonomous Communities, each of which has its own Government and a Parliament with legislative capacities. Six of these communities have Statutes of Autonomy, which establish a second language as a co-official language along with Spanish. In Catalonia and the Balearic Islands, this language is Catalan, in Valencia, Valencian (the regional variety of Catalan), in Galicia, Galician, in the Basque country, Basque (or, *euskera*), and in Navarre, as well, the Basque language is officially used, although only in parts of the region.

To complete this panorama one must mention the Statute of Asturias, which recognises the existence of *bable* – the current nomenclature for Asturian – and proposes its protection, although without granting it a co-official status. The Statute of Aragon similarly recommends the protection of Aragonese, a language that has been maintained in several valleys of the Pyrenees. Finally, the Statute of Catalonia recognises the existence of Aranese, a language native to the Val d'Aran (Valley of Aran) – also in the Pyrenees – which is a variety of the Occitan language spoken in the south of France.

And so the Constitution of 1978 marked a new era in the linguistic situation of Spain. The central government has taken measures in response to this situation, and, above all, the different Autonomous Communities with their own languages have written laws to define their linguistic policies, and created governmental bodies to put those laws into practice. Before discussing those linguistic policies in greater depth, it will be useful to provide an overview of the languages currently present in Spain.

Spanish

The official and principal language of the Spanish State, which has a current population of 40 million people, is Spanish. It is also the official language of 24 states in South and Central America, former colonies of Spain. The political independence of these countries did not end their linguistic unity with Spain; in the majority of the new States, national Academies of the Language were created, declaring their solidarity with each other and with the Spanish Royal Academy (RAE). Although originally it was the RAE that dictated the linguistic norms – the official dictionary and grammar – now all decisions are made by consensus, with the norms reflecting the language throughout the whole of its territories, and demonstrating awareness of variation in each country.

The Spanish language has also been expanding its dominion in other territories. In the United States, an uninterrupted current of immigration proceeding from Latin America has converted Spanish into the country's second language. For reasons of continental solidarity, Spanish is also gaining ground in Brazil. In Europe and even the Far East, the number of people who are learning Spanish as a second language is increasing rapidly. It has reached the point where, on a global level, Spanish is the second most studied language, after English.

Catalan

Catalan is the co-official language in Catalonia, the Balearic Islands, and Valencia (in the latter taking the form of the regional variety, Valencian). It is also spoken in parts of Aragon, parts of southwestern France (most of the Eastern Pyrenees) and in the city of Alghero on the island of Sardinia, Italy. It is the official language of Andorra, a small country situated in the Pyrenees that was recently incorporated into the United Nations. An estimated six million people speak Catalan, making it a more widely spoken language than over half of those officially recognised by the European Union.

At the beginning of the 20th century the Institute of Catalan Studies established official linguistic norms for modern Catalan, which are generally accepted in all regions where the language is used. These norms recognise various dialects, among them Valencian.

Catalan has a central role in the educational systems of all those communities that claim the language as their own. In Catalonia it is the primary language used at all levels of education, including the university level. The language also has a growing literature and a significant presence in all forms of media: written press, radio, TV, and Internet.

Galician

Galician is the co-official language in Galicia (population: 2,700,000). It is also spoken in the neighbouring regions of Asturias and Castile-Leon, and in emigrant communities in South America. Modern linguistic norms have been established by the Academy of the Galician Language. There is a minor current, called Lusitanism, which defends a linguistic standard closer to that of Portuguese. Galician also has an important presence in the community's educational system and in the media.

Basque, or Euskera

The co-official language of the Basque Country (2,100,000 inhabitants) and portions of Navarre is Basque (or *Euskera*); it is also spoken in parts of southern France. As mentioned above, Basque is a very old language, which has survived in isolation and been splintered into a number of diverse dialects. Around 1970, the Academy of the Basque Language proposed a modernised linguistic standard, which has permitted the unification of the language, under the name *euskera batua* ('common Basque'). Although Spanish, Catalan, and Galician are all derived from Latin, thus sharing many similarities and allowing for the relatively easy acquisition or comprehension of one another, Basque is completely different, and its acquisition by speakers of Spanish, or other romance languages, is much more difficult. Like Catalan or Galician, Basque currently has an important presence in the educational system and media of its territories.

Other languages
Aranese, spoken in the Valley of Aran (6000 inhabitants) is a dialect of Gascon (which is, in turn, a dialect of the Occitan language group). Despite the very small number of people who speak this language, the protection it has received from the government of Catalonia has allowed for its standardisation and habitual use in education, which is not true for the Occitan spoken in French territories.

Finally, there is Bable, the current form of the old Asturian language, which has been maintained in Asturias, where the regional government has granted it a certain protection; this has allowed for some literary growth and the possibility of its future use in education.

The New Linguistic Policies and Their Results

In accordance with the text of the new constitution, the Spanish government has taken certain measures with regard to minority languages. Furthermore, those Autonomous communities with languages other than Spanish have taken their own political action – making laws and establishing linguistic policies to protect and encourage the use of the regional language. Before discussing these policies in detail, it may be useful to examine the data available on the knowledge and use of each of these languages in their respective Autonomous Communities. These data, presented in the following, are extracted from a poll on the 'Knowledge and use of languages' in Spain, carried out by the CIS (Center for Sociological Research) in 1998.

The data in Table 1 indicate linguistic knowledge and distinguish between (1) those who are able to speak the regional language, (2) those who do not speak but can understand the language, and (3) those who do not understand the language. The data in Table 2 indicate the language that the subjects consider their primary or habitual language and distinguish between (1) those whose primary language is the regional language of the community, (2) those who consider themselves completely bilingual, and (3,4) those whose primary language is Spanish,

Table 1 Knowledge of the regional languages in each Autonomous Community

	Region					
	Catalonia	Balearic Islands	Valencia	Galicia	Basque Country	Navarre
(1) Able to speak the language	79.1%	71.7%	55.6%	89.2%	28.6%	15.6%
(2) Understand the language	18.3%	20.7%	33.6%	9.6%	14.7%	7.1%
(3) Do not understand the language	2.6%	7.6%	10.8%	1.2%	56.6%	77.3%

distinguishing between (3) those who are also able to speak the community language, and (4) those who are not.

The Spanish government has taken measures in accordance with the Constitution, which proposes the recognition and promotion of linguistic diversity. The Official Bulletin of the State, the publication that explains

Table 2 Primary language of the inhabitants in each Autonomous Community

	Region					
	Catalonia	Balearic Islands	Valencia	Galicia	Basque Country	Navarre
Community language	39.6%	41.3%	29.1%	46.1%	21.4%	6.2%
Completely bilingual	14.4%	11.7%	8.6%	16.6%	4.8%	3.6%
Spanish, but able to understand the community language	20.8%	18.4%	18.6%	26.4%	11.4%	5.6%
Spanish, and unable to understand the community language	25.2%	28.5%	43.4%	10.9%	62.4%	84.6%

the statutory provisions valid throughout the country, is published in the different regional languages; it also allows for the possibility, although it is currently only in the conceptual phase, that the regional languages be used in Congress and in the Senate. Additionally, the Spanish government has proposed to the European Union that Catalan, Galician, and Basque receive the same treatment as the official languages of the member states.

Catalonia (6,100,000)

The Law of Linguistic Normalisation approved by the Parliament of Catalonia in 1983, and which has been more or less intact since then, states that Catalan and Castilian are co-official languages in Catalonia, and that a document written in either of these two languages has the same legal value; it adds, however, that Catalan is Catalonia's own language, and is therefore considered the primary language of the government and its administrative bodies. In terms of education, the law establishes that at the end of the period of obligatory education all students must be able to use both languages, both orally and in writing. Earlier regulations had already established Catalan as the primary language of education, at least in the public schools. The law also instructs the government to encourage the presence of the language in the media, especially in radio and television.

The widespread knowledge and use of Catalan in Catalonian society, the language's brilliant literary history, and, above all, the fact that since the democratic transition the government of Catalonia has been controlled by nationalistic political parties, have all infused the linguistic policies designed to protect Catalan with an exceptional energy, although naturally the promotion of Catalan has also encountered obstacles. As has been noted above, Spanish is not only the language of the Spanish state; it is also an international language with more than 300 million speakers, and in many ways the world's most popular language after English, which assures it, among other things, a strong presence in the media, both written and audiovisual. In addition, due to the high level of economic activity in the region, Catalonia has attracted a great deal of immigration from Spanish-speaking regions: both the historical internal immigration of Spaniards from the south as well as a recent wave of immigration from Latin America.

Out of proportion to the number of speakers of other languages, the data on the presence of Catalan in public life illustrates its significant presence in university education. In the universities of Catalonia it is taken for granted that the students know both Castilian and Catalan and the professors are free to provide instruction in either. The proportions in which both languages are actually used varies depending on the university, and, within each university, depending on the department. On the whole, however, it is estimated that around 60% of university classes are given in Catalan, and 40% in Castilian.

The data offered thus far describe the situation at a specific moment in time. Naturally, in the nearly 30 years since Spain's return to democracy, the linguistic situation of Catalonia has changed considerably. These changes can be summarised as in the following.

The population's knowledge of Catalan has increased considerably, in large part due to its presence in the educational system, and this increase has occurred in two directions. Traditionally, Catalans learned to speak Catalan at home, as the habitual language of the family, whereas in school they learned to read and write in Spanish. The majority of people, therefore, were only literate in one language: Spanish. With the introduction of Catalan into the educational system, the proportion of the population who can be considered literate in Catalan has increased dramatically. Furthermore, those Catalan citizens who are native Spanish-speakers, and the children of immigrants from a variety of backgrounds, make contact with Catalan when they enter into the school system and thus are soon able to understand and speak the language.

Of course, although the tendency thus far has been movement towards the society's greater knowledge of Catalan, at the same time there are signs of movement in the opposite direction. Specifically, there is a tendency towards a greater use of Castilian in oral communication, and therefore in social life. This is attributed to the increase in immigrants whose first language is Castilian; although these immigrants are generally able to understand Catalan after a short time, they tend to continue using their first language. This has led to a decrease in the number of citizens for whom Catalan is the primary language of communication, and an increase in those who consider themselves to be completely bilingual.

Balearic Islands (800,000)

The law that establishes the Linguistic Policy of the Balearic Islands is very similar to that of Catalonia, although the Balearic government's political commitment to this law has been much weaker. Furthermore, the increasing dedication to tourism in the Balearic Islands (Mallorca, Menorca and Ibiza) is producing a cosmopolitan society that uses German and English, heavily while also attracting Spanish-speaking immigrants from the south of Spain. Notwithstanding this, as indicated by the data above, the population's knowledge of Catalan is not very different from that of Catalonia.

Valencia (4,000,000)

The linguistic laws in Valencia are similar to those of the other communities with their own languages; however, not only is there less commitment to the language from the Valencia Parliamentary representatives, but there is also a reactionary current that rejects the classification of Valencian as a dialect of Catalan and seeks to establish linguistic independence – an aim that is difficult to justify but which represents a great obstacle for the promotion of the language, due to the challenges that it provokes. The language is present in the educational system, although in a different way than in Catalonia and the Balearic Islands. In Valencia, families can choose between a system of primary education primarily or exclusively in Spanish or a system with a strong presence of Catalan/Valencian.

As we have seen in the statistics offered above, the population's knowledge of the language is slightly lower than in Catalonia and the Balearic Islands. Additionally, the presence of the regional language in the universities of Valencia is considerably lower than in the universities of the other Catalan-speaking communities: Catalan is present in around 15% of the classes at the Univerisity of Castellon, slightly less at the University of Valencia, and is scarcely witnessed in the others.

Galicia (2,700,000)

Although Catalonia has historically been a highly developed region, which has led to the prestige of its language, Galicia has traditionally been an underdeveloped region in which emigration was obligatory for a large part of the population. Under such conditions the Galician language seemed tied to poverty and ignorance, and social ascent began with the renunciation of Galician and the adoption of Spanish. Since the transition to democracy in the 1970s, this situation has somewhat changed. Galicia has been on the path of economic development and the Galician language has benefited from the change. Although the region's government has not been politically nationalistic, it has promoted the use of the language in the media and in education.

As illustrated by the data above, the percentage of the population with knowledge of the language is even higher than in Catalonia. The reason for this is easy to deduce: in Catalonia more than a third of the population was born outside Catalonia, or to parents who were born outside Catalonia and whose first language is Spanish. In Galicia the reverse is true; immigration has been minimal, and emigration has been predominant.

Despite this difference, the public presence of the Catalan language in Catalonia is far superior than that of Galician in Galicia, as illustrated by the example of university education. At the University of Santiago, the Galician university most committed to the regional language and culture, only around 10% of classes are taught in Galician. In the other two major Galician universities, those of Coruña and Lugo, the presence of Galician is scarcely worth mentioning.

The Basque Country (2,100,000)

The laws for Linguistic Policies in the Basque Country are highly similar to those of Catalonia and the other regions with neo-Latin languages discussed thus far, but the situation is completely different. In the other communities, a large part of the population has continued to use the regional language but also knows Spanish, whereas in the Basque Country the regional language, Basque or *euskera*, has remained isolated within largely monolingual populations in determined areas, while in the rest of the territory the population is largely monolingual in Spanish. The data on the population's knowledge of the Basque language illustrate this trend. Under these circumstances the first priority should be to increase the knowledge of Basque by means of the educational system. This project has already been undertaken in two ways. There is a network of schools, called *ikastoles*, which take in children from Spanish-speaking families and provide linguistic immersion, using Basque as the primary language of education. There are also public schools that use Spanish has the primary language of education, but offer Basque language classes and, as much as possible, other instruction in Basque. In addition to those measures for school-aged children, there are programmes of intensive Basque instruction for adults. The existence of Basque media, among them a television channel that broadcasts exclusively in Basque, helps to increase the presence of the language, and includes efforts such as an educational Basque language programme for adults.

The other indicator that we have used so far, the use of the language at the university level, has also been modified in the context of the Basque Country. Given that it cannot be assumed that the majority of the students understand the Basque language, is has been necessary to establish parallel tracks in Spanish, sometimes in separate centres. Although there exist some undergraduate institutions where education is exclusively in Basque, in the majority of cases the different university departments have established Basque educational programmes alongside academic classes given in Spanish, so that the students can choose the language in which they receive their education. Currently, around a quarter of university classes are available in Basque.

Navarre (500,000)

The area in which Basque has been maintained in Navarre is even smaller than that of the Basque country, and the linguistic policies of Navarre establish the co-officiality of the two languages only in this area. In Navarre, unlike the Basque country, Basque nationalists have never been a presence in the regional government, which explains the lower level of attention to the language. In the time since the linguistic laws were passed, the government of Navarre has sensitively increased its attention to the Basque language and it is now present to some extent in the school system, including through the establishment of several *ikastoles*. Notwithstanding this, the level of knowledge and public use of the Basque language is minimal, as is shown clearly in the statistics at the beginning of this section.

The languages of immigrants

To the linguistic diversity already present in the school systems of the officially bilingual communities, one must add the ever-increasing numbers of students who come to school speaking a foreign language.

Spain has traditionally been an emigrant country, but in recent years this tendency has been inverted and now a great number of immigrants from underdeveloped countries come to Spain in search of an improved standard of living. As a result of this recent wave of immigration, nearly 10% of the Spanish population is of foreign origin: from Morocco, Sub-Saharan Africa, Eastern Europe, South America, China, and so on. The proportion of foreign residents varies greatly throughout the Autonomous Communities and reaches its height in Madrid and in Catalonia. Because these immigrants include children, and because the birth rate among foreigners is greater than among native Spaniards, the presence of immigrants in the public schools reaches, in many cases, around 15% of the student body, and, in extreme cases, more than 50%. Frequently, the immigrants attending a single school come from diverse backgrounds and speak different languages. This is a well-documented problem in many European countries; however, in the case of Catalonia and the other Autonomous Communities with their own languages, it is aggravated by the fact that these immigrants, except for those of South American origin, have to familiarise themselves with not one, but two new languages.

Among the Autonomous Communities, this problem is most grave in Catalonia, because the educational system is completely bilingual and because the number of immigrants is the highest. Many efforts have been dedicated to resolving the problem, both with methods that facilitate the learning of Catalan and also by producing informative material that familiarises teachers with the most common characteristics of the different languages spoken by immigrant students.

An influx of immigrants from underdeveloped countries is common in many countries in Western Europe; however, in certain parts of Spain, specifically on the Mediterranean coast, the Balearic and Canary Islands, there has been another important current of immigration, less common in other places, comprised of European citizens from countries like Germany, the UK, Holland, and so on, who establish second residences that, in practice, become primary residences. This has meant the presence of students of these nationalities, who arrive at school speaking only the languages of their home countries. These students, like the rest, must learn the language or languages of the community in school, although, unlike those immigrants from underdeveloped regions, they tend to speak languages that have a high level of social prestige.

Acquisition of Foreign Languages

Added to this panorama of linguistic diversity in the school system, there is a mounting pressure to promote the acquisition of foreign languages during the period of obligatory education. As in the rest of Europe, secondary education in Spain – given this name for its role of preparing students for entry into university – traditionally included instruction in Latin, and sometimes Greek, as the bases of classical culture. Throughout the 19th century, the pressure to learn classical languages decreased in tandem with an increased interest in 'living' foreign language, most notably French. In certain regions, such as Catalonia, the knowledge of French extended beyond the university context and was considered part of being a generally cultured person.

As noted at the beginning of this section, today, as in the mid-20th century, there is a rapidly increasing interest in learning foreign languages, which has provoked a greater focus on languages in education. Even before this surge, the authorities of the European Union insisted that citizens of the Union should know two languages besides their own, a proposal that, in the case of bilingual communities, signifies the knowledge of four languages. The available data indicate that the reality is still far from this ideal and that in Spain, and in the Southern European countries in general, the population's knowledge of foreign languages is far less than in Northern countries (with the sole exception of the UK, where this knowledge is also minimal).

Despite the initial delay, the current pressure to learn foreign languages is very strong, and one indicator of the attention to this issue is that in certain Autonomous Communities, specifically those that could be considered the most dynamic – the Basque country, Madrid, and Catalonia – the past two years have seen the introduction of experimental programmes introducing English in the preschool years, through different methods of immersion; this means that within a certain period of time these regions will be able to use English as a language of instruction, beyond simply teaching the language, and as part of a plan for genuinely bilingual education (or, to be more exact in the case of Catalonia or the Basque Country, trilingual education).

As one might imagine, this project is difficult to carry out and even more difficult to generalise throughout the entire educational system. Currently there is an excess of superfluous French teachers, but there is a lack of English language teachers, and an even greater lack of teachers capable of teaching other academic subjects in English.

Research on Bilingualism and Bilingual Education

The abundance of bilingual and multilingual situations in Spain, and the ensuing importance of bilingual and multilingual education, explains the great interest that has been awoken in the study of childhood language acquisition and bilingual education, and has sparked considerable research activity among Spanish scholars. In the following, an attempt is made to summarise the main characteristics of the principal lines of research in these fields.

One might, without exaggeration, situate the beginning of this heightened interest in language development in Barcelona in 1977, at a meeting of the Society of Scientific Psychology of the French Language that was dedicated to the origin of child language (at which I gave a presentation entitled 'From gesture to language', proposing a genetic interpretation of both). After that point, a research group dedicated to the topic was formed at the University of Barcelona, with a genetic orientation and influenced by Vigotsky. Soon after, other researchers took positions closer to cognitivism and functionalism. Years later, the book *La Adquisición del lenguaje* ['The Acquisition of Language'], by Serra, Serrat, Solé, Bel and Aparici, published in 2000, reflected the activity of this Barcelona nucleus quite nicely. In other parts of Spain, independently from the Barcelona current, efforts were under way to empirically describe the acquisition of language, best illustrated by the pioneering work by López Ornat, *La adquisición de la española* ['The Acquisition of

Spanish']. It was, however, specifically in those territories with languages other than Spanish and where, as a result, children were in contact with two languages, where the study of language development awoke the greatest interest. One of the first manifestations of this interest was the meeting in Santiago de Compostella in 1995, the results of which can be found in Perez Pereira (ed.) *Estudios sobre la adquisicion castellano, catalan, euskera y gallego* ['Studies on the acquisition of Spanish, Catalan, Euskera, and Galician']. Even before that, meetings were held in other places and an association had been created linking scholars throughout Spain with interest in the topic.

The study of language acquisition in children who are exposed to two languages asks, among other questions, whether children are able to separate their two linguistic systems from the beginning, or whether they treat them as a single system during a certain initial period. Because Spanish, Catalan, and Galician are all romance languages, which are highly similar with regard to lexis and especially syntax, it has been difficult to determine an answer to this question with data from subjects learning these languages. The opposite has occurred with those children who are in contact with Basque and Spanish at the same time. One study with many participants, led by Meisel (1994), *The Acquisition of Basque and Spanish by Bilingual Children*, clearly showed that children maintain two separate systems from the beginning of acquisition. Idiazabal, who participated in that same study, noted that if children have two clearly different syntactic systems, the knowledge that they acquire with regards to specific language use – in different personal situations, to achieve certain purposes – is easily transferred from one language to another.

Of course, whether or not a child is able to acquire two different linguistic structures and keep them separate is quite a different question from whether or not the child *realises* that he or she is in possession of two different but equivalent systems, and is able to communicate the same meanings with both languages; arguably, it is precisely this latter ability that makes him or her a bilingual, and capable of translation. Observations (Siguan & Vila, 1987; Vila & Siguan, 1998) of children growing up in contact with both Catalan and Castilian in different contexts indicate that during a first stage a child may know what, for us, is the same word in Catalan and Castilian and yet which has different meanings for the child; that is, because children have learned these words in different contexts, they may resist considering the words equivalents. It appears, however, that at the moment in which they accept the equivalence they generalise this transferability and quickly become capable of asking for the translation of any word in the other language. One might say that there is a specific moment in which these children become aware that they have two equivalent systems.

Although the theoretical debate over the separation of languages in bilingual acquisition has been focused on morpho-syntactic and lexical elements, it is important to mention that a bilingual child whose languages have clear phonetic differences is able to perceive these very early on. Bosch and Sebastián-Gallés (2001) have shown that children as young as 3 months of age react with greater attention to the sounds of their mother tongue, so that, for example, children who are raised in Catalan-speaking families pay greater attention to the phonemes of this language, and not to the Spanish language, whereas for children raised in Spanish-speaking families the reverse is true. Those children who are raised in bilingual families show interest in phonemes from both languages, seemingly without confusing or mixing the two. We are led to assume, then, that children raised in bilingual environments are able to separate their two linguistic systems from very early on based on their phonetic differences.

Research on bilingual education began even before the study of bilingual language acquisition. When General Franco was still in power, the Institute of Educational Sciences at the University of Barcelona took advantage of a relative permissiveness in the final years of the regime regarding the use of other languages in education, and led an experimental bilingual education project. Shortly after, in 1974, a seminar was held to present and discuss the results obtained. Since then, this seminar, entitled 'Languages and Education', has met regularly – first annually, and now biannually – and the material presented at each session has been compiled and edited into various volumes. The seminar quickly became a meeting point for all those in Spain who were formulating bilingual education initiatives.

Among the different studies presented in these seminars, some of the most significant were those that found that children from Spanish-speaking families who received Catalan classes throughout the length of their educational careers were easily able to understand Catalan, but encountered difficulties in speaking, whereas it was only after Catalan was used as the primary language of instruction in other academic subjects that these students were able to develop their oral competence. It has been necessary to provide experimental evidence that linguistic immersion models, in which Catalan or Basque become the primary vehicular languages of education, are feasible and effective and do not endanger the scholastic success of those students who come from families with different linguistic backgrounds.

Finally, concern over the early introduction of foreign languages, principally English, into the educational system has posed the question of whether or not this might produce an excessive linguistic burden, or whether it would be better to abandon one of the two community languages. Different research (Sanz, 2005) has indicated, however, that this concern is unfounded, and that early bilingual education does not obstruct, but actually facilitates, the early acquisition of English.

To finish this overview of the research inspired by the linguistic diversity of Spain, it is important to note that the official recognition of languages other than Spanish has not only led to linguistic policies designed to protect these languages, but has also provoked periodic censuses to obtain data on the linguistic characteristics of the population, including a large number of polls, diverse in nature, that have led to a flourishing branch of sociolinguistic studies. It is no exaggeration to say that Spain, specifically those Autonomous Communities with their own languages, is an exceptional terrain for research on bilingualism, as evidenced by the book that you hold in your hands.

References

Bosch, L. and Sebastián-Gallés, N. (2001) Early language differentiation in bilingual infants. In J. Cenoz and F. Genesee (eds) *Trends in Bilingual Acquisition* (pp. 71–93). Amsterdam: John Benjamins.

Lagasabaster, D. and Huguet, A. (eds) (2006) *Multilingualism in European Bilingual Contexts. Language Use and Attitudes*. Clevedon, UK: Multilingual Matters.

Sanz, C. (ed.) (2005) *Adult Second Language Acquisition. Methods, Theory, and Practice*. Washington: Georgetown University Press.

Siguan, M. (1992) *España plurilingüe*. Madrid: Alianza Editorial (*Multilingual Spain*. Amsterdam, Sweets & Zeitlinger).

Siguan, M. (1998) *La escuela y los inmigrantes*. Barcelona: Paidós.

Siguan, M. (1999) *Conocimiento y uso de las lenguas*. Madrid: CIS (Centro de Investigaciones Sociológicas).

Siguan, M. (2001) *Bilingüismo y lenguas en contacto*. Madrid: Alianza Editorial.

Siguan, M. and Vila, I. (1987) Bilingüismo y educación. In A. Alvarez (ed.) *Psicología y Educación: realizaciones y tendencias actuales en la investigación y en la práctica: actas de las II Jornadas Internacionales de Psicología y Educación*. Madrid: Centro de Publicaciones del MEC/Visor.

Turell, M.T. (2001) *Multilingualism in Spain. Sociolinguistic and Psycholinguistic Aspects of Linguistic Minority Groups*. Clevedon, UK: Multilingual Matters.

Vila, I. (2000) Inmigración, educación y lengua propia. In *La inmigración extranjera en España. Los retos educativos* (pp. 145–166). Barcelona: Fundación La Caixa.

Vila, I. and Siguan, M. (1998) *Bilingüisme i educació*. Barcelona: Proa.

Chapter 1
Issues in the Acquisition of Two or More Languages in Multilingual Environments

CARMEN PÉREZ-VIDAL, MARIA JUAN-GARAU
and AURORA BEL

Introduction

This book is about children and young people becoming bilingual or multilingual in the context of multicultural Spain. The eleven chapters present a series of studies of the acquisition of the different official languages in Spain (Spanish, Catalan, Basque and Galician), and also a representative sample of the languages of several communities, both European and non-European. As a whole, the studies seek to address the central issues in bilingual and trilingual language acquisition, focusing on different linguistic phenomena and language levels. The objective of this chapter is to provide the reader with an overview of the main issues in the field and the different angles of analysis in the studies that follow.

Definitions and Challenges

Contrary to what is often believed, bi- or multilingualism seems to be the norm in numerous parts of the world. According to the web version of *The Ethnologue* (Gordon, 2005), over 6000 different languages are spoken in roughly 160 nation states, and it is estimated that almost half of the world's population is functionally bilingual. These facts help explain the current research interest in both the benefits and challenges of growing up multilingual, and why this phenomenon has been approached from a variety of perspectives, linguistic, psychological, and sociological (see Wei *et al.*, 2002, for a review).

In the different accounts of bilingualism (and multilingualism), many definitions are deemed necessary. Among these is the rather idealistic characterisation of a bilingual as someone who is fully competent in two languages. A more pragmatic definition, however, might simply describe someone who can function in two languages according to given needs (Bialystok, 2001), and indeed it seems that in many cases, bilinguals do not necessarily feel equally at ease in each of their languages or in every domain, and may use them differently depending on interlocutors, communicative contexts, or other factors. A further layer of definitions deals with categorising different types of bilingual acquisition, generally based on the age at which the languages are acquired. Infant acquisition of two languages is known as *simultaneous* bilingual acquisition, or bilingual first language acquisition (BFLA), and tends to be defined as the exposure to two languages from birth. When one of the languages is acquired from birth and the other at a later stage, the phenomenon is defined as *successive* bilingual acquisition, or bilingual second language acquisition (BSLA). Recent empirical evidence suggests that if bilingual acquisition begins before approximately five years of age, the course of acquisition often appears indistinguishable from BFLA (Meisel, 2004). In the present volume, Part 1 is devoted to studies of BFLA and Part 2 to cases of BSLA in different kinds of formal instructional (FI) settings, ranging from nursery to university.

A final level of definitions in bilingual acquisition relates to whether a bilingual child receives comparable amounts of input (and produces comparable amounts of output) in both languages, thereby becoming a *balanced bilingual*, or whether the child receives substantially more input (and produces substantially more output) in one language than in the other, thereby becoming a *dominant*, or *unbalanced, bilingual*. In this respect, the vision we would like to offer in this book is that the contrast between balanced and unbalanced bilingualism cannot be defined in terms of *degrees of competence* but rather in terms of *differences in profiles*. Indeed, even in cases of simultaneous balanced bilingualism, although Genesee (2003) has observed that bilingual children's strategies are not really different from those of monolingual children acquiring their first language, a number of researchers have shown that those 'balanced' bilinguals differ somewhat from monolingual native speakers. Furthermore, when analysing successive bilingualism, even when L2 learners reach a degree of competence at which their usage may be comparable to that of native speakers, their knowledge of the language is not exactly equivalent. In other words, there is a specific nature of bilingual or multilingual development that has inspired concepts such as 'multicompetence'

(Cook, 2002). This notion recognises that a multilingual speaker's first language competence is different from that of a monolingual peer, and indicates the dangers of using a 'native-speaker' standard in SLA research. This is compatible with a holistic view of multilingualism, like that proposed by Grosjean (1994, 2004).

As for concerns about the challenges of establishing bilingualism, a standing issue has been whether bi/multilingual acquisition affects *cognitive development*, positively or negatively and whether, in the latter case, there is evidence of developmental disadvantages for bilingual children in comparison to monolingual children. Despite negative theories proposed at the onset of the 20th century, there is abundant research nowadays showing that bilingual and monolingual children follow parallel paths, and that bilingual children do not show signs of cognitive delay. Early attempts to attribute the relative underachievement of bilinguals to interference or fossilisation (Peal & Lambert, 1962) have been contrasted with later attempts by Cummins (1979) to explain contradictory evidence of the effects of bilingualism on cognitive and linguistic development (through the Threshold Hypothesis and the model of Common Underlying Proficiency, Basic Interpersonal Cognitive Skills, and Cognitive Academic Language Proficiency) as recently revisited by Baker and Hornberger (2001). Indeed, many studies dealing with bilingualism over past years have tried to provide an answer to the crucial question of how bi- or multilingual children's progress in each of their languages compares to monolingual norms. According to Meisel (2004), comparisons between monolinguals and bilinguals can accomplish a two-fold aim. On the one hand, they can help to dismiss alleged problems frequently associated with child bilingualism. On the other, they present an opportunity to explain the capacity for multilingualism within theoretical language frameworks. The study of bilingual children offers an excellent chance to investigate general and language-specific mechanisms during the acquisition process, and to explore whether and how two developing linguistic systems interact with one another; furthermore, bilingual children provide an ideal backdrop to investigate the cognitive and social factors that may affect the acquisition process (Meisel, 1989; De Houwer, 1990). For these reasons, studies of bilingual children have proved important in validating theories of monolingual first language acquisition. Recent studies have also revealed that bilingualism has a significant impact on a speaker's ability to selectively attend to relevant information (Costa *et al.*, 2007). Similarly, the advantages for bilingual children as far as cognitive flexibility are reported by Viberg (2001). This type of advantage is discussed in the studies in Part 1 of this volume, which draws comparisons between monolingual and bilingual children (in carrying out such comparisons, of course, one must not lose sight of Grosjean's (1989) caveat that 'the bilingual is not two monolinguals in one person'). Overall, no major differences are found between these two groups, although some of the studies report performance differences in certain areas, often reflecting exposure patterns, and certain advantages for bilinguals. In Part 2, additional advantages for bilinguals with regard to the acquisition of a third language are reported.

Finally, in each part of the book the studies consistently address the input patterns relevant to the language acquisition taking place, and it is felt that, as a general rule, the *one person, one language strategy* may promote balanced bilingualism, which in turn may eventually provide the best conditions for functioning in two or more languages in a larger variety of contexts. Moreover, it is suggested that by keeping languages separate in the input, parents and caretakers make it easier for the child to keep their two linguistic systems separate and to avoid mixing, two issues that we will now address in greater detail.

Central Themes in the Field

There are three questions that have attracted the special attention of researchers interested in bilingual acquisition, including those whose work is represented in this volume. The first one, as Meisel (2004: 95) describes, revolves around whether people growing up in bi/multilingual environments acquire the languages they are exposed to as separate systems. The second involves the impact of the linguistic *context* in which such acquisition takes place, and the third addresses the extent to which mixing may be the result of the first two factors.

Language separation

According to Baker (2006: 98), in order to acquire two languages successfully from birth, babies need to be able to differentiate them and to store them effectively, thus developing two different capacities. With regard to differentiation, infants' ability to discriminate between languages reportedly starts very early on in development, and possibly even before birth. Maneva and Genesee (2002), for example, have shown that a child raised with two languages from birth may show evidence in the pre-linguistic stage of language-specific babbling patterns, as well as a tendency to babble in the stronger language. The fact that bilingual children normally exhibit a certain amount of mixing in their language production has led some scholars to question these children's capacity to initially keep their two language systems separate. However, closer examination of young bilinguals' mixing has revealed that children as young as two-and-a-half years of age do not just *mix* languages randomly, but rather are *code-switching* in much the same way as adult bilinguals do – pragmatically adjusting their language choices to the interlocutor and the communicative context. With regard to language storage, a review of the early research on the storage of two languages in the developing bilingual mind shows that, until the mid-1980s, BFLA was characterised by theories postulating an initial period during which children form a single (fused/mixed) language system – with a single lexicon and grammar – until they eventually succeed in separating their two systems. This position was known as the unitary or single-system hypothesis and was defended most notably by Volterra and Taeschner (1978), who drew from and were supported by other researchers (Leopold, 1970; Redlinger & Park, 1980; Saunders, 1982; Swain, 1977; Taeschner, 1983; Vihman, 1985). More recent research on this issue, however, has provided a wealth of evidence in favour of a dual-system hypothesis, and made a convincing argument that, 'the languages of the bilingual child are represented in underlying differentiated ways' (Genesee 2001: 158), at least from the moment that productive use of morphology and syntax begins (e.g. De Houwer, 1990; Genesee, 1989; Juan-Garau & Pérez-Vidal, 2000; Lanza, 1997; Meisel, 1989). In this scenario, the study of cross-linguistic influence has come to the forefront, as it can clarify the extent to which bilingual children acquire their two languages autonomously (i.e. in ways that are not qualitatively different from the monolingual acquisition of each language), or interdependently, which would entail essential differences between monolingual and bilingual development.

Two of the chapters in Part 1 of this volume address the question of language separation in BFLA by focusing on grammatical phenomena that are formally different in the subjects' two target languages. Liceras *et al.* (Chapter 5, this volume) examine the null subject parameter to see whether the distribution of subject pronouns in their Spanish data shows evidence of interference from English. Their results clearly point to the existence of two separate systems in the bilingual. Álvarez (Chapter 7, this volume) provides one of the few studies that explore the interaction of a bilingual's two languages in the later stages of acquisition, once core grammar has been established. The author investigates the degree of autonomy or interdependence of her subject's two developing referential systems and finds that they appear to evolve separately.

Context of acquisition

With regard to the second central issue, recent research on bilingualism and multilingualism has paid increasing attention to the contexts in which languages are acquired and used, because the familial, educational and social contexts in which SLA takes place have been seen to have a bearing on acquisition outcomes (Siegel, 2003).

In cases of early child bi- and multilingualism, when parents speak more than one language there is the possibility of choosing which language(s) to use with the child. This element of choice is what Piller (2001) refers to as private language planning. Nevertheless, many couples' language choices are not consciously made (Piller, 2002). Subconscious and spontaneous decisions are often made at both general and specific levels (Pavlenko, 2004). Parents' language choices may be affected by a myriad of factors including their preferred identity, attitude to languages, expected benefits, extended family and friends, and their children's own preferences (Tuominen, 1999). Emotions have also been considered influential (Pavlenko, 2004). A common strategy among parents has been to keep the two languages separate by adhering to the 'one-parent-one-language' approach mentioned in the first section, with each parent consistently speaking a different language to the child (see Barron-Hauwert, 2004). Mixed patterns of exposure, however, where one or both parents speak both languages to the children, are also common (Romaine, 1995). Finally, sometimes parents exclusively use the minority (i.e. non-community) language, leaving the child to acquire the majority language formally or informally outside the home (Deuchar & Quay, 2000). Of these three types of exposure, the use of mixed language with children has generally been less positively regarded than the other two strategies. In addition to the language that parents use with a child, many other factors are considered to play an important role in language acquisition, including the language parents use with one another, the language choices of siblings and caretakers, and environmental influences such as neighbours and friends, extended family, mass media, nursery school (Baker, 2006).

In Part 1 of this volume, Barnes (Chapter 3, this volume) provides a case study of a child (1;11–3;6) in the Basque country who is consistently addressed in three languages from birth: English from her mother, Basque from her father, and Spanish from her caretaker. It is thus a case of family trilingualism, which is far less common than trilingualism achieved through schooling (Baker, 2006). Other studies have approached trilingualism in the Basque country from the educational and sociolinguistic perspective (e.g. Cenoz, 2004; Etxeberría, 2004; Lasagabaster, 2000). Liceras *et al.* (Chapter 5, this volume) present another longitudinal study, in this case of bilingual English/Spanish twins (1;1–6;3) raised in a monolingual-Spanish social context. As in Barnes' contribution, the parents follow a systematic one-person-one-language policy, a pattern that is also present for the Spanish/English subject of study in Álvarez (Chapter 7, this volume). Pérez-Pereira and Barreña *et al.* (Chapters 2 and 4, this volume, respectively), on the other hand, include cross-sectional data from familial bilingual and monolingual contexts in Galicia and the Basque country respectively. In Pérez-Pereira's study, most of the bilingual children (0;8–2;6) come from Spanish-Galician- speaking families that either followed the one-parent-one-language approach or mixed languages. Barreña *et al.* concentrate on two features of parental input: the degree to which a given language is present in the child's immediate environment and the parents' knowledge of each language. Finally, in Chapter 6, the perspective on acquisition contexts widens, as Sanz-Torrent *et al.* study six Catalan-Spanish early successive bilinguals with diagnosed specific language impairment (SLI) over a three-year span (ages 3 to 6), the majority of whom have Spanish as their family language, with Catalan present in their preschool and re-education environment.

Part 2 considers bi- and multilingual acquisition in instructional or formal including immersion bilingual education, mainstreaming/submersion, and mainstreaming with conventional foreign language instruction. One of the contributions in this section also deals with the university Stay Abroad (SA) context.

The contemporary forms of bilingual education established in the 1950s and 1960s have become increasingly popular and more geographically widespread over the years. Bilingual education refers to education in which two languages (or sometimes more than two) are used as the medium of instruction. There is an additional distinction, as addressed by Baker (2006), between *strong* and *weak* forms of bilingual education (see also Skutnabb-Kangas, 2000); the former aim at additive bilingualism (i.e. the acquisition and maintenance of both languages), biliteracy and biculturalism, and the latter do not explicitly work towards such outcomes. Among strong bilingual education programmes, the term *bilingual immersion* applies to language programmes where at least 50% of the curricular content is taught using the L2 (for a characterisation of immersion programmes, see Swain & Johnson, 1997; Swain & Lapkin, 2005). Research evidence has attested to the effectiveness of immersion bilingual education on eventual L2 competence (e.g. Johnstone, 2002;

Swain & Johnson, 1997); that is, immersion students generally succeed in gaining competence in a second language at no cost to their L1 or other curricular areas. Two of the chapters in the present volume report on children in immersion programmes. Llinares García study (Chapter 8) draws on classroom speech data from a number of five-year-old Spanish-speaking children living in Madrid and learning English as an L2 in a total immersion programme, with only one hour of Spanish per day. This chapter analyses task types that can make classroom settings resemble natural contexts of L2 acquisition.

Mainstreaming and mainstreaming with foreign language teaching are included among the weak forms of bilingual education (Baker, 2006). In mainstreaming, or submersion education, children who speak minority languages are placed in L2 mainstream classes without L1 support. The main goal of mainstreaming is the assimilation of children with minority languages, especially in immigration situations. In this instruction context, dealing with an undeveloped language may prove difficult for children and teachers alike (Carrasquillo & Rodríguez, 2002; Skutnabb-Kangas, 2000). In Chapter 9, Serrat *et al.* analyse speech data from immigrant children with L1 Soninke, Tagalog or Chinese who are learning Catalan as an L2 in Catalonia, where both Catalan and Spanish are official languages. These children attend Catalan-speaking public schools following a curricular model for children from immigrant communities; however, Catalan is scarcely present in their familial and social environments. In mainstreaming with foreign language teaching, on the other hand, the L1 is the medium of instruction and the L2 is the subject of classroom study. In this context, the emphasis is on language learning rather than the learning of other academic content. As Lotherington (2006: 711) notes, 'Exposure to the L2 is limited in this model, and traditionally focused on form rather than meaning'. Consequently, enrichment tends to be limited as well. The acquisition of English (L3) through formal instruction is tackled by Sanz (Chapter 10, this volume) and Gutierrez and García Mayo (Chapter 12, this volume), with Catalan/Spanish and Basque/Spanish students in immersion programmes in their respective communities. Finally, Mora (Chapter 11, this volume) contrasts content-based EFL formal instruction in the home university (see Pérez-Vidal & Campanale-Grilloni, 2005) with a Stay Abroad (SA) in an English-speaking country. The SA context allows L2 learners to take part in linguistic exchanges, often embedded in target culture situations and involving interaction with native speakers, and the classroom context induces learners to attend to form with the goal of improving their linguistic expertise. Although the acquisition of an L2 during a SA has been compared and contrasted to instruction in the home country (e.g. Collentine & Freed, 2004), no conclusive evidence has yet been presented supporting the advantages of SA over formal at-home contexts for all students, language levels, and language skills (see DeKeyser, 2007).

Language transfer/cross-linguistic influence

The term 'cross-linguistic influence' was coined in the 1980s by Kellerman and Sharwood-Smith (1986: 1) to refer to Contrastive Analysis, transfer, interference, or language mixing in the two languages of a bilingual speaker. In the past decade, the study of language mixing in bilingual acquisition underwent a shift in focus, and the inevitability of interaction, in the form of mixing, between the two otherwise independently developing linguistic systems of a bilingual child came to be accepted (Cenoz et al., 2001; Groot & Kroll, 1997; Larsen-Freeman & Long, 1991; Odlin, 2003). Prior to this new outlook, particularly for the proponents of the unitary hypothesis (see section 'Language separation' on p. 21), mixing by bilingual children was regarded as failure to separate the two linguistic systems and, consequently, it was viewed differently from adult mixing. Now, within the perspective of the dual-system hypothesis, mixing, although labelled 'inappropriate language', is viewed as the result of choice, just as adult mixing, prompted by various linguistic and sociolinguistic factors. Proposed causes of mixing include the features of semantic domain (De Houwer, 1990), patterns of input difference (Genesee, 1989), relief strategy (i.e. unavailability of an item) (Saunders, 1988), a Gap Filling Hypothesis (as defined by Sanz-Torrent et al. in this volume); and caretaker discourse patterns (Juan-Garau & Pérez-Vidal, 2001; Lanza, 1992).

When analysing mixing, scholars have focused not only on the possible causes, but also on the strings and levels of mixing, and certain constraints and patterns have been identified. Meisel (1994: 414), for example, draws a *de facto* distinction between intrasentential and intersentential mixing, the former consisting of linguistic units from two syntactic systems mixed within a sentence (also called code-mixing, CM), and the latter (code-switching, CS) consisting of the same phenomenon but across sentence boundaries. In CM, phonemes, free morphemes and bound morphemes, syntactic patterns and lexis of one language – typically the weaker one in unbalanced bilingualism – appear in the other language, although subject to systematic constraints. With regard to these constraints, the discussion has revolved around identifying the boundaries of mixed strings. Research has also focused on different degrees of mixing, and whether function words and grammatical words are mixed, presenting sound evidence for a U-shaped model of mixing (Köppe & Meisel, 1995; Pérez-Vidal, 1998: 197; Vihman, 1985: 317). Finally, as Vihman explains: '[mixing] may increase again, once the child has acquired sufficient knowledge in order to use adult-like code-switching [...] a step forward in metalinguistic pragmatic sophistication'. In spite of certain patterns observed, however, the reasons for mixing remain difficult to establish, as high rates of individual variability for this phenomenon impede easy generalisations.

Several chapters in this book address the issues of mixing and crosslinguistic influence as part of larger studies. Sanz-Torrent et al.'s (Chapter 6, this volume) data from Catalan-Spanish bilingual SLI children shows that they do not follow a different code-mixing pattern than average bilinguals, nor mix in higher degrees. Insertions contain borrowings of phonology, lexis and regularisation patterns mostly from Spanish into Catalan, the majority language at school where data have been collected. This study has the additional interest of dealing with two typologically similar languages, Catalan and Spanish. Álvarez's study of Spanish-English development of narratives (Chapter 7, this volume) finds a developmental pattern in the pragmatics of space reference, which she characterises as the 'in-between style' of narrating, particularly with respect to verbs of movement, and which appears to hinder predicted development. Serrat et al. (Chapter 9, this volume) analyse data from children in Catalonia acquiring Catalan along with Tagalog, Soninke and Chinese to investigate morphological transfer in both nominal and verbal phrases, and find evidence of different developmental patterns from those found in monolinguals. Mora (Chapter 11, this volume) reflects on the interaction between a group of Catalan-Spanish bilinguals' phonetic subsystems within a single phonological space, and the nature of the resulting phonetic categories reflecting the input received in English in two different contexts of acquisition, FI and SA. Finally, Gutierrez and García Mayo's results from Basque/Spanish learners of EFL (Chapter 12, this volume) indicate that both UG and the learners' first languages interact with the L3 acquired through formal instruction.

With specific regard to bilinguals' acquisition of third languages – a phenomenon that has been explored in several recent publications (e.g. Cenoz et al., 2001; Herdina & Jessner, 2002) – the initial findings seem to point to bidirectionality as a distinct feature of influence between a speaker's several languages, and the relevance of typological distance, L2 status, recency, context and proficiency. In this vein, Sanz

(Chapter 10, this volume) finds that the order of acquisition of her subjects' majority and minority languages (Catalan and Spanish, respectively) has no significant impact on their L3 competence (as developed through FI), yet that there is a positive relationship between the ability to read and write in both languages and the more efficient development of L3 structural knowledge.

Having reviewed the central issues in the field, let us now turn to specific linguistic phenomena that have attracted the attention of the scholars represented in this volume.

Linguistic Phenomena

In SLA research, attempts to explain bilingual and multilingual acquisition have been characterised by several different *approaches*. Most of the chapters in this volume use descriptive, communicative or psychological approaches in order to account for both internal and external factors in linguistic development. Two of the chapters (5 and 12), however, use the perspectives of nativism and generative linguistics, focusing on internal factors to make predictions about universal and language-specific features of bilingual acquisition.

Lexis and phonology

One of the aspects of bilingual development that has attracted the most attention over the years is lexical acquisition. Research on this issue has addressed a number of crucial questions, including bilingual children's ability to keep their two lexicons separate and the size of bilinguals' receptive and productive vocabularies in comparison with those of matched monolinguals. Four of the chapters in this volume tackle these, and related, issues of lexical acquisition. To begin with, Pérez-Pereira's contribution (Chapter 2) sheds new light on the acquisition of Galician, and on Galician-Spanish bilingualism, two areas scantly research thus far. The author analyses the effects of this bilingualism on lexical comprehension and production. He also focuses on the relationships between measures of vocabulary development and different grammatical development scores in order to test Marchman *et al.*'s (2004) specificity hypothesis. Early lexical development has been found to correlate with the amount of exposure to each language (Huttenlocher *et al.*, 1991). Barreña *et al.* (Chapter 4, this volume) examine different levels of exposure to Basque input as well as parental linguistic competence in that language as factors directly influencing children's acquisition of Basque lexical items; a threshold value is suggested for the degree of language exposure required to ensure monolingual-like development. Álvarez (Chapter 7) discusses the lexical items used to encode references to space, including motion/posture verbs, prepositions, particles, and certain adjectives and adverbials. Research has found young children to be sensitive to the lexicalisation patterns of their native language, and Álvarez's study provides further insight into this question by showing how differences in the lexicalisation patterns of motion events in Spanish and English affect the development of her bilingual subjects' two languages.

As regards the other level of linguistic analysis, phonology, one chapter in the book deals with phonological development from a specific standpoint. Indeed, although recent research on the effect of study abroad on the acquisition of L2 phonology has focused on native speakers of English learning Spanish, Mora (Chapter 11) tackles this issue from the inverse perspective. SA learners' ability to approximate the target norms for specific measures such as voice onset time for voiceless stops (Díaz-Campos, 2004; Stevens, 2001) has been compared to that of learners in domestic contexts. The results of such research have been mixed and have suggested the importance of considering not just learning context, but also individual learner factors and contact variables in order to account for differences in learners' pronunciation performance (Dufon & Churchill, 2006). Mora explores the differential effects of SA and FI contexts on the perceptual and productive phonological competence of a group of advanced L2 learners of English.

Syntax and morphology

Regarding bilingual grammatical acquisition, much attention has been paid to the study of syntactic and morphological development in relation to the differentiation process and cross-linguistic influence discussed in sections 'Language separation' on p. 21 and 'Language transfer' on p. 26. In comparing bilingual and monolingual development, research has shown that a good number of morphosyntactic phenomena observed in bilingual acquisition can be accommodated within analogous parameters of monolingual acquisition (see in particular Genesee & Nicoladis, 2006, or Meisel, 2004, for a review of the literature on bilingual development of word order, interrogatives, verbal affixes, and so on and Bel 2001). Previous studies of BFLA have shown that even though bilingual children's language systems develop separately at the morphosyntactic level (see DeHouwer, 1990), the possibility of the two languages influencing each other is not excluded, and there is contact between the two languages (Müller, 1998). For these authors, cross-linguistic influence is caused by structural aspects, and not by external factors such as language dominance. For instance, Paradis and Genesee (1996: 3) label this mutual influence 'interdependent development' and describe it as 'the systemic influence of the grammar of one language on the grammar of the other language during acquisition, causing differences in a bilingual's patterns or rates of development in comparison with those of a monolingual. Studying interdependence in Spanish-English bilingual acquisition in the specific domain of subject realisation, Paradis and Navarro (2003) attested to patterns of subject use in a child's Spanish that could be interpreted as due, to a certain extent, to the cross-linguistic influence of English. In Chapter 5 of this volume, Liceras *et al.* challenge the interpretation of Paradis and Navarro (2003) by arguing that if there were a cross-linguistic influence from English, Spanish data from bilinguals should contain a higher percentage of subject pronouns than the corresponding monolingual data. However, their study demonstrates that no transfer is found for this specific grammatical feature, which implies that, at least in this domain, the two grammars are kept separate. In Chapter 6, Sanz-Torrent *et al.* provide data from the acquisition of different syntactic categories (verbs, prepositions, pronouns and articles) by children with SLI, and show that the two languages (Catalan and Spanish) present similar deficits and that, in accordance with previous research (Genesee *et al.*, 2004), the development is not challenged by the language impairment. Chapter 9 by Serrat *et al.* addresses first language transfer at the morphological level of nominal and verbal categories, examining the Catalan and Spanish developing systems of immigrant children from different linguistic backgrounds. Finally, Gutierrez and García Mayo (Chapter 12) aim to explain the developmental path of bilingual Basque-Spanish learners' acquisition of long-distance *wh-* questions in English, a structure that differs in both first languages.

Discourse and pragmatics

In order to be 'competent' in two or more languages, speakers need knowledge not only of the vocabulary, syntax, morphology and phonology of each language, but also of how to use language appropriately in sociocultural contexts (Butler & Hakuta, 2004). The study of this pragmatic competence, and the aspects of language-specific discourse that embody it, has gained increasing prominence in bilingualism research, and is accordingly represented in this volume. The analysis carried out by Álvarez (Chapter 7) seeks to document the development of referential structures in the narrative discourse of a bilingual Spanish-English child from the ages of 6 to 11. Her subject must learn to construct narrative texts in accordance with the specific ways in which his two languages encode universal principles of text organisation. Using the well-known "Frog" re-telling task, Álvarez focuses on the developing use of person, time and reference at the discourse-syntax level of language growth. The linguistic forms used to refer to person, time and space are analysed as the specific discourse organisers that contribute to narrative cohesion. In Chapter 8, in a different vein, Llinares García examines the communicative functions, both mathetic and pragmatic, realised by 5-year-old Spanish learners of English as a foreign language. The author aims to identify the classroom tasks that are conducive to the most 'natural', functional, L2 production. The types of functions generated by different activities are analysed, with special attention paid to those activities that encourage the children's higher use of discourse initiations. The teacher's role in learners' functional production is also considered. Along similar lines, Barnes (Chapter 3, this volume) provides us with one of the very few studies that address the developing pragmatic competence of early bilinguals, specifically exploring the acquisition of the functional aspects of the interrogative in English by a small child, and finding that questions serve different pragmatic functions from an early age. Finally, Liceras *et al.* (Chapter 5, this volume) acknowledge the importance of taking into account the user's intended semantic/pragmatic effects in order to explain the distribution of null and overt subjects in pro-drop languages such as Spanish.

Conclusions

To anyone wanting to explore aspects of language acquisition, and specifically bilingual acquisition, this chapter should serve as a guide to link different topics to specific research designs, languages, phenomena and methods of analysis. To those who have an interest in the specific language combinations and phenomena studied in this volume, we hope that the background offered here, as well as that of the preface and introduction, will help place these studies in perspective. Finally, for the researcher acquainted with both the issues and the studies addressed here, we hope that viewing them as a whole may reveal a composite image: a portrait of the complex and multiple linguistic reality facing the young in the new multilingual Spain.

References

Baker, C. (2006) *Foundations of Bilingual Education and Bilingualism* (4th edn). Clevedon: Multilingual Matters.

Baker, C. and Hornberger, N.H. (2001) *An Introductory Reader to the Writings of Jim Cummins*. Clevedon: Multilingual Matters.
Barron-Hauwert, S. (2004) *Language Strategies for Bilingual Families. The One-Parent-One-Language Approach*. Clevedon: Multilingual Matters.
Bel, A. (2001) *Teoría lingüística i adquisició del llenguatge. Anàlisi comparada dels trets morfológics en català i en castellà. Premi Pompeu Fabra de Gramàtica 2000*. Barcelona: Institut d'Estudis Catalans, Biblioteca Filològica, XLIV.
Bialystok, E. (2001) *Bilingualism in Development: Language, Literacy, and Cognition*. New York: Cambridge University Press.
Butler, Y.G. and Hakuta, K. (2004) Bilingualism and second language acquisition. In T.K. Bathia and W.C. Ritchie (eds) *The Handbook of Bilingualism* (pp. 114–144). Oxford: Blackwell Publishing.
Carrasquillo, A.L. and Rodríguez, V. (2002) *Language Minority Students in the Mainstream Classroom* (2nd edn). Clevedon: Multilingual Matters.
Cenoz, J. (2004) Teaching English as a third language: The effect of attitudes and motivation. In C. Hoffman and J. Ytsma (eds) *Trilingualism in Family, School and Community* (pp. 202–218). Clevedon: Multilingual Matters.
Cenoz, J., Hufeisen, B. and Jessner, U. (2001) *Cross-Linguistic Influence in Third Language Acquisition: Psycholinguistic Perspectives*. Clevedon: Multilingual Matters.
Collentine, J. and Freed, B. (2004) Learning context and its effect on second language acquisition. *Studies in Second Language Acquisition* 26, 153–171.
Cook, V. (ed.) (2002) *Portraits of the L2 User*. Clevedon: Multilingual Matters.
Costa A., Hernández, M. and Sebastián-Gallés, N. (2007) Bilingualism aids conflict resolution: Evidence from the ANT task, and cognition, doi:10.1016/j.cognition.2006.12.013.
Cummins, J. (1979) Cognitive/academic language proficiency, linguistic interdependence, the optimum age question and some other matters. *Working Papers on Bilingualism* 19, 121–129.
De Houwer, A. (1990) *The Acquisition of Two Languages from Birth: A Case Study*. Cambridge: Cambridge University Press.
DeKeyser, R. (2007) Study abroad as foreign language practice. In R. DeKeyser (ed.) *Practice in Second Language: Perspectives from Applied Linguistics and Cognitive Psychology* (pp. 208–226). Cambridge: Cambridge University Press.
Deuchar, M. and Quay, S. (2000) *Bilingual Acquisition: Theoretical Implications of a Case Study*. Oxford: Oxford University Press.
Díaz-Campos, M. (2004) Context of learning in the acquisition of Spanish second language phonology. *Studies in Second Language Acquisition* 26(2), 249–273.
Dufon, M.A. and Churchill, E. (2006). *Language Learners in Study Abroad Contexts*. Clevedon: Multilingual Matters.
Etxeberría, F. (2004) Trilinguals at four? Early trilingual education in the Basque country. In C. Hoffman and J. Ytsma (eds) *Trilingualism in Family, School and Community* (pp. 185–201). Clevedon: Multilingual Matters.
Genesee, F. (1989) Early bilingual development: One language or two? *Journal of Child Language* 16, 161–179.
Genesee, F. (2001) Bilingual first language acquisition: Exploring the limits of the language faculty. *Annual Review of Applied Linguistics* 21, 153–168.
Genesee, F. and Nicoladis, E. (2006) Bilingual first language acquisition. In E. Hoff and M. Shatz (eds) *Handbook of Language Development* (pp. 324–342). Oxford: Blackwell.

Genesee, F., Paradis, J. and Crago, M. (2004) *Dual Language Development & Disorders. A Handbook on Bilingualism & Second Language Learning*. Baltimore: Paul H. Brookes Publishing.
Genesee, F. (2003) Rethinking bilingual acquisition. In J.M. Desaekem, A. Housen and L. Wei (eds) *Bilingualism: Beyond Basic Principles* (pp. 204–228). Clevedon: Multilingual Matters.
Gordon, R.G. (ed.) (2005) *Ethnologue: Languages of the World* (15th edn). Dallas, TX: SIL International. On WWW at http://www.ethnologue.com.
Groot, M.B. and Kroll, J.F. (eds) (1997) *Tutorials in Bilingualism*. New Jersey: Lawrence Erlbaum Associates, Publishers.
Grosjean, F. (1989) Neurolinguists beware! The bilingual is not two monolinguals in one person. *Brain and Language* 36, 3–15.
Grosjean, F. (1994) Individual bilingualism. In *Encyclopedia of Language and Linguistics* (pp. 1656–1660). Oxford: Pergamon Press.
Grosjean, F. (2004) Studying bilinguals: Methodological and conceptual issues. In T.K. Bhatia and W.C. Ritchie (eds) *The Handbook of Bilingualism* (pp. 32–63). Oxford: Blackwell Publishing.
Herdina, P. and Jessner, U. (2002) *A Dynamic Model of Multilingualism: Perspectives of Change in Psycholinguistics*. Clevedon: Multilingual Matters.
Huttenlocher, J., Haight, W., Bryk, A., Seltzer, M. and Lyons, T. (1991) Early vocabulary growth: Relation to language input and gender. *Developmental Psychology* 27, 236–248.
Johnstone, R. (2002) *Immersion in a Second or Additional Language at School: A Review of the International Research*. Stirling, Scotland: Scottish Centre for Information on Language Teaching.
Juan-Garau, M. (1996) *Language Development in a Catalan-English Bilingual Between the Ages of 1 and 3*. Barcelona: PPU.
Juan-Garau, M. and Pérez-Vidal, C. (2000) Subject realization in the syntactic development of a bilingual child. *Bilingualism: Language and Cognition* 3, 173–191. (Special edition on Syntactic Development. F. Genesee (ed.)).
Juan-Garau, M. and Pérez-Vidal, C. (2001) Mixing and pragmatic parental strategies in early bilingual acquisition. *Journal of Child Language* 28(1), 59–86.
Kellerman, E. and Sharwood-Smith, M. (eds) (1986) *Crosslinguistic Influence in SLA*. Oxford: Pergamon Press.
Köppe, R. and Meisel, J.M. (1995) Code-switching in bilingual first language acquisition. In L. Milroy and P. Muysken (eds) *One Speaker; Two Languages: Cross-Disciplinary Perspectives on Code-Switching* (pp. 276–301). Cambridge: Cambridge University Press.
Lanza, E. (1992) Can bilingual two-year olds code-switch? *Journal of Child Language* 19, 633–658.
Lanza, E. (1997) *Language Mixing in Infant Bilingualism: A Sociolinguistic Perspective*. Oxford: Oxford University Press.
Larsen-Freeman, D. and Long, M. (1991) *An Introduction to Second Language Acquisition Research*. London: Longman.
Lasagabaster, D. (2000) Three languages and three linguistic models in the Basque country. In J. Cenoz and U. Jessner (eds) *English in Europe: The Acquisition of a Third Language*. Clevedon: Multilingual Matters.

Leopold, W.F. (1970) *Speech Development of a Bilingual Child: A Linguist's Record* (4 volumes). New York: AMS Press.

Lotherington, H. (2006) Bilingual education. In A. Davies and C. Elder (eds) *The Handbook of Applied Linguistics* (pp. 695–718). Oxford: Blackwell.

Maneva, B. and Genesee, F. (2002) Bilingual babbling: Evidence for language differentiation in dual language acquisition. In B. Skarabela, S. Fish and A. Do (eds) *BUCLD 26: Proceedings of the 26th Annual Boston University Conference on Language Development* (Vol. 1, pp. 383–392). Somerville, MA: Cascadilla Press.

Marchman, V.A., Martínez-Sussmann, C. and Dale, P.S. (2004) The language-specific nature of grammatical development: Evidence from bilingual learners. *Developmental Science* 7(2), 212–224.

Meisel, J.M. (1989) Early differentiation of languages in bilingual children. In K. Hyltenstam and L. Obler (eds) *Bilingualism Across the Lifespan: Aspects of Acquisition, Maturity, and Loss* (pp. 13–40). Cambridge: Cambridge University Press.

Meisel, J.M. (1994) Code-switching in young bilingual children. *Studies in Second Language Acquisition* 16, 413–439.

Meisel, J.M. (2004) The bilingual child. In T.K. Bhatia and W.C. Ritchie (eds) *The Handbook of Bilingualism* (pp. 91–112). Oxford: Blackwell.

Müller, N. (1998) Transfer in bilingual first language acquisition. *Bilingualism: Language and Cognition* 1, 151–171.

Odlin, T. (2003) Cross-linguistic influence. In C.J. Doughty and M.H. Long (eds) *The Handbook of Second Language Acquisition* (pp. 436–486). Oxford: Blackwell Publishing.

Paradis, J. and Genesee, F. (1996) Syntactic acquisition in bilingual children: Autonomous or interdependent? *Studies in Second Language Acquisition* 18, 1–25.

Paradis, J. and Navarro, S. (2003) Subject realization and crosslinguistic interference in the bilingual acquisition of Spanish and English. *Journal of Child Language* 30, 1–23.

Pavlenko, A. (2004) 'Stop doing that, ia komu skazala!': Language choice and emotions in parent–child communication. *Journal of Multilingual and Multicultural Development* 25 (2/3), 179–203.

Peal, E. and Lambert, W.E. (1962). The relation of bilingualism to intelligence. *Psychological Monographs* 76, 1–23.

Pérez-Vidal, C. (1995) La adquisición del inglés de un niño bilingüe catalán/inglés. PhD thesis, University of Barcelona.

Pérez-Vidal, C. (1998) La adquisición bilingüe infantil sin mezclas. In M. Pujol, L. Nussbaum and M.M. Llobera (eds) *La Adquisición de Lenguas Extranjeras: Nuevas Perspectivas en Europa*. Madrid: SGEL.

Pérez-Vidal, C. and Campanale-Grilloni, N. (eds) (2005) *Content and Language Integrated Learning in Europe. Teaching Materials for the Secondary Classroom*. Barcelona: UPF-European Commission.

Piller, I. (2001) Private language planning: The best of both worlds? *Estudios de Sociolingüística* 2 (1), 61–80.

Piller, I. (2002) *Bilingual Couples Talk: The Discursive Construction of Hybridity*. Amsterdam: John Benjamins.

Redlinger, W.E. and Park, T. (1980) Language mixing in young bilinguals. *Journal of Child Language* 7, 337–352.
Romaine, S. (1995) *Bilingualism* (2nd edn). Oxford: Basil Blackwell.
Saunders, G. (1982) *Bilingual Children: Guidance for the Family.* Clevedon: Multilingual Matters.
Saunders, G. (1988) *Bilingual Children: From Birth to Teens.* Clevedon: Multilingual Matters.
Siegel, J. (2003) Social context. In C.J. Doughty and M.H. Long (eds) *The Handbook of Second Language Acquisition* (pp. 178–223). Oxford: Blackwell Publishing.
Skutnabb-Kangas, T. (2000) *Linguistic Genocide in Education – or Worldwide Diversity and Human Rights.* Mahwah, NJ: Erlbaum.
Stevens, J.J. (2001) The acquisition of L2 Spanish pronunciation in a study abroad context. PhD thesis, University of Southern California, 2000. *Dissertation Abstracts International*-A 62 (6), 2095.
Swain, M. (1977) Bilingualism, monolingualism, and code acquisition. In Mackey, W. and Andersson, T. (eds) *Bilingualism in Early Childhood.* Rowley, MA: Newbury.
Swain, M. and Johnson, R.K. (1997) Immersion education: a category within bilingual education. In R.K. Johnson and M. Swain (eds) *Immersion Education: International Perspectives* (pp. 11–16). Cambridge: Cambridge University Press.
Swain, M. and S. Lapkin (2005) The evolving sociopolitical context of immersion education in Canada: Some implications for program development. *International Journal of Applied Linguistics* 15(2), 169–186.
Taeschner, T. (1983) *The Sun is Feminine: A Study on Language Acquisition in Bilingual Children.* Berlin: Springer.
Tuominen, A. (1999) Who decides the home language? A look at multilingual families. *International Journal of the Sociology of Language* 140, 59–76.
Viberg, A. (2001) Age-related and L2-related features in bilingual narrative development in Sweden. In L. Verhoeven and S. Strömqvist (eds) *Narrative Development in a Multilingual Context* (pp. 87–128). Amsterdam/Philadelphia: John Benjamins.
Vihman, M. (1985) Language differentiation by the bilingual infant. *Journal of Child Language* 12, 297–324.
Volterra, V. and Taeschner, T. (1978) The acquisition and development of language by bilingual children. *Journal of Child Language* 5, 311–326.
Wei, L., Dewaele, J.M. and Housen, A. (2002) *Opportunities and Challenges of Bilingualism.* Berlin/New York: Mouton de Gruyter.

Part 1
The Early Acquisition of Two or More Languages Within the Family Context

Chapter 2
Early Galician/Spanish Bilingualism: Contrasts with Monolingualism

MIGUEL PÉREZ-PEREIRA

Introduction

The effect of bilingualism on the development of language was and still continues to be a controversial topic. There are several important works on the acquisition of language by children born in a bilingual family environment – what has been called *bilingual acquisition* (Deuchar & Quay, 2000). Generally speaking, it is considered that bilingual acquisition takes place when the child is regularly exposed to two languages from birth or during the first year of life (Deuchar & Quay, 2000). In a more restrictive conception, De Houwer (1990) maintains that *bilingual first language acquisition* takes place when the child is exposed to two languages from the first month of life.

Many of the studies carried out on this topic are single case studies, or studies on a few subjects. Although they offer information of great value on bilingual children's development (De Houwer, 1990; Deuchar & Quay, 2000; Döpke, 1992; Lanza, 1997; Taeschner, 1983), if we take into consideration that important differences exist in language development (Bates *et al.*, 1995), it is difficult to draw reliable and valid conclusions on the comparison between bilingual and monolingual children from these single case studies.

In order to reach firm conclusions we need to perform comparisons between numerically large samples of bilingual and monolingual children, or, to be more precise, children who live in bilingual contexts and children who live in monolingual contexts.

Previous studies

The very first studies on the effects of bilingualism on cognitive development (Saer, 1923), which presented a dark panorama for bilingual children, came to determine the existing conceptions of the effects of bilingualism on the acquisition of language for many years.

The first comparative cross-sectional studies on the acquisition of vocabulary by bilingual and monolingual children pointed out that bilinguals showed a more reduced lexical development than monolinguals. In the majority of these studies (Ben Zeev, 1977; Doyle et al., 1978; Rosenblum & Pinker, 1983), in which comparisons of the vocabulary comprehended by the bilingual and monolingual children were performed by using the Peabody picture vocabulary test, the results agreed that bilingual children between 5 and 7 years of age obtained significantly lower results than same-aged monolingual children. The only exception was the study carried out by Umbel et al. (1992), who found that first-grade Spanish-English bilingual children showed a non-significant slight delay in their receptive vocabulary as measured through the Peabody test in comparison to the receptive vocabulary of English-speaking monolingual children from similar socioeconomic status (SES).

One of the problems with these previous studies is that they only took into account the receptive vocabulary of bilingual children in only one of the two languages. Generally speaking, when we compare monolingual to bilingual children who speak very different languages, if we only count the words that are known by bilingual children in only one of the two languages, the results show that bilingual children exhibit a more reduced vocabulary than monolingual children. In contrast, if we add up the words known by bilingual children in both languages, bilingual children's vocabularies are larger than those of the monolingual children. Finally, when simultaneous words in the two languages, or terms with equivalent meanings, are counted only once, the results obtained by bilingual and monolingual children are similar (Siguan, 2001).

However, this point is controversial, as the study carried out by Pearson and colleagues shows (Pearson et al., 1993, 1995). In this study Pearson and others compared the lexical development of 25 simultaneously bilingual Spanish-English children from Florida (USA) between 8 and 30 months of age with 35 monolingual children of a similar age, whose parents had a similar educational level. The authors used the English and Mexican-Spanish versions of the MacArthur scales (Communicative Development Inventories: CDI) (Fenson et al., 1993; Jackson-Maldonado et al., 2003), which allowed them to assess the comprehension of vocabulary between 8 and 15 months, and the production of vocabulary between 8 and 30 months of age. Pearson *et al.* found that the bilingual children did not show lower results than the monolingual ones when the researchers took into account the whole vocabulary produced in the two languages together. The same result was obtained when they compared their subjects' conceptual vocabulary. This measure was obtained by adding the bilinguals' vocabularies in each language, and then dividing the vocabulary shared between the two languages (equivalent terms) by two, in other words, counting the equivalent terms only once. This comparative procedure is considered by Hamers and Blanc (2000: 35) to be 'the only valid one when bilinguality is measured on the "additive–subtractive" dimension' (see also Marchman & Martínez-Sussmann, 2002, who consider that an adequate language assessment of bilingual children requires an examination of lexical and grammatical skills in both languages). Nevertheless, Pearson *et al.* (1993, 1995) found that the bilingual children had a significantly lower vocabulary than the monolinguals when the comparisons were performed in only one language, unless the bilingual children were clearly dominant in one language (Spanish or English) and were compared to monolingual children who spoke the bilinguals' dominant language.

Regarding vocabulary understanding, the bilingual children understood a larger number of words than the monolinguals, regardless of whether comparisons were performed on their total vocabulary (English plus Spanish) or on their conceptual vocabulary. Differences, however, did not reach significance. If comparisons were focused on the dominant language of those bilingual children with a clear dominance of one language over the other, these bilingual children even got better results than their monolingual peers. However, if comparisons were focused on the bilinguals' non-dominant language, the bilingual children understood fewer words than their monolingual peers.

From these data the authors concluded that, contrary to former studies, the bilingual children show vocabularies that are comparable to those of the monolingual children in comprehension when comparisons are focused on the dominant language of bilingual children, and higher than those of the monolinguals when comparisons are performed on the two languages together (total vocabulary and conceptual vocabulary). In relation to production, the results obtained by the bilingual and the monolingual children are comparable provided the words produced by the bilinguals in the two languages are taken into account together.

In a related study, the measures of language environment and the percentage of vocabulary in each language obtained by 25 bilingual

Spanish-English children were correlated (Pearson et al., 1997). Parent estimates of language exposure to both languages (in percentages) were used as a language environment measure, and CDI scores for English and Spanish were used as the basis for obtaining the percentage of vocabulary in English and Spanish. Pearson et al. (1997) observed a substantial relation between the quantity of input in a given language and the amount of vocabulary produced in that language, indicating that the number of words learned in each language is proportional to the amount of time spent with speakers of the language (see also Juan-Garau & Pérez-Vidal, 2001).

Similar results to those of Pearson et al. (1993, 1995) were obtained by Junker and Stockman (2002). These authors measured the vocabulary skills of 10 German-English bilingual 24-month-old children both in German and in English, using the Language Development Survey (Rescorla, 1989). They then compared the results with the vocabulary produced by two groups of monolingual German- and English-speaking children of the same age. Junker and Stockman (2002) found that bilingual children were not inferior in conceptual vocabulary size when words in both languages were pooled. In addition, they found that bilingual children seem to have both languages separated, because 43% of bilingual conceptual vocabulary was associated with lexical forms in both languages, contrary to Taeschener's claim (Taeschner, 1983).

Marchman and Martínez-Sussmann (2002) investigated the current validity of the MacArthur–Bates scales in English (Fenson et al., 1993) and Mexican Spanish (Jackson-Maldonado et al., 2003) with 26 English-Spanish bilingual children in order to extend the validity of the instrument, already established with monolingual children, to a bilingual population. The authors found a very high correlation between the measures of vocabulary obtained with the CDI in each language and behavioral measures of vocabulary obtained in an object naming task. However, the correlations were much higher for measures within each language than between languages, indicating a specific process of acquisition for each language and not a general linguistic process. At the same time the authors found a significant, but somewhat lower, correlation between measures of grammar development obtained through the CDI and behavioral measures of grammar (MLU in words obtained in a free play conversation). As occurred with vocabulary, within-language correlations were much higher than between-language correlations, supporting the specific language learning view. Therefore, the CDI seems to be a valid and useful instrument for assessing bilinguals' language acquisition.

Recently, Marchman et al. (2004) carried out a study with 113 Spanish-English bilingual children. The authors applied the CDI in English and Spanish, and performed correlation and multiple regression analysis on the results. The most important finding was that there were very high correlations between vocabulary in English and grammatical complexity in English, and between vocabulary in Spanish and grammatical complexity in Spanish (0.78 and 0.80, respectively). However, the correlations between languages were much lower (not significant). Within-language associations of lexical and grammatical development were similar to those found in monolingual learners. Multiple regression analyses showed that vocabulary within each language accounted for the highest variance in predicting grammar development in each language, but composite vocabulary (the whole vocabulary produced in Spanish and English together) did not contribute to grammar development (although composite vocabulary scores showed a high correlation with vocabulary scores in each language). Input or exposure to the language accounted for a relatively low variance. These results suggest that, although general (non-language-specific) factors influence progress in language development in both languages, 'there is an independent and more substantial contribution of specific lexical progress in the specific language' (Marchman et al., 2004: 219). These results were also confirmed in new analyses that Marchman et al. (2004) performed on the data obtained with the sample of 26 children from the study cited above (Marchman & Martínez-Sussmann, 2002).

The overall results obtained by Marchman et al. (2004) indicate that bilingual children display grammatical skills in a given language that are strongly linked to vocabulary growth in that language. Therefore, the relationship between vocabulary and grammar is best viewed as a language-specific, rather than a language-general phenomenon. This hypothesis may be considered an extension or specification of the *critical mass hypothesis* stated by Bates and others (Bates & Goodman, 1997; Marchman & Bates, 1994).

Aspects of the Galician language

Galician is a Romance language spoken in Galicia, a community located in the North West of Spain, to the north of Portugal, which is spoken by 86% of the population of Galicia (2,700,000 inhabitants), and understood by 97% of the population (Fernández et al., 1994). In relation to Spanish, Galician is the minority language, with a lower status and prestige. Most of the population speak both languages. With respect to the initial language of the Galicians, 62.4% learn Galician as their first language, 25.6% learn Spanish as the first language, 11.4% learn both languages at the same time (bilinguals), and 0.6% learn another language as their first language. Across generations there is a progressive loss of speakers of Galician as the usual language, although an increase in written knowledge also exists (Fernández et al., 1994). Both Galician and Spanish have been the official languages of Galicia since 1983. The Galician educational system may be considered as a variety of maintenance bilingualism (Siguan, 2001).[1]

Generally speaking, Galician is a language both close to Spanish and Portuguese, with important influences of Spanish throughout the last 500 years. Galician has morphological gender marking (masculine/feminine; a few neutrals) and gender agreement (determiner–noun–adjective). Plural morphological marking is simple and regular (two specific allomorphs, with a few exceptions). There is also augmentative and diminutive marking on nouns, and adjectives. Verb morphology is rich, with person, number, tense-aspect, and mood marking. In contrast to Spanish no composite past verbal forms exist. Galician is a pro-drop language, with non-obligatory specification of subject, thanks to its rich verbal morphology. Subject–verb agreement is a common characteristic with other Romance languages. The pronoun usually follows the verb (enclitic pronoun) in simple declarative or interrogative sentences, although in other clauses (negative, subordinate, and so on) the pronoun precedes the verb. This is a distinctive characteristic in relation to Spanish, and a similarity with Portuguese. As has been previously stated, lexically, there are many words that are the same or very similar in Spanish and Galician.

Aims of the study

Although the aforementioned study by Pearson et al. (1995) is interesting, it seems reasonable to carry out comparative studies with larger samples of subjects. Indeed, 25 and 35 participants do not seem enough in order to obtain generalised results. This is one of the aims of the present research.

Another aim is to extend the comparisons not only to vocabulary comprehension and production, but also to the morphological and syntactic knowledge of children, in particular, and to their prelinguistic communicative behaviours. In this way we can find out how the bilingual condition affects children's non-linguistic communicative capabilities in comparison to their linguistic ones, as well as analyse in detail the effects of bilingualism on different dimensions of language development, such as morphology, syntax, and vocabulary.

The analysis of the relationships between measures of vocabulary development and different grammatical development scores will also be an aim of the present research, seeking to test the hypothesis of Marchman *et al.* (2004). In this case, the test of the specificity hypothesis will be performed under interesting new conditions, given the closeness between Spanish and Galician, two languages not studied until now. These languages, unlike English and Spanish, are very close, and many words are the same or very similar in both languages. As both languages are used in contact, there are mixed uses of Spanish and Galician. This is particularly so in young children because of their phonological difficulties, which may make it difficult to distinguish between different, but phonologically similar, words of the two languages (such is the case of *cabalo* and *caballo* 'horse' in Galician and Spanish respectively).

Finally, an obvious aim of the research is to study how Galician children learn to talk, with particular reference to the question of bilingualism. There is a lack of research focusing on this population and on Galician-Spanish bilingualism.

Method

Subjects

The subjects were 706 Galician children between 8 and 30 months of age. Of these, 431 (61%) lived in a family bilingual environment, and 275 (39%) lived in a family monolingual environment. These data are very close to the data offered by the survey of the Galician Government (IGE, 2004) on the use of these languages. According to this survey, 42.62% of the people usually speak in Galician. In our sample 39% were Galician-speaking families. Information about the languages used at home was obtained through eight questions from the Galician CDI (see next section). Parents were questioned about the languages they used, and how frequently they used each one. They were also asked whether the child was in contact with other languages different from Galician, and if so, for how many hours a day and from what age, and who spoke the other language, and so on. Most of the bilingual children lived in Spanish-Galician-speaking families (96%), where one of the parents spoke Galician and the other Spanish, or both of them simultaneously used both languages, or one spoke one language (either Spanish or Galician) and the other both languages. The rest of the bilingual children (4%) lived in families who used Galician and another language different from Spanish (mainly Portuguese and French). Most of the children came from families with only one child, or with two

Table 2.1 Mean age comparison between the monolingual and bilingual groups

Age	Bilingual mean age	Monolingual mean age	t-value	p-value	Degree of freedom
8–15 months	11.96	12.11	−0.478	0.633	222.192
16–30 months	23.63	23.22	1.015	0.311	365.931

children (93.8%). Consequently, 56.5% of the children were first born and 33.5% were second born.

Regarding the mothers' education, 42.1% had primary education, 36.5% secondary education, and 17.8% university studies; 0.8% did not even receive primary education, and 2.8% did not answer the question. The data on the fathers' education are very similar (41.8%, 36%, 18.7%, 0.7%, and 2.8%, respectively). These data indicate a lower level of education of this sample than the estimates for the Galician population (IGE, 2004), which is probably due to a higher rural origin in the sample. In any case, the sample is quite representative of the population, in contrast to other CDI samples in which there is a bias towards higher education, with a very high percentage of mothers or fathers with university degrees (Fenson et al., 1994; López Ornat et al., 2005).

There were no significant differences in age between the monolingual and the bilingual groups, as shown in Table 2.1.

Instruments

The Galician version of the MacArthur–Bates inventories (Pérez Pereira & García Soto, 2003) was used to evaluate the children's communicative and linguistic development. This test is a parental report, originally developed in the USA (Fenson et al., 1993, 1994), which shows very good reliability, internal consistency, and validity scores. There are now over 25 adaptations to different languages, with the Galician adaptation being the first one developed in Spain. The Galician version, called *Inventario para o Desenvolvemento de Habilidades Comunicativas* (IDHC), has two different forms, just as the original North-American version does. The first one, called *Palabras e Xestos* (words and gestures), is for children between 8 and 15 months of age, and the second one, called *Palabras e Oracións* (words and sentences), is for children between 16 and 30 months. The enormous changes in communicative and linguistic abilities that children show between 8 and 30 months of age made it necessary to develop two different instruments so as to appropriately reflect these changes.

The Words and Gestures (*Palabras e Xestos*) form (8–15 months) has two parts. The first part, called Early words (*Primeiras palabras*), assesses early comprehension and production of words by children. This part has four sections:

(1) *Early understanding of language*: which tries to explore initial understanding of certain very simple phrases, such as 'The child answers when he/she is called by his/her name?' This part has three items.
(2) *Phrases*: a list of 27 simple phrases. The parents are asked to mark those phrases that are understood by their children in context: for instance, 'sit down!' or 'throw the ball!'
(3) *Ways of speaking*: this section tries to detect the learning style of the children, whether imitative or referential (two items).
(4) *List of words*: 384 words sorted into 19 categories (animals, body parts, toys, verbs, and so on). The parents are asked to mark in separate columns those words that their children understand (comprehension) and those that their children understand and say (production). This last section is considered to give a clear glimpse of the children's overall linguistic development.

The second part, Gestures and Actions (*Xestos e accións*), assesses the use of communicative gestures by children, as well as the existence of behaviours such as imitation of adult actions, participation in joint play, symbolic play, and so on, which are related to the communicative capacity of children (Bates *et al.*, 1979). This second part is made up of six sections:

(1) *First communicative gestures*: gestures commonly used by children to convey communicative intentions, such as 'The child stretches his/her arm to show something he/she has in his/her hand' (16 items).
(2) *Games and routines*: this explores children's abilities to participate in everyday routines and social play, such as 'Does the child play peekaboo?' (13 items).
(3) *Actions with objects*: assesses children's capacities to carry out functional actions with objects, such as 'Does the child eat with a spoon?' (17 items).
(4) *Acting as parents do*: assesses children's performance of parental-like actions, such as 'Does the child feed a doll?' (14 items).
(5) *Imitation of other adults' activities*, such as 'Does the child hit with a hammer?' (15 items).

(6) *Symbolic play*: the parents are asked if the child plays with an object as if it were a different thing (for instance, a shoebox as if it were a crib), and are asked to give a few examples.

The Words and Sentences (*Palabras e oracións*) form (16–30 months) includes two different parts. The first one, First Words (*Primeiras palabras*), has two sections:

(1) There is a Vocabulary checklist (719 items), from which the parents are asked to mark those words that the child says (production). Words are organised into 22 different categories (animals, furniture, verbs, question words, auxiliary verbs, connectives, and so on). In this form there is no assessment of comprehension because it is considered that at this point the parents may have difficulties in knowing how many words their children understand. This is the principal part for the assessment of children's linguistic development.

(2) How does the child understand language? (five items) (hereafter *use of language*). The intention is to explore whether the child uses language in a flexible way, unconnected to the here and now, in reference to events that took place in the past, to non-present objects, or to the owner of a recently discovered object, for instance.

The second part, Sentences and Grammar (*Oracións e Gramática*), is composed of five sections whose intention is to assess children's degree of knowledge of morphology and syntax:

(1) Word endings/Part 1 (nine items), in which the parents have to indicate if their children produce different regular nominal and verbal suffixes, such as plurals, gender marking, past perfect, future, verb person marking, etc.

(2) Word forms (15 items), in which the parents are asked whether the children correctly produce irregular forms (for instance, *aberto, sei*).

(3) Word endings/Part 2 (14 items), in which the parents are asked to mark whether their children produce irregular forms in an incorrect over-regularised way (for instance, *abrido, sabo*).

(4) Phrases, in which the parents are asked if their children already produce phrases by combining two or more words, and if so, they are asked to give examples of the three longest utterances they heard from their children. The MLU (mean length of utterances) in morphemes is obtained from these phrases.

(5) Sentence complexity (38 items), in which the parents are asked to mark which one of two forms presented is the nearest to their children's

productions (for instance, *nene quere* (baby wants)/*eu quero* (I want)). In every item, one form is more developed than the other.

Table 2.2 shows a summary of the different sections of the MacArthur–Bates scales.

Table 2.2 Summary of the different sections of the Galician CDI

Words and gestures (8–15 months): Sections
(1) Early words
(A) Early understanding of language (3 items)
(B) Phrases (27 items)
(C) Ways of speaking (2 items)
(D) List of words:
Word comprehension (384 words; 19 categories)
Word production (384 words; 19 categories)
(2) Gestures and actions
(A) First communicative gestures (16 items)
(B) Games and routines (13 items)
(C) Actions with objects (17 items)
(D) Acting as parents do (14 items)
(E) Imitation of other adults' activities (15 items)
(F) Symbolic play (examples)
Total gestures and actions = (A + B + C + D + E)
Word and sentences (16–30 months): Sections
(1) First words
(A) Word production (719 words; 22 categories)
(B) How does the child understand language? (Use of language) (5 items)
(2) Sentences and grammar
(A) Word endings I (regular suffixes) (9 items)
(B) Forms of words (irregular suffixes) (15 items)
(C) Word endings II (over-regularisations) (14 items)
(D) Phrases: MLU of the three longest utterances
(E) Sentence complexity (38 items)

Procedure

The children were assessed only through the Galician version of the CDI, for different reasons: first, when the study took place, the (European) Spanish adaptation of the CDI (López Ornat *et al.*, 2005) did not exist; second, it would be very odd for the Galician parents to apply identical instruments in two such close languages. Regarding this latter point, the list of words comprised 67% of words that were exactly identical to the Spanish corresponding term (*casa* = casa 'house', *mesa* = mesa 'table', *pan* = pan 'bread'), and 21% of words that were very similar to the Spanish equivalent word (*auga* = agua 'water', *chaves* = llaves 'keys'). As was pointed out above, the way children pronounce makes it even more difficult to distinguish between words when they are producing the Galician or the Spanish terms.

The inventories were given to one of the parents (usually the mother), who – in most cases – completed them in the presence of a person trained to deal with any queries that might arise.

In total, 127 parents of bilingual families and 104 of monolingual Galician-speaking families returned the Words and Gestures (8–15 months) inventory, and 304 parents of bilingual families and 171 of monolingual families (706 in all) returned the Words and Sentences (16–30 months) form. It should be noted that there was no significant difference in average age between children from monolingual and bilingual families.

Analysis performed

Comparisons of the mean scores obtained by the groups of bilingual and monolingual children (Student's *t*-test) were carried out for each of the main sections of the two forms of the MacArthur–Bates scales (Words and Gestures and Words and Sentences). MANOVA were performed in order to test the influence of different factors on the measures obtained. Correlations between scores in vocabulary production and grammar scores were also obtained.

Results

Tables 2.3 and 2.4 show the average score obtained in every section by the monolingual and bilingual children, as well as the results of the Student's *t*-test, indicating the degree of significance. The results found with the Words and Gestures form (8–15 months of age) indicate that no significant difference was found between the monolingual and the bilingual children, although the bilingual children show slightly higher

Table 2.3 Comparison between the mean results obtained by the bilingual and the monolingual groups in the Words and Gestures form (8–15 months)

Section	Bilingual mean score	Monolingual mean score	t-value	p-value	Degree of freedom
Understanding of phrases	18.06	17.13	0.995	0.321	229
Communicative gestures	9.72	9.51	0.412	0.680	229
Gestures and actions	34.76	33.72	0.480	0.631	229
Word understanding	120.35	106.26	1.276	0.208	229
Word production	19.12	15.47	0.887	0.376	229

results than the monolingual ones. The differences are higher in those sections that evaluate language knowledge (such as understanding of phrases, word comprehension, and word production), in contrast with those that evaluate the use of first communicative gestures, or gestures and actions, which is the total score for the use of gestures plus games and routines, actions with objects, acting as parents do, and imitation of adult actions. Figures 2.1 and 2.2 (Understanding, 8–15 months) show these results.

In the results found with the Words and Sentences form (16–30 months of age), the bilingual children always attained higher scores than the monolingual children. However, this time, differences reach significance in the sections on 'Use of language' ($t = 2.293$, $p < 0.023$), 'MLU of the 3 longest utterances' (henceforth MLU3) ($t = 2.452$, $p < 0.015$), and 'Sentence complexity' ($t = 1.994$, $p < 0.047$), while in the section on 'Word endings I (Regular suffixes)', differences reach near significance ($t = 1.906$, $p < 0.057$). Figures 2.2 (Production 16–30) and 2.3 show these results in a graphic way.

Even though there is a significant difference between the monolingual and bilingual children in relation to the mothers' level of education ($\chi^2 = 34.67$, $p < 0.001$, and $\chi^2 = 23.28$, $p < 0.001$ for children 8–15 and 16–30 months old, respectively, which indicate that families with mothers who have higher levels of studies tend to use both languages), a significant effect of bilingualism still exists when controlling the effect

Table 2.4 Comparison between the mean results obtained by the bilingual and monolingual groups in the Words and Sentences form (16–30 months)

Section	Bilingual mean score	Monolingual mean score	t-value	p-value	Degree of freedom
Word production	303.51	279.43	1.291	0.197	388.109
Use of language	4.08	3.77	2.293	0.023	320.591
Regular suffixes	3.70	3.16	1.906	0.057	387.642
Irregular suffixes	2.11	1.83	1.101	0.272	386.640
Over-regularisations	3.46	2.91	1.426	0.155	365.977
MLU3	4.50	3.84	2.452	0.015	397.356
Sentence complexity	11.00	8.51	1.994	0.047	370.903

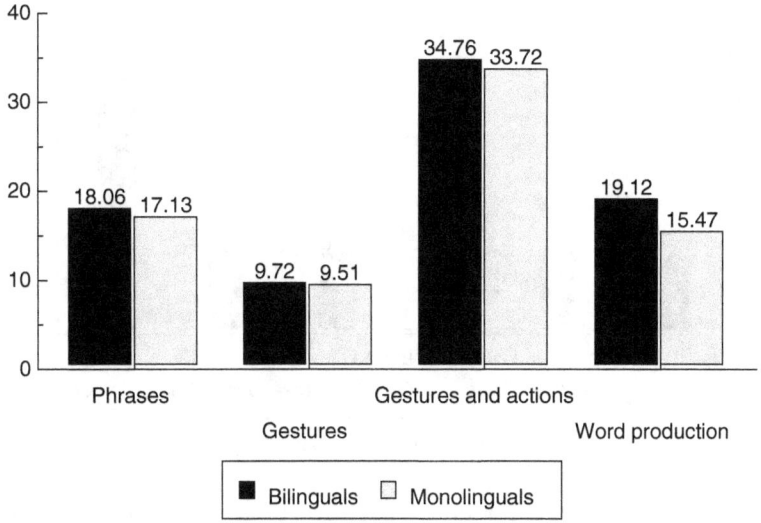

Figure 2.1 Mean scores obtained by the bilingual and monolingual children in different sections of the Words and Gestures form

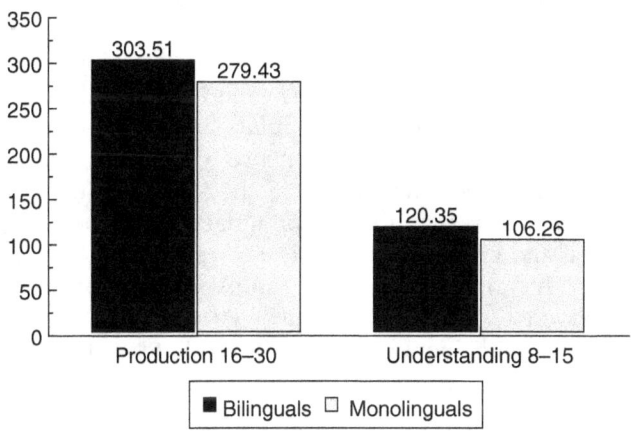

Figure 2.2 Mean scores obtained by the monolingual and bilingual groups in word understanding (8–15 months), and word production (16–30 months)

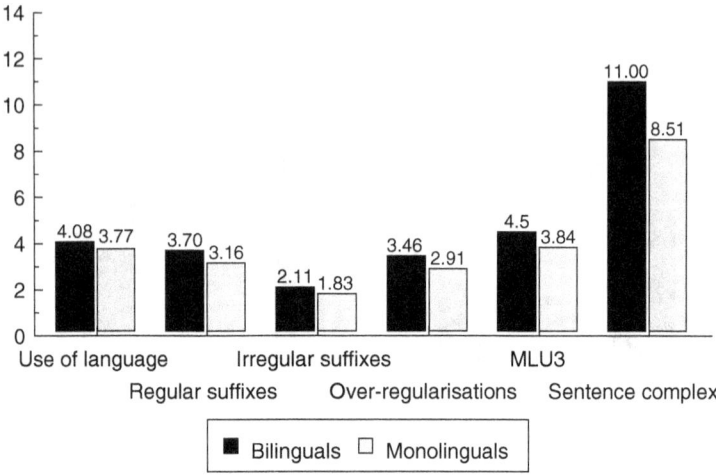

Figure 2.3 Mean scores obtained by the bilingual and monolingual children in different sections of the Words and Sentences form

of mothers' education on MLU3, Sentence complexity, and word endings I ('Regular suffixes'), as Table 2.5 shows. Differences nearly reach significance in the case of 'Irregular suffixes'. Differences this time do not reach significance in the case of 'How children use language', the scores of which seem to be affected by a joint effect of bilingualism and mothers' studies.

As much for the bilingual children as for the monolingual ones, very high significant correlations were found among all the following variables: vocabulary production, regular suffixes, irregular suffixes, over-regularisations, MLU3, and sentence complexity, as shown in Table 2.6. As can be observed in Table 2.6, the bilingual children obtained even higher correlations than the monolingual children between vocabulary production and grammar scores. The correlations observed between vocabulary production and sentence complexity are within the range of those observed by Marchman *et al.* (2004) with bilingual children and other studies with monolingual children (Bates & Goodman, 1997; Fenson *et al.*, 1994).

Discussion

From these results, it clearly appears that lexical development of the bilingual children between 8 and 15 months of age is not below their

Table 2.5 Multivariate analysis: effect of bilingualism on dependent measures controlling the effect of mothers' education

Section	Bilingual mean score	Monolingual mean score	F-value	p-value	Degree of freedom
Word production	303.51	279.43	2.093	0.149	1
Use of language	4.08	3.77	2.471	0.117	1
Regular suffixes	3.70	3.16	3.989	0.046	1
Irregular suffixes	2.11	1.83	3.715	0.055	1
Over-regularisations	3.46	2.91	1.941	0.164	1
MLU3	4.50	3.84	5.756	0.017	1
Sentence complexity	11.00	8.51	4.110	0.043	1

Table 2.6 Pearson's correlations between vocabulary production and grammar scores: differences between bilingual and monolingual children

	Bilingualism	N	Regular suffixes	Irregular suffixes	Over-regularisation	MLU3	Sentence complexity
Vocabulary production	Bilingual	304	0.867	0.839	0.703	0.738	0.815
	Monolingual	171	0.764	0.818	0.561	0.661	0.757

All correlations reach 0.01 level of significance (bilateral).

monolingual counterparts, either in comprehension or production. Thus, these results do not give support to the earlier studies that indicate that older bilingual children show lexical comprehension delay as compared to monolingual children when using the Peabody test of vocabulary comprehension. Probably, the differences found were due to the fact that bilingual children who learn two separate languages, such as Spanish and English, or Hebrew and English, were assessed using a test in only one language. Therefore lexical knowledge in the other language is not taken into account, and, thus, bilingual children's lexical knowledge may be underestimated.

When assessment considers both languages, and bilingual children's lexical development is the sum of the two languages, the results obtained by researchers are much more favourable to bilinguals as compared to monolinguals (Junker & Stockman, 2002; Pearson et al., 1993, 1995). In the case of the present research, the closeness of Spanish and Galician, and their simultaneous use, make it difficult for parents to differentiate between the Galician and Spanish words produced or understood by their children. Although the assessment was performed in only one language (Galician), it could be said that, given their proximity, both languages were in fact assessed.

It is noticeable that those communicative abilities that are to a lesser extent related to language competence (use of communicative gestures, gestures and actions) are the ones in which bilingual children show results that are close to those obtained by the monolingual children. This probably indicates that the bilingual condition particularly affects the knowledge of language (of both languages) in the strict sense of the word, although at this early age the knowledge children may have is still very incipient.

Differences between the bilingual and monolingual children in their knowledge of language seem to increase with age, if we look at the results obtained with the children between 16 and 30 months of age. Bilingual children get higher scores than monolingual children in vocabulary production, use of irregular suffixes, and production of overregularisations, although these differences do not reach significance. The bilingual children show nearly significantly higher scores than the monolingual ones in the use of first nominal and verbal regular morphemes, and significantly higher scores in sentence complexity and MLU3, both of which show that bilingual children use longer and more complex utterances than their monolingual peers. In addition, the results obtained regarding how the children use/understand language indicate that the bilingual children use and understand language with greater flexibility than the monolingual children of the same age; that is, they use language more abundantly than the monolingual children in reference to a time different from present (past or future), in reference to non-present objects or people, and in reference to the owner of a found object. Generally speaking, all this indicates that the bilingual children use language in a form that is more distant from reality than the monolingual children, and in a clearly symbolic way. The complement of this more flexible use of language by the bilingual children is their more advanced use of morphology and syntax as compared to the monolingual children. For instance, the use of verbs in the past facilitates the reference to past events, and vice versa the need to talk about non-present events leads the children to learn grammar. This higher mastery of morphology and syntax allows bilingual children a more flexible and 'separated from reality' use of language.

What is surprising is that the main differences between the bilingual group and the monolingual group are not in vocabulary production, but in grammar. It would be expected that the bilingual children have an advantage over the monolinguals, because nearly any word they produce in Galician or Spanish could be recognised by their parents. This does not happen to monolingual children, who only produce words in Galician, or to bilingual children who learn two distant languages, such as the case of children who live in the Basque country (Arratibel *et al.*, 2005). However, the main differences between the two groups of children were found in those sections of the CDI that assess grammatical development, in which bilingual children are not favoured by this instrument. These results seem to indicate that being exposed to two languages may promote underlying linguistic development, and that differences between the children are not an artifact of the inventory. The fact that significant differences between monolingual and bilingual children were found in the mean length of the three longest utterances spontaneously produced by the children is particularly important. It could be argued that as the bilingual children were not assessed in Spanish as well, their real grammar performance was under-represented. However, in the case of the MLU3 this argument has no effect, because the parents reported the spontaneous utterances produced by their children (with no limitation), and the MLUs were scored from these reported utterances, were they in Spanish or in Galician.

The fact that bilingual children obtained higher correlations between vocabulary production and grammar scores than their monolingual peers (see Table 2.6) apparently points to a general effect of vocabulary on grammar, because the vocabulary of our bilingual sample might be considered as a kind of composite vocabulary. This result is not in agreement with that found by Marchman et al. (2004), according to which composite vocabulary (the whole vocabulary produced in Spanish and English together) did not contribute to grammar development in regression analysis. Therefore, general factors could be mediating the acquisition of both languages by bilingual children. Another possibility, related to Cummins' (1979) hypothesis of the interdependency between languages, is that when the two languages a bilingual child is learning are very similar, the relationships between languages may vary in comparison to other children learning two different languages. The interdependence hypothesis poses a core of skills common to both languages, such that learning in one language can advance learning in the other. Low correlations were found between oral skills in English and Spanish in school-age bilingual English-Spanish children, but high correlations between both languages were found when comparing writing and reading skills (Cobo-Lewis et al., 2002). These results suggest that oral language transfer between English and Spanish, two distant languages, is reduced. Unfortunately, we do not know of similar studies carried out with children speaking two closer languages at earlier ages.

The hypothesis that common skills in both languages are present in children who learn two close languages does not contradict the well-established differentiation of languages effected by bilingual children at a very early stage (Almgrem & Barreña, 2005; Barreña & Almgrem, 2000; Juan-Garau & Pérez-Vidal, 2000).

Conclusions

Regarding vocabulary comprehension in early infancy (8–15 months), bilingual children are not at a disadvantage in relation to monolingual children. The same may be stated concerning vocabulary production, in which the bilingual children show results similar to those of the monolingual children, and even slightly higher scores.

The results found also show that bilingual children seem to have more highly developed grammatical development than the monolingual children of a similar age (16–30 months).

In all, these results indicate that being exposed to two languages does not have negative effects on language development and may even have a positive effect on the acquisition of language during the age period studied. The bilingual children seem to show an earlier mastering of first grammar than the monolingual children.

Correlations between vocabulary production and grammar scores seem to be slightly higher in bilingual children than in monolingual children. This finding does not support the language-specific hypothesis, because vocabulary in bilingual children can be considered as composite or conceptual vocabulary. The main argument in favour of the language-specific hypothesis (Marchman et al., 2004) is that vocabulary in one language correlates with and explains grammar scores to a greater extent than composite vocabulary. In any case, the results seem to be related to the characteristics of the particular languages studied, which were very close, and would need further evidence.

Obviously, the study of bilingual children (the same as for monolinguals) through the MacArthur–Bates scales has its limits (Pearson, 1998). Like any standardised test, the CDI can only analyse those aspects that are included in it, but not the immense creativity of language used by children. The CDI does not allow us to explore phonology, nor the appropriate use of linguistic rules in communicative settings. In this regard, the MacArthur scales are a limited, albeit useful, way of exploring linguistic competence, something that probably requires a combination of methods and techniques.

Future research should investigate the relationships between lexical and grammatical components in Galician-Spanish bilinguals using at the same time parts of the inventories in Galician and Spanish (European Spanish), of which the latter has recently appeared (López Ornat et al., 2005).

Acknowledgements

The present chapter was supported by grant XUGA21102B98 from the Galician Autonomous Government and grant PB97-0526 from the Ministry of Education and Culture of the Spanish Government.

Notes

1. Children are educated in their first language when they enter the school (preschool or *infant education*), and both Spanish and Galician are used in a balanced way from the beginning of primary school until the end of secondary school.

References

Arratibel, N., Barreña, A., Pérez Pereira, M. and Fernández, P. (2005) Comparaciones interlingüísticas euskara-gallego del desarrollo léxico y gramatical. In M.A. Mayor, B. Zubiauz and E. Díez (eds) *Estudios sobre la Adquisición del Lenguaje* (pp. 983–997). Salamanca: Ediciones Universidad de Salamanca.

Almgren, M. and Barreña, A. (2005) El desarrollo de la morfología de futuro en castellano y euskara en niños monolingües y bilingües. *Cognitiva* 17 (2), 127–142.

Barreña, A. and Almgren, M. (2000) Marcas de sujetos y objetos en euskara y español y separación de códigos lingüísticos. *Infancia y Aprendizaje* 91, 31–54.

Bates, E., Benigni, E., Bretherton, I., Camaioni, L. and Volterra, V. (1979) *The Emergence of Symbols. Cognition and Communication in Infancy*. New York: Academic Press.

Bates, E., Dale, P.S. and Thal, D. (1995) Individual differences and their implications for theories of language development. In P. Fletcher and B. MacWhinney (eds) *The Handbook of Child Language* (pp. 96–151). Oxford: Blackwell.

Bates, E. and Goodman, J. (1997) On the inseparability of grammar and the lexicon: Evidence from acquisition, aphasia, and real-time processing. *Language and Cognitive Processess* 12 (5/6), 507–584.

Ben-Zeev, S. (1977) The influence of bilingualism on cognitive strategy and cognitive development. *Child Development* 48, 109–118.

Cobo-Lewis, A., Eilers, R.E., Pearson, B.Z. and Umbel, V.M. (2002) Interdependence of Spanish and English knowledge in language and literacy among bilingual children. In K.D. Oller and R.E. Eilers (eds) *Language and Literacy in Bilingual Children*. (pp. 118–132) Clevedon: Multilingual Matters.

Cummins, J. (1979) Linguistic interdependence and the educational development of bilingual children. *Review of Educational Research* 49, 222–251.

De Houwer, A. (1990) *The Acquisition of Two Languages from Birth: A Case Study*. Cambridge, UK: Cambridge University Press.

Deuchar, M. and Quay, S. (2000) *Bilingual Acquisition: Theoretical Implications of a Case Study*. New York: Oxford University Press.

Döpke, S. (1992) *One Parent One Language. An Interactional Approach*. Amsterdam: John Benjamins.

Doyle, A., Champagne, M. and Segalowitz, N. (1978) Some issues in the assessment of linguistic consequences of early bilingualism. In M. Paradis (ed.) *Aspects of Bilingualism* (pp. 13–21). Columbia, SC: Hornbeam Press.

Fenson, L.O., Dale, P.S., Reznick, S., Thal, D., Bates, E., Hartung, J.P., Pethick, S. and Reilly, J.S. (1993) *MacArthur Communicative Development Inventories. User's Guide and Technical Manual*. San Diego: Singular Publishing.

Fenson, L., Dale, P.S., Reznick, J.S., Bates, E., Thal, D.J. and Pethick, S.J. (1994) Variability in early communicative development. *Monographs of the Society for Research in Child Development* Serial No. 242, 59(5).

Fernández, M., Fernández, F., Fernández, M., Recalde, M., Rei, G. and Rodríguez, M. (1994) *Lingua Inicial e Competencia Lingüística en Galicia*. Santiago: Real Academia Galega.

Hamers, J.F. and Blanc, M.H.A. (2000) *Bilinguality and Bilingualism*. Cambridge: Cambridge University Press.

IGE (Instituto Galego de Estatística) (2004) On WWW at http://ige.xunta.es/

Jackson-Maldonado, D., Thal, D., Marchman, V., Newton, T., Fenson, L. and Conboy, B. (2003) *Inventarios del Desarrollo de Habilidades Comunicativa. User's Guide and Technical Manual*. Maryland: Brookes.

Juan-Garau, M. and Pérez-Vidal, C. (2000) Subject realization in the syntactic development of a bilingual child. *Bilingualism: Language and Cognition* 3 (3), 173–191.

Juan-Garau, M. and Pérez-Vidal, C. (2001) Mixing and pragmatic parental strategies in early bilingual acquisition. *Journal of Child Language* 28, 59–86.

Junker, D.A. and Stockman, I.J. (2002) Expressive vocabulary of German-English bilingual toddlers. *American Journal of Speech and Language Pathology* 11 (3), 381–394.

Lanza, E. (1997) *Language Mixing in Infant Bilingualism. A Sociolinguistic Perspective.* Oxford: Clarendon Press.

López Ornat, S., Gallego, C., Gallo, P., Karousou, S., Mariscal, S. and Martínez, M. (2005) *MacArthur, Inventario de Desarrollo Comunicativo.* Madrid: TEA Ediciones.

Marchman, V. and Bates, E. (1994) Continuity in lexical and morphological development: A test of the critical mass hypothesis. *Journal of Child Language* 21, 339–366.

Marchman, V.A. and Martínez-Sussmann, C. (2002) Concurrent validity of caregiver/parent report measures of language for children who are learning both English and Spanish. *Journal of Speech, Language, and Hearing Research* 45, 983–997.

Marchman, V.A., Martínez-Sussmann, C. and Dale, P.S. (2004) The language-specific nature of grammatical development: Evidence from bilingual learners. *Developmental Science* 7 (2), 212–224.

Pearson, B.Z. (1998) Assessing lexical development in bilingual babies and toddlers. *The International Journal of Bilingualism* 2(3), 347–372.

Pearson, B.Z., Fernández, S.C., Lewedeg, V. and Oller, D.K. (1997) The relation of input factors to lexical learning by bilingual infants. *Applied Psycholinguistics* 18, 41–58.

Pearson, B.Z., Fernández, S.V. and Oller, D.K. (1993) Lexical development in bilingual infants and toddlers: Comparison to monolingual norms. *Language Learning* 43(1), 93–120.

Pearson, B.Z., Fernández, S.C. and Oller, D.K. (1995) Lexical development in bilingual infants and toddlers: Comparison to monolingual norms. In B. Harley (ed.) *Lexical Issues in Language Learning* (pp. 31–57). Ann Arbor, MI: John Benjamins.

Pérez Pereira, M. and García Soto, X.R. (2003) El diagnóstico del desarrollo comunicativo en la primera infancia: Adaptación de las escalas MacArthur al gallego. *Psicothema* 15 (3), 352–361.

Rescorla, L. (1989) The language development survey: A screening tool for delayed language in toddlers. *Journal of Speech and Hearing Disorders* 54, 587–599.

Rosenblum, T. and Pinker, S.A. (1983) Word magic revisited: Monolingual and bilingual children's understanding of the word–object relationships. *Child Development* 54, 773–780.

Saer, D.J. (1923) The effect of bilingualism on intelligence. *British Journal of Psychology* 14, 25–38.

Siguan, M. (2001) *Bilingüismo y Lenguas en Contacto.* Madrid: Alianza Editorial.

Taeschner, T. (1983) *The Sun is Feminine. A Study on Language Acquisition in Bilingual Children.* Berlin: Springer-Verlag.

Umbel, V.M., Pearson, B.Z., Fernández, M.C. and Oller, D.K. (1992) Measuring bilingual children's receptive vocabularies. *Child Development* 63, 1012–1020.

Chapter 3
Early Trilingualism: The Development of Communicative Competence in English Alongside Basque and Spanish

JULIA BARNES

Introduction

This chapter discusses how it is possible for a child to acquire a third language with limited exposure, within a bilingual community in Spain where Spanish and Basque are spoken. It describes the development of several aspects of communicative competence (Hymes, 1972) as revealed in samples from recordings from a longitudinal study of the acquisition of English by a child who is trilingual from birth. The child is exposed to English from her mother, Basque from her father, and Spanish is the language of the community. The study, which focuses on the formal and functional aspects of the interrogative in English of the child communicating with her mother, is described in full in Barnes (2006). However, the focus here is the way that the child is able to express quite sophisticated ideas in English at an early age through the pragmatic use of a limited number of words, specifically in questions.

Communicative competence consists of the ability to use language effectively to perform tasks not only at a linguistic level but also pragmatically. Chomsky defines this capacity as follows:

> We may [...] distinguish 'grammatical competence' from 'pragmatic competence', restricting the first to the knowledge of form and meaning and the second to the knowledge of conditions and manner of appropriate use, in conformity with various purposes. (Chomsky, 1980: 224)

In the following pages we will see how pragmatic competence can develop in a small child, specifically the functional knowledge that forms the relationships between utterances and the intentions or communicative purposes behind them (Halliday, 1975). Austin's (1962) speech act theory provides a framework for the understanding of how this can work. According to Austin (1962), linguistic realisations actually perform communicative acts termed speech acts, such as promising, requesting or ordering. These acts have three components, namely the locutionary act, the illocutionary act and the perlocutionary act:

- The locutionary act refers to the words actually said by the speaker.
- The illocutionary act is the intention that the speaker has in saying these words (this may be to give a literal message or to have a hidden agenda).
- The perlocutionary act is the effect that the words may have on the listener (in other words whether that are interpreted literally or whether the hidden message is perceived and acted upon).

Speech acts simultaneously manifest the structure, content and function of language, where 'the structure of the speech act is its grammar, the content consists of the conceptual substance of the proposition and [...] constitutes what is talked about, (and) its function is its illocutionary force which consists of the speaker's intentions and expectations' (Dore, 1978: 108).

Communicative competence is a very broad term, which, as well as implying knowledge of rules of language use without which grammar would be useless (Hymes, 1972), includes the sociolinguistic knowledge of how to choose between different varieties of speech to be used according to the context. In the case of bilinguals this also includes the ability to choose to use a language in relation to the addressee or context (Genesee *et al.*, 1996); however, this will not be addressed by the present study, which focuses solely on English-speaking contexts. In fact there are few studies that address the acquisition of pragmatics and communicative competence in early bilinguals (but see De Houwer, 1990: 310–337, for a fascinating account of the development of metalinguistic behaviour in a bilingual English/Dutch child), so much of what we have to say will be based on findings from monolingual children.

Nevertheless, although we will be examining pragmatic competence in the development of English, we should not overlook the fact that the small child who is the subject of our study has been exposed equally to three languages from birth (Barnes, 2006). In the view of Cook (1995: 94), in order to understand trilingualism it is necessary to imagine what is going on inside a mind where the three systems co-exist as 'a single mind with more than one language has a totality that is very different from a mind with a single language'. Cook terms such language capacities 'multi-competence' and points out that although the languages in a multi-competent individual may develop as separate systems, one should not overlook the fact that they also share points in common. Multilinguals should therefore be viewed as possessing a personal multi-competent knowledge that is not measurable in terms of monolingual standards (Hoffmann, 1991) rather than as having two (or three) first languages added together. Here it is pertinent to ask whether this multi-competent knowledge extends to aspects of pragmatics that may either be specific to each language or which may overlap between two or more of the languages known to the multilingual.

Although their language may be extremely limited, children have the ability to make themselves understood to those closest to them from a very early age. Early functional acts (Bates, 1976; Bruner, 1975; Dore, 1979) and similar notions such as Halliday's (1975) 'act of meaning' have been proposed as the primary unit of pre-speech communication. In order to assist communication, caregivers make rich interpretations of the child's early utterances and gestures in relation to context (Brown, 1973), and this simple language already shows characteristics such as proposition and illocutionary force (Austin, 1962; Carter, 1974; Dore, 1973, 1979; Halliday, 1975; Searle, 1969). As more language forms emerge, these 'primitive' speech acts (Dore, 1973) increase in complexity and type (Ervin-Tripp, 1977) until, by the age of three, children's 'intentions and propositions become grammaticalised as full speech acts' (Dore, 1975, 1978: 94). Caregivers perform a facilitative role throughout this process and interact with the child to undertake 'the collaborative construction of meaning' (Döpke, 1992; Stubbs, 1983; Wells, 1985). Early pragmatic and communicative competence is based on the child's understanding of meaning in contexts and the ability to understand utterances in context forms the very basis of language acquisition (Macnamara, 1972).

A number of analyses of monolingual children's pragmatic competence in directives, requests and question requests have been carried out within functional frameworks (Ervin-Tripp, 1970, 1977; Ervin-Tripp & Gordon, 1986; Gordon & Ervin-Tripp, 1984; Holzman, 1972; James & Seebach, 1982; Prinz, 1982; Przetacnik-Gierowska & Ligeza, 1990). Functional taxonomies for describing speech acts and the pragmatic use of language in children's speech have also been proposed by Dore (1974, 1977, 1978, 1979, 1986), Tough (1977), McShane (1980), Halliday (1975), Wells (1985), Ninio and Wheeler (1984) and others. It is important to be clear about what is meant here by function within the theory of speech acts. In Dore's view, function characterises the utterances of children at an early age and captures what they know about using language. He suggests that 'perhaps the most significant development in terms of language acquisition is the three-year-old's control of form and functions' (Dore, 1979: 353).

James and Seebach (1982: 3) summarise the findings of earlier studies of function in children's questions:

> The results of studies of both adults' and children's questions seem to indicate that questions serve different pragmatic functions. The functional categories used in these studies have varied but three general pragmatic functions appear in every classification system: the information function, the directive function and the conversational function. Although there may be subcategories, these three functions appear to be the basic ones served by questions.

The present chapter first describes a taxonomy of question functions that was designed and applied to the English questions of a trilingual child (English/Basque/Spanish). It then goes on to give examples of how the child makes use of these question functions pragmatically as part of her developing communicative competence.

Method

The subject

The subject is a trilingual girl, Jenny, who was recorded between the ages of 1;11.23 and 3;6.17.[1] She is the youngest of three children in a trilingual family and has two elder brothers, Mikel and Jon, who were aged 5;10–7;4 and 3;11–5;5 respectively, during the period of recording. The family live in a small industrial town in the Basque Country where both Basque and Spanish are spoken. As is the case throughout the Basque Country, Basque is the minority language. However, the family live in the province of Guipúzcoa in an area where Basque is widely used.

Jenny was exposed to English, Spanish and Basque in equal amounts from birth, and her relationship with each of these languages will be described in turn. Jenny's main source of English has been the family environment, principally her English mother and to a lesser extent her brothers and the interaction of the four of them. Jenny's father uses Basque with the children. During the period of data collection Jenny had never been abroad but was frequently in touch with English due to visits from English-speaking family and friends. Since a baby she was also exposed to English through educational and entertainment videos and television programmes, games, songs and rhymes, and was read stories in English by her mother. Television viewing for the family consisted mainly of English-language videos and satellite programmes.

Jenny was introduced to her Spanish-speaking caregiver within hours of being born and therefore can be considered trilingual from birth (De Houwer, 1990: 11). The caregiver had been the family's domestic helper for six months before the birth and continued to be present throughout Jenny's mother's maternity leave. She was a monolingual speaker of Spanish who cared for Jenny all day in her own surroundings until the age of 2;5, when she started Basque medium nursery school. We can estimate that, excluding holidays and weekends, Jenny was receiving at least a third of her language input in Spanish between the ages of 0;5, when her mother returned to work, and 2;5 when she began nursery. The input was related to feeding, dressing, the daily routine and domestic tasks. It did not involve play and story-telling like the parental input. Jenny went on holiday for two weeks to the south of Spain with her family at 1;1 and one week at 2;3 and 3;3. The type of holiday involved plenty of contact with monolingual Spanish speakers.

Jenny was exposed to Basque from birth through her father, his family, and the local Basque-speaking community, having access to Basque videos, television programmes, games, songs and storybooks both at school and at home. At the age of 2;5 Jenny began to attend Basque medium nursery school in the mornings and at 3;5 Jenny began to stay at Basque speaking nursery school all day. This meant that the time she was exposed to Spanish was reduced to only an hour a day, apart from when she had contact with Spanish outside the home and with her Spanish-speaking playmates.

From her birth until the age of 2;5, when she started nursery school, Jenny had been living in a trilingual environment where she received input from her three languages in similar proportions. From 2;5 and then 3;5 onwards her exposure to Spanish and Basque began to change and we would expect that from then on her Basque would continue to develop ahead of Spanish as is suggested in Cenoz and Barnes (1997) and Barnes (2001). Several recordings have been made of Jenny using Spanish and Basque. MLU and TTR have been calculated for these recordings and give an indication of the child's balanced proficiency in all three languages, and in relation to peers (Barnes, 2006).

Of the patterns of exposure proposed by Döpke (1992: 12), the closest description for Jenny's case would be 'the parents have different native tongues, neither of which is spoken in the wider community' (Basque is a minority language, and Spanish is the majority language). 'Each parent speaks his/her own language to the child. The parents speak one of the minority languages (English) to each other'.

Instrument and procedure

Analyses of interrogative behaviour (question length, form and function) were carried out on the 32 half-hour recordings made of the child at play with her mother as follows. The transcripts of the recordings were examined and classified using a protocol according to the following criteria and in the following order.

Exchange

The first step in the analysis of the data was to identify the discourse units containing one or more questions from either participant or both. These units are referred to as *exchanges* in the present study, a term used by Döpke (1992: 88) and adapted from Stubbs' (1983) model based on the basic category of the *move* proposed by Sinclair and Coulthard (1975):

> Verbal interaction consists of chains of moves which are related to each other. These chains are called exchanges. An exchange is a series of subsequent moves, each of which is conditioned by the move which immediately precedes it [...] A minimal exchange consists of an initiation and a response or an initiation and a follow up. (Döpke, 1992: 88)

Interlocutor

For each interlocutor and in every transcript, six identical protocols were filled in.

Functional category

The six protocols corresponded to a taxonomy as described below, which consisted of six functional categories and which formed the basis for the pragmatic research in this study:

(1) Real Information
(2) Known Information
(3) Confirmation
(4) Clarification
(5) Interactive
(6) Affective

Piaget (1926: 202) in the introduction to his taxonomy of non *why*-question groups describes the task of classifying by function:

> In the main [...] these groups correspond to certain fundamental functions of the mind, which are distinct from one another and for which when we come to examine them in greater detail, we shall find it quite possible to establish reliable criteria.

The present taxonomy has aspects of this psychological perspective and intuition when assigning the categories, although it is also based on linguistic principles and on previously designed functional classifications.

The Real Information, Known Information, Confirmation, and Clarification categories are standard and can be compared with each other and across studies, but the Interactive category cannot be contrasted except within itself. Confirmation and Clarification were designated two categories for the purposes of our study. However, for purposes of comparison with other studies, the two categories can also be collapsed into one, as in Corsaro (1977: 185). Incidentally, these two categories coincide respectively with *expressed guess* and *minimal grasp* questions in Lanza's (1992) taxonomy for parental reactions to mixing in child bilinguals. The fifth category, called Interactive, collected those questions that were not clearly definable as any of the previous four. In fact it is a unifying characteristic of the Interactive questions that they do not form part of the other four categories and this is borne in mind when analysing the data.

After the data had been analysed, it became clear that only the mother used the Affective category and, as this was not relevant for the findings about pragmatic use by the child, it was excluded. Furthermore, detailed data from the mother are not included in the present study, which focuses on the child's production. Once the questions had been placed in a functional category, they were then described quantitatively in terms of form, length, and type of feedback.

A second more qualitative phase of the analysis was aimed at describing the development of the child's communicative competence, and involved the detection of and interpretation of exchanges considered rich in content by the researcher. In such exchanges, which were often more extended, the child could be observed using one or more of the five question functions in her discourse. Many of the questions asked by the child were used pragmatically to initiate topics, to ask about new words, to avoid the truth, and even to display a sense of humour. Some of these involved repetition and reformulation, others the use of

Known Information questions to initiate an exchange. Ten such examples will be described in the results section of this chapter.

A third phase (which will not be mentioned here) dealt with the analysis of cross-linguistic influence from Basque and Spanish in the child's questions in English.

Examples are given below of the type of question asked by the child and classified into each functional category.

A. Real Information

This category is used for questions considered to be seeking information the questioner does not have and that she presumably needs or wants to know. Mother and child (C) are playing with a toy farm.[2]

(1)   C: Ooh lovely one.   S28. 3;1.22
       C: Do you want t' help me with other ones?
       M: Let's put the animals on the farm then.

Questions that require a response, such as offers, suggestions including 'we' and 'do you want...' and requests for permission, were also included in this category. The respondent's answer to such questions, either in the affirmative or negative, will affect the asker, who takes action on the basis of this information. Therefore the asking of the question results in the asker being provided with the information she needs or wants to know.

B. Known Information

This category is used for questions where the asker is presumed to already know the answer. The communicative purpose of the question is to pretend to seek novel information in order to initiate or maintain conversation or elicit answers. Mother and child are looking at photos, and the photo is clearly of the aunt's house, not the child's own home.

(2)   M: Who's that?   S31. 3;5.18
       C: Nicola who is this?
       M: That's Aunty Sally isn't it?
       C: Where in our house or him house?
       C: Him house.

C. Confirmation (checking)

This category is used for questions referring back to something that was said before by one of the participants where the original utterance has clearly been understood. Therefore these questions do not have the full illocutionary force of a request for information but rather that of checking information already received.

(3)   **M:** So let's sort it out then (it = the child's hair)   S25. 3;0.19
      M: Right
      C: Ah, here it is hairbrush.
      C: *What is # hairbrush?*
      M: Hairbrush, yes, that's right.

The aim of such questions is to maintain the conversation or to show interest in the interlocutor's words. This category also includes expressions such as *alright?* and *okay?* for checking approval that has already been shown or is taken for granted.

D. Clarification (repair)

This category is used when a previous utterance or utterances have not been understood and further explanation or repetition are required by the hearer.

(4)   **M:** It's like feeding a dog, isn't it?   S31. 3;5.18
      C: *Eh?*
      M: You're like my little dog.

This category also contains requests for further explanation and requests for repetition such as: *Hmm? Pardon? What? Uhh?*

E. Interactive

This umbrella category contains a variety of question functions that clearly do not fit into the other four categories. They are termed 'interactive', because their use covers a variety of functions that will keep the interaction going rather than seeking information. In the example below, the main purpose of the child's questions is to attract the mother's attention to the book the child clearly sees, so that the mother will get the book and give it to her; therefore the questions are classified as Interactive.

(5)   **C:** Er what's.   S14. 2;7.9
      C: *Oh what's that?*
      C: *Mum what's that ## book?*
      M: What darling?
      C: The book.
      C: Where is it?
      C: *Mum where's that book?*
      M: What book?
      M: What book are you looking at love?

Jenny's own questions to herself were also coded as interactive, because they lacked the illocutionary force of 'request' of the four previous categories above.

Results

The results of the qualitative analysis of the child's questions in English, shown in Table 3.1, demonstrate that the functional category most used by the child was Real Information (53.98%). Known Information (12.42%), Confirmation (10.88%) and Clarification (14.45%) questions showed similar percentages, and the Interactive category (8.20%) was the smallest.

It has been reported elsewhere (Barnes, 2006), and can be seen in Table 3.1, that within the classification of functional categories for the questions of this child, Real Information questions showed the greatest increase over time. Known Information questions appeared at the start of data collection at 1;11 and again at 2;2.24 and were used sporadically but in increasing amounts. Interactive questions were also infrequent but showed growth. Confirmation and Clarification questions decreased, presumably as Jenny's command and understanding of the language became stronger.

In the course of the quantitative analysis of the data, both from a primarily functional but also formal perspective, it became apparent that Jenny followed a range of questioning patterns consistently (see Barnes, 2006). Through the second phase of qualitative analysis, it was also possible to observe how her communicative competence was developing as she became increasingly involved in and proficient at negotiating meaning with her mother through the use of a variety of questioning strategies based around functional use. It seemed that the child had in some way learned what was expected of her as a participant in the discourse and was eager to take the lead.

In this section we will examine ten samples based on exchanges in which the child displays such communicative strategies in the light of what has been presented in relation to question functions. The samples will be described chronologically so that the growth in her communicative competence can be observed. Their titles are for guidance only, and are not intended to constitute a classification as the samples were chosen at random on the basis of the interest of the communicative competence demonstrated in their content.

Table 3.1 Number of questions (Jenny)

Tape	Real Information	Known Information	Interactive	Confirmation	Clarification
1	8	2	4	0	1
2	31	0	5	9	3
3	8	0	2	3	9
4	13	0	1	1	9
5	0	0	1	1	3
6	29	11	1	5	26
7	13	1	0	6	8
8	14	0	0	7	11
9	10	6	0	6	16
10	23	7	2	1	3
11	14	7	8	2	0
12	26	14	2	5	9
13	23	2	11	12	0
14	14	8	6	6	3
15	11	5	3	2	9
16	35	7	5	4	1
17	12	21	1	5	9
18	20	2	0	8	3
19	13	3	4	3	5
20	22	0	0	3	5
21	16	1	4	3	1
22	25	6	3	6	2
23	11	6	2	3	0
24	20	1	0	4	5
25	18	10	8	3	2
26	22	0	7	0	10
27	12	10	5	3	4
28	35	1	0	7	10
29	25	3	5	1	5
30	87	6	10	12	2

(*Continued*)

Table 3.1 (*Continued*)

Tape	Real Information	Known Information	Interactive	Confirmation	Clarification
31	33	9	1	0	2
32	22	4	0	3	2
Total	665	153	101	134	178
Total %	53.98	12.42	8.20	10.88	14.45

(1) S2 (2;0.6) Feeding a doll

In the following exchanges, when she is just two and with an MLU (Mean Length of Utterance) of 1.8, the child's full involvement in the discourse can be seen. She uses a variety of question functions such as Real Information (lines 5, 6, 8, 20), Confirmation (2, 3, 23, 29) and Interactive (line 17) to find things out, to maintain the interaction with her mother and to attract her attention respectively. *Bib?* at lines 23 and 29 are echo questions that allow the child to participate in the interaction by echoing in a question her mother's utterance, and thus returning the turn to her.

```
1   M:   Go and give dolly a yogurt.
2   C:   Yogurt?
3   C:   Yogurt?
4   M:   Hmm give dolly a yogurt.
5   C:   Like this?
6   C:   Like this?
7   M:   Yes.
8   C:   Here?
9   M:   Is that a yogurt?
10  C:   This yogurt.
11  M:   What about a spoon?
12  M:   She needs a spoon doesn't she?
13  M:   Can you see one?
14  M:   Well go and get it then?
15  M:   Get a spoon for the dolly's yogurt.
16  C:   Is here.
17  C:   Here here?
18  M:   That's it.
19  M:   Well done Jenny.
```

20	C:	Here?
21	M:	Oh go on please.
22	M:	What about a bib?
23	C:	Bib?
24	M:	Does she need a bib?
25	C:	Yes bib.
26	M:	Does dolly need a bib?
27	C:	She need a bib.
28	M:	Does the dolly need a bib?
29	C:	Bib?
30	M:	Yes.

(2) S7 (2;4.17) Choosing socks

In the following exchanges Jenny uses a limited variety of two-word declarative questions to show her mother a variety of possible socks she could wear. Although she says very little, her involvement in the interaction at a pragmatic level is total. *Eh?* (line 5) asks for Clarification of the mother's comments, to which Jenny replies with indignation (line 7). The questions in lines 12, 20, 27, 33, and 35 all request Real Information relating to the sock's suitability or not. For example in lines 20 and 27 the meaning of *this one?* could be glossed as *'what about this one?'* Similarly in line 35, when Jenny asks *this is # this?*, the meaning of the sentence is something like *'does this match?'*

1	M:	Give me some socks.
2	C:	I like it this one.
3	M:	No no they're not nice.
4	M:	They don't look nice with your dress.
5	C:	Eh?
6	M:	They don't look very nice.
7	C:	Yes (with intonation 'yes, they do')
8	M:	No they don't.
9	M:	They are pink and your dress is green.
10	C:	Yes green.
11	C:	Okay green.
12	C:	Like this?
13	M:	Show me.
14	M:	Which ones are they?
15	C:	This.
16	M:	No no those are stripy ones.

17	C:	Yes.
18	M:	You don't want to wear stripy ones.
19	C:	Okay.
20	C:	This one?
21	M:	Those ones are a bit too thick.
22	C:	Yes.
23	M:	I don't like those ones.
24	M:	Put them back.
25	M:	They're not very nice.
26	C:	Eh # on the floor.
27	C:	This one?
28	M:	Hmmm could be.
29	M:	I don't like them.
30	M:	They don't go with your dress darling.
31	M:	You need white ones white ones.
32	M:	You got any nice white ones.
33	C:	This one?
34	M:	Could be but where's the other one ?
35	C:	This is # this?
36	M:	They are different darling.

(3) S9 (2;5.5) Attracting attention

In this sample we see Jenny using the strategy of asking a Known Information question (line 1) to initiate an exchange, in this case about a flower her panda is wearing. When she has no response from her mother she uses the strategy of repeating (line 3) and reformulating (lines 2 and 4) the question until she gets a reply. This is the earliest example of Jenny initiating discourse by means of a Known Information question. She later becomes very proficient at it.

1	C:	Mummy what's doing Panda?
2	C:	Mummy what's doing?
3	C:	Mummy what's doing Panda?
4	C:	What's doing?
5	M:	What's the panda doing love?
6	M:	What's he doing to the flower?

(4) S10 (2;5.19) Initiating play

In the following exchanges we observe how Jenny uses Known Information questions (lines 1, 4, 5) first to initiate play with her mother, involving plastic bath animals that both of them can see, and then to continue the game (lines 10, 11, 13, 15). We also see how the child reformulates the question (lines 1, 4, 5) until she has obtained her mother's participation in the game.

1	C:	Mummy where's Eeyore?
2	C:	Heyo.
3	M:	What love?
4	C:	Eeyore what's that?
5	C:	Where's Eeyore?
6	M:	Where's Eeyore?
7	M:	Here he is.
8	C:	Eh?
9	M:	Here he is.
10	C:	Yes and Pooh?
11	C:	And Pooh?
12	M:	There's Pooh.
13	C:	And Piglet?
14	M:	And Piglet.
15	C:	And er Tigger?
16	C:	Heehee.
17	M:	There he is.
18	C:	Yes.

(5) S11 (2;6.3) Seeking a new lexical item

Here we also find a case of Jenny asking explicitly for a lexical item in English by means of Real Information questions (lines 1, 2, 4, 6).

1	C:	I'm # what's that?
2	C:	Mummy what's that?
3	M:	What's what love?
4	C:	What's that?
5	M:	Oh here.
6	C:	What's that?
7	M:	You know what that is.
8	M:	What is it?
9	C:	Olloa (Basque)
10	M:	A chicken # a chicken.
11	C:	A chicken.
12	C:	Hello chicken.

(6) S17 (2;8.19) Re-seeking a lexical item

In the next example Jenny again uses questions, this time indirectly, as a strategy to obtain a lexical item she does not have in English. In line 3 the mother supplies the new word but during the play of utterances 4 and 5 Jenny appears to forget. Lines 6 and 7 are therefore Real Information questions directed at the toy but requiring a response from the mother as demonstrated by the reproachful *Mummy* in line 8. The mother supplies the word (lines 9 and 10) and play continues (line 11).

1	**M:**	And this # what's this?
2	**C:**	I don't know.
3	**M:**	It's a hedgehog.
4	**C:**	Yes it's going up there.
5	**C:**	Is going jump.
6	**C:**	Hello # who are you?
7	**C:**	Who are you is name?
8	**C:**	Mummy.
9	**M:**	It's hedgehog.
10	**M:**	Say hedgehog.
11	**C:**	Hello hedgehog.

(7) S18 (2;9.5) Seeking lexical items

By this age Jenny is able to use a series of fairly well formed Real Information (lines 2, 3, 5, 10, 11) and Confirmation questions (line 7) to obtain new information.

1	**M:**	Do you know what colour they are?
2	**C:**	What's this?
3	**C:**	What's this colour?
4	**M:**	That's blue # blue.
5	**C:**	And what's this colour?
6	**M:**	That's yellow colour.
7	**C:**	And this is a yellow one?
8	**M:**	No that's a white one.
9	**C:**	Oh white.
10	**C:**	And this is not?
11	**C:**	And this?
12	**M:**	That's red and that's yellow.

(8) S29 (3;3.8) Showing interest and enthusiasm

The following exchange demonstrates how Jenny has grasped the use of questioning for a variety of functional purposes. Jenny is unwrapping the pieces of a toy tea set. In lines 2 and 6 she answers her own Interactive questions. In line 9 the mother responds to Jenny's Interactive question. Jenny then asks for Clarification with an echo question (line 11) immediately followed by two reformulated Real Information questions on the same theme (lines 12 and 13), putting pressure on her interlocutor to reply. The exchange ends with a simple Real Information question formed by the declarative *and more?* said with disappointment to mean 'isn't there anything more?'

1	C:	And this is look like a cup of tea.
2	C:	What's this?
3	C:	A plate.
4	C:	A schwimt of cuppa tea.
5	C:	Another cup of tea.
6	C:	Ah what's in?
7	C:	Another one.
8	C:	Another plate.
9	C:	Now what's in there?
10	M:	A tray.
11	C:	A tray?
12	C:	What's the tray do?
13	C:	Mum what's the tray do?
14	M:	You put the cup of tea on like that.
15	C:	And there and there and there.
16	M:	Isn't that pretty?
17	C:	And more?

(9) S31 (3;5.18) Initiating and maintaining discourse

Jenny and her mother are looking at photos together. In line 1 Jenny initiates the exchange with a question that could relate either to Real or Known Information. She is now able to initiate exchanges by asking questions based on shared knowledge, or lack of it, because her mother's answer implies that she does not know either (lines 2, 3 and 4). This does not seem to matter to either participant as Jenny does not repeat or reformulate to get an answer and the conversation proceeds to the next photograph in line 8, where Jenny again initiates the exchange.

1	C:	What's Grandad doing over here?
2	M:	I don't know what he's doing.
3	M:	What is he doing?
4	M:	### What's he doing?

5	M:	Oh look at you.
6	M:	Don't you look sweet.
7	C:	And what he got here Grandad?
8	M:	Ah well that tells you the date.
9	M:	Who's that?
10	C:	Nicola.
11	C:	Who is this?

(10) S32 (3;6.18) Expressing surprise

Jenny is able to use a formulaic *what's this?* with appropriate intonation to express surprise when the building bricks are emptied out onto the floor.

1	C:	Ooh what's this?
2	C:	### ooh ###ooh.
3	C:	One ## two ### three ### xxx four.
4	C:	Five ### three. (counting pieces)
5	C:	Mum Mummy can you take this out?
6	C:	Mummy can you take this all out?

Discussion and Conclusion

These findings on the acquisition of question function English by a trilingual child have been compared with other studies on the acquisition of question function in monolingual English children of the same age in Barnes (2006). Studies on early bilingual and trilingual children in English were not available for comparison of this area. Jenny's results as a trilingual were found to be consistent with those of James and Seebach (1982) for numbers of questions in the Informative (Real Information)[3] category, although a decrease in these questions as children get older was reported by them. Holzman (1972) also found growth in Real (Real Information) questions, as did Przetacnik-Gierowska and Ligeza (1990), who relate this to cognitive development and quality of questioning interaction.

Barnes (2006) found that Jenny became increasingly proficient at using Known Information questions to initiate and maintain conversations. This is consistent with the findings of Holzman (1972), who reported that Test (Known) questions in monolinguals could serve as conversation initiators. In James and Seebach (1982) it was found that Conversational (Known) questions were present from age two and that they decreased in the age three group, which is not in agreement with Barnes (2006), where a slight increase was found.

James and Seebach (1982) found that the, Directive (Interactive) function was not used until age three, but in Barnes (2006) it is present from age 1;11. Results relating to children's questions in the Confirmation and Clarification functions with which to make comparisons were not available from other studies, but in relation to the functional categories of Real Information, Known Information, and Interactive it can be seen that, by and large, Jenny's progress, as a trilingual learner, is consistent with that of monolingual development.

Jenny's use of question functions became more sophisticated over time, as is also described by Gordon and Ervin-Tripp (1984). Her use also seems to fulfil the criteria of solving the five problems of getting attention, clarity, persuasiveness, maintaining social relations and performing repairs mentioned by Ervin-Tripp and Gordon (1986).

Trilingual Jenny made use of reformulation and repetition to modify the function of the questions so as to achieve her communicative aim, as has been reported for monolinguals elsewhere (Ervin-Tripp, 1988; Gordon & Ervin-Tripp, 1984; Newcombe & Zaslow, 1981; Ochs-Keenan, 1977). She also copied functional use by her mother by repeating questions from part of her mother's earlier exchange, for instance to make a 'joke' (Barnes, 2006: 163) Retracing at a lexical level has been reported by Bloom *et al.* (1982) but has not, as far we know, been described at a functional level.

The findings of Prinz (1982) for monolinguals that form and function appear in a parallel fashion are not in agreement with those for Jenny reported by Barnes (2006). Barnes (2006) shows that, although Jenny may not have had many forms available in the early recordings, she was, in fact, able to make some use of all of the functions except Known Information, which, although it appeared in the first recording, was not found again until three months later. Furthermore, her use of function became increasingly sophisticated as her language developed. This is consistent with language behaviour reported by Dore (1977: 148) who says that 'children interpret forms as having a variety of functions and functions as having a variety of forms'.

The ten samples presented here illustrate Jenny's communicative competence (Hymes, 1972) and show that she is able to use questions for functional purposes from an early age and to express a variety of communicative intents. It may be that such routines are a type of training for strategies she will later apply in conversation, for example that of using questions to obtain lexical items. She also shows evidence of metalinguistic awareness in her strategies to find out how to express concepts in English for which she may already have the word(s) in her other languages. Many other samples could have been included (see Barnes, 2006) and even with an MLU of 2.0–2.5 for question form, she makes use of all five question functions in the taxonomy. Here we have seen how she is able to attract attention, make a choice, initiate play, initiate and maintain conversation, ask for and about new words, show surprise, interest and enthusiasm, as well as use strategies to obtain information she needs through the pragmatic use of questions. She is also able to avoid and manipulate the truth, initiate and extend play, express humour and attract attention (Barnes, 2006). A similar published selection of language samples for monolingual children has not been found with which to compare, but nonetheless it is remarkable that a child who has only been exposed to English in the home as one of three languages in her linguistic microcosm is able to do this.

The fact that Jenny is able to use questions (rather than statements) in all the functional categories by age 1;11 and shows pragmatic growth equivalent to or more than that reported in other studies on groups of monolingual children can be considered evidence of considerable pragmatic flexibility. This may be explained by a combination of factors. First, Przetacnik-Gierowska and Ligeza (1990) relate question use and pragmatic function to the quality of questioning interaction in which the child is a participant and suggest that it is superior in home dyads than in kindergartens with teachers. On the one hand, as most of Jenny's questioning interaction in English has taken place with her mother, this may explain in part her apparent flexibility. The same applies to her Spanish with her caregiver and Basque with her father. On the other hand, Dore (1986) has found that flexibility in function can be a result of fantasy play with peers. Apart from playing at home with her brothers and friends, Jenny has attended kindergarten (in Basque) from the age of 2;5 where this type of play took place. It is also possible that any resulting pragmatic growth in Basque will also be seen in English, because pragmatic skills may be transferred across languages (Barnes, 2001; Blum-Kulka & House, 1989). From the point of view of developing pragmatic flexibility, it would therefore seem that Jenny has had the best of both worlds both at home and in kindergarten. If we tentatively include the possibility of the influence of her three languages upon one another as a factor, we have further justification for the pragmatic flexibility revealed both by the taxonomy and in the examples of her communicative competence, although personality factors may also have a part to play. In sum, Jenny demonstrates through her communicative competence here that she has not only been acquiring knowledge of the forms of English, but also the ability to use them appropriately pragmatically, albeit with a single interlocutor in the home context with her siblings, and along with Basque and Spanish in the community outside.

Notes

1. The use of the abbreviation *year;month.day* to show a child's age is an established convention throughout the literature on child language acquisition. Thus 1;10 indicates that the child is 1 year and 10 months old, and 3;1.9 would indicate an age of 3 years, 1 month and 9 days.
2. S28, refers to the script number, and 3;1.22 to the child's age at the time of recording the script.
3. The name of functional category used in the present study is placed in parentheses after the name used in a particular study. As has been pointed out above, the amount of correspondence between functional categories across studies is open to discussion.

References

Austin, J. (1962) *How to Do Things with Words*. New York: Oxford University Press.
Barnes, J. (2001) Politeness in English, Basque and Spanish: Evidence from a trilingual child. *Jakingarriak* 45, 40–45.
Barnes, J. (2006) *Early Trilingualism: A Focus on Questions*. Clevedon: Multilingual Mattters.
Bates, E. (1976) *Language and Context: The Acquisition of Pragmatics*. New York: Academic Press.
Bloom, L., Merkin, S. and Wootten, J. (1982) *Wh-* questions: Linguistic factors that contribute to the sequence of acquisition. *Child Development* 53, 1084–1092.
Blum-Kulka, S. and House, J. (1989) Variation in requesting behaviour. In S. Blum-Kulka, J. House and G. Kasper (eds) *Cross-Cultural Pragmatics: Requests and Apologies* (pp. 123–153). New Jersey: Ablex.
Brown, R. (1973) *A First Language: The Early Stages*. London: Allen and Unwin.
Bruner, J. (1975) The ontogenesis of speech acts. *Journal of Child Language* 2, 1–19.
Carter, A. (1974) Communication in the sensorimotor period. Doctoral dissertation, University of California, Berkeley.
Cenoz, J. and Barnes, J. (1997) Early trilingualism: Basque, English and Spanish. ERIC Document Reproduction Service No. ED413761.
Chomsky, N. (1980) *Rules and Representations*. New York: Columbia University Press.
Cook, V. (1995) Multi-competence and the learning of many languages. *Language, Culture and Curriculum* 8, 93–98.
Corsaro, W. (1977) The clarification request as a feature of adult interactive styles with young children. *Language in Society* 6, 183–207.
De Houwer, A. (1990) *The Acquisition of Two Languages from Birth: A Case Study*. Cambridge: Cambridge University Press.
Döpke, S. (1992) *One Parent–One Language: An Interactional Approach*. Amsterdam: Benjamins.

Dore, J. (1973) The development of speech acts. Doctoral dissertation. City University of New York.
Dore, J. (1974) A pragmatic description of early language development. *Journal of Psycholinguistic Research* 3, 343–350.
Dore, J. (1975) Holophrases, speech acts and language universals. *Journal of Child Language* 2, 21–40.
Dore, J. (1977) Oh them sheriff: a pragmatic analysis of children's responses to questions. In S. Ervin-Tripp and C. Mitchell-Kernan (eds) *Child Discourse* (pp. 139–163). New York: Academic Press.
Dore, J. (1978) Conditions for the acquisition of speech acts. In I. Markova (ed.) *The Social Context of Language* (pp. 87–111). Chichester: Wiley.
Dore, J. (1979) Conversation and preschool language development. In P. Fletcher and M. Garman (eds) *Language Acquisition* (pp. 339–361). Cambridge: Cambridge University Press.
Dore, J. (1986) The development of conversational competence. In R.L. Schiefelbusch (ed.) *Language Competence: Assessment and Intervention* (pp. 3–60). London/Philadelphia: Taylor and Francis.
Ervin-Tripp, S. (1970) Discourse agreement: how children answer questions. In J.R. Hayes (ed.) *Cognition and Development of Language* (pp. 79–107). New York: Wiley.
Ervin-Tripp, S. (1977) Wait for me, roller skate. In S. Ervin-Tripp and C. Mitchell-Kernan (eds) *Child Discourse* (pp. 165–188). New York: Academic Press.
Ervin-Tripp, S. (1988) Request retries. *Lenguas Modernas* 15, 25–34.
Ervin-Tripp, S. and Gordon, D. (1986) The development of requests. In R.L. Schiefelbusch (ed.) *Language Competence: Assessment and Intervention* (pp. 61–95). London/Philadelphia: Taylor and Francis.
Genesee, F., Boivin, I. and Nicoladis, E. (1996) Talking with strangers: A study of bilingual childrens communicative competence. *Applied Psycholinguistics* 17, 427–442.
Gordon, D. and Ervin-Tripp, S. (1984) The structure of children's requests. In R.L. Schiefelbusch and J. Pickar (eds) *The Acquisition of Communicative Competence* (pp. 295–321). Baltimore, MD: University Park Press.
Halliday, M.A.K. (1975) *Learning How to Mean.* London: Edward Arnold.
Hoffmann, C. (1991) *An Introduction to Bilingualism.* London: Longman.
Holzman, M. (1972) The use of interrogative forms in the verbal interaction of three mothers and their children. *Journal of Psycholinguistic Research* 1 (4), 311–336.
Hymes, D. (1972) *Towards Communicative Competence.* Philadelphia: University of Pennsylvania Press.
James, S. and Seebach, M. (1982). The pragmatic function of children's questions. *Journal of Speech and Hearing Research* 25, 2–11.
Lanza, E. (1992) Can bilingual two-year-olds code-switch? *Journal of Child Language* 19, 633–658.
Macnamara, J. (1972) The cognitive basis of language learning in infants. *Psychological Review* 79, 1–13.
McShane, J. (1980) *Learning to Talk.* Cambridge: Cambridge University Press.

Newcombe, N. and Zaslow, M. (1981) Do 2 1/2-year-olds hint? A study of directive forms in the speech of 2 1/2-year-old children to adults. *Discourse Processes* 4, 239–252.

Ninio, A. and Wheeler, P. (1984) A manual for classifying verbal communicative acts in mother–infant interaction. *Working Papers in Developmental Psychology*, no. 1. Jerusalem: The Martin and Vivian Levin Center, Hebrew University. Reprinted in *Transcript Analysis* (1986) 3, 1–82.

Ochs-Keenan, E. (1977) Making it last: repetition in children's discourse. In S. Ervin-Tripp and C. Mitchell Kernan (eds) *Child Discourse* (pp. 125–131). New York: Academic Press.

Piaget, J. (1926) *The Language and Thought of the Child*. London: Routledge and Kegan Paul.

Prinz, P. (1982) 'Requesting' in normal and language-disordered children. In K. Nelson (ed.) *Children's Language* (Vol. 3, pp. 139–203). Hillsdale, NJ: Erlbaum.

Przetacnik-Gierowska, M. and Ligeza, M. (1990) Cognitive and interpersonal functions of children's questions. In G. Conti-Ramsden and C. Snow (eds) *Children's Language* (Vol. 7, pp. 69–101). Hillsdale NJ: Erlbaum.

Searle, J.R. (1969) *Speech Acts*. Cambridge: Cambridge University Press.

Sinclair, J. and Coulthard, R. (1975) *Towards an Analysis of Discourse: The English Used by Teachers and Pupils*. London: Oxford University Press.

Stubbs, M. (1983) *Discourse Analysis. The Sociolinguistic Analysis of Natural Language*. London: Blackwell.

Tough, J. (1977) *The Development of Meaning*. New York: Halsted Press.

Wells, G. (1985) *Language Development in the Pre-School Years*. Cambridge: Cambridge University Press.

Chapter 4
Influence of the Linguistic Environment on the Development of the Lexicon and Grammar of Basque Bilingual Children

ANDONI BARREÑA, Mª JOSÉ EZEIZABARRENA and IÑAKI GARCÍA

Introduction

The study of early, simultaneous acquisition of two languages by bilingual children has led researchers to defend different positions with regard to children's ability to develop both languages separately from the very beginning. Several authors, such as Volterra and Taeschner (1978) or Redlinger and Park (1980), concluded that bilingual children are not able to distinguish both languages at first. Instances of syntactic errors and mixed utterances illustrated these claims, and children's mixed utterances were found to reflect adult mixing rates (Tabouret-Keller, 1969). Many other researchers have provided different kinds of evidence that lead them to defend the opposite position, namely the *separation hypothesis*, which states that children acquiring two languages simultaneously develop both languages separately, from a very early age (Bel, 2001; De Houwer, 1995; Deuchar & Quay, 2000; Genesee *et al.*, 1995; Meisel, 1994, 2001). Similarly, research carried out on early language production by balanced bilingual children acquiring Basque and Spanish simultaneously showed that the development of each language takes place in bilingual children in a very similar way to that shown by monolinguals, as similar stages and similar errors have been found (Almgren & Barreña, 2001; Barreña, 1995, 1997, 2001; Ezeizabarrena, 1996). It should be noted that most evidence for this hypothesis has been found in cases of balanced bilingualism, that is to say, in cases of children exposed equally to both languages from birth onwards, and most of them when growing up follow the Grammontian principle of 'one person, one language'. Both languages may also develop separately in cases of unbalanced input, and one language may develop earlier than the other (Pérez-Vidal, 1995).

The results mentioned so far do not exclude the possible existence of some cross-linguistic influence on bilingual acquisition. For instance, Müller and Hulk (2000) predict syntactic conditions where one language may influence the other language being acquired. Moreover, Lleo *et al.* (2003) present data on the acquisition of codas in Spanish and German by monolingual and bilingual children and conclude that one language may positively (accelerate) influence the acquisition of the syllable structure in the other language.

Most of the longitudinal studies referred to here are based on spontaneous production data by a small number of children recorded from their first words until age 3 or later.

The use of cross-sectional methodologies such as the MacArthur–Bates test allows the collection and comparison of early data (until 30 months)[1] for hundreds of children at the same ages, and across several languages. Some very interesting results have been found in the production of lexicon and grammar in monolingual and bilingual corpora. On the one hand, such research has shown that lexical development precedes grammatical development (Arratibel *et al.*, 2005; Bassano, 2000; Pérez-Pereira & García Soto, 2003; Serrat *et al.*, 2004). Thus, the high correlation between grammatical and lexical development, at least until the age of 30 months (Bassano, 2000; Bates & Goodman, 1997), has led many authors to argue for the existence of a causal relation between the two, and to formulate the notion of *critical mass*, as the minimum number of words needed in order for grammatical development to take place (Bates *et al.*, 1988; Marcham & Bates, 1994). For instance, Bates *et al.* (1994) have even quantified this critical mass as being 400 items for English, whereas Pérez-Pereira *et al.* (2006) found a very high correlation between the production of 100 words and the production of grammatical suffixes in other languages such as Galician and Basque. Moreover, Marchman and Bates (1994) found a nonlinear correlation between the lexical mass and the development of verb morphology, which led them to suggest the possibility that different grammatical (nominal/verbal) elements correlate with different values of lexical mass. Results on early Romance languages studied by Caselli *et al.* (1999), Devescovi *et al.* (2005) and Pérez-Pereira and García-Soto (2003) confirm such a proposal.

On the other hand, the MacArthur–Bates test may also be used to assess the language development of bilingual children. De Houwer and Bornstein (2005), for instance, found that 13-month-old bilingual children may produce different test scores for Dutch and French. Furthermore, Galician-Spanish bilingual children seem to produce longer and more complex sentences than monolingual Galician children (Pérez-Pereira & García-Soto, 2003).

Other kinds of research such as the study of early speech category perception have shown that monolingual and bilingual children do not follow a similar developmental pattern. The discrimination of some phonemic contrasts that exist in only one of the two languages being acquired takes longer for bilingual children than for the monolinguals. In contrast to monolingual children, bilingual children undergo an intermediate stage where they seem to be 'less able' to discriminate some speech sound pairs than they were some months earlier, prior to the acquisition of adult-like discrimination ability (Sebastián-Gallés, 2006).

So far, we may conclude that studies on language production where no major differences have been found between monolingual and bilingual children do not seem to show the whole picture on early bilingual acquisition. In general, it seems reasonable to think that as the input (amount and quality of exposure to each language) may influence the kind of bilingualism, balanced and unbalanced bilinguals may show different developmental patterns in early language production, and there may even be degrees of difference within the different kinds of bilinguals.

In this paper we present production data for children exposed to different levels of Basque input, in order to determine the level of influence this input has on both lexical and grammatical development (three nominal suffixes for plural and case marking).

Two variables related to the input will be distinguished: the degree to which a given language is present in the immediate environment of the monolingual and bilingual children, and their parents' knowledge of the language. In relation to these variables, the following predictions can be made:

(1) *Degree of exposure to the language*: The more Basque input is present in children's linguistic environment, the more extensive lexical and grammatical production children will show.
(2) *Linguistic competence of parents*: Children of Basque-speaking parents will show more extensive lexical and grammatical knowledge at earlier ages than children of mixed couples (Basque-speaker + Romance-speaker).

Subsequent sections deal with an analysis of the influence these two input-related variables have on the lexical and grammatical development of monolingual and bilingual children up to the age of 30 months. First, previous results of longitudinal studies on the grammatical development of monolingual and bilingual children acquiring Basque will be presented. Second, cross-sectional data for children aged between 16 and 30 months will be presented with regard to both lexical and grammatical development. Finally, results from both kinds of studies will be discussed in terms of the influence of input on such results.

Methodology

Two kinds of data constitute the corpus of this study. We will first present data from previous longitudinal studies on the acquisition of Basque and then some recent data collected using the Basque version of the MacArthur–Bates Inventory of Communicative Development (CDI).

Longitudinal studies

Most of the Basque longitudinal data refer to children brought up in families where Basque is either the only or a very frequently used language at home, together with Spanish.[2,3] Children were video-recorded fortnightly, in sessions of about 30 minutes per language, from 15 months (the youngest child) to 30 months. Recording sessions took place at children's homes, in spontaneous interaction with another child or adult, usually one or both parents.

Three of the children considered to be monolingual (M) are offspring of native speakers of Basque. The other three children, brought up in bilingual families, show a greater variability in relation to the presence of Basque, although for them, it is the predominant language in their immediate social environment, that of their families. Thus, they are considered Basque-dominant bilinguals (BB). In two of the cases, the father speaks to the child in Spanish, his mother language; in the third, there is a monolingual Spanish caregiver who spends many hours a day with the child during his first years (Table 4.1).

Cross-sectional study

The MacArthur–Bates CDI has been adapted for use in Basque by the KGNZ Research Group.[4] The CDI consists of a questionnaire on the linguistic and grammatical knowledge of children. For the present study,

Table 4.1 Longitudinal corpus of three monolingual and three bilingual Basque children

Child	Number of recordings	Age range (months)	Basque in the input	Language of the parents	Interparental language
Oitz (M)	17	18–30	100%	B–B	B
Egoitz (M)	31	15–30	100%	B–B	B
Bianditz (M)	27	18–30	100%	B–B	B
Mikel (Bi)	15	19–30	70%	B–S	S
Kerman (Bi)	19	23–30	70%	B–S	B
Peru (Bi)	8	23–30	70%	B(L2)–B	B

M, Monolingual; Bi, bilingual; B, Basque; S, Spanish.

data for the CDI-2, which correspond to children of 16–30 months of age, have been taken into account.

In general, the CDI-2 contains three kinds of information: (1) The lexical section of the Basque version contains 657 lexical items, divided into 21 semantic fields, which the parents mark if their child has started producing them; (2) The grammar section contains 88 items divided into 5 subsections, plus one other where the parents are asked to write down the three longest utterances produced by the child recently (this last piece of information is necessary in order to estimate the mean length of utterance, although the calculation is based on the three longest sentences (MaxLU), and not on the total number of sentences the child produces (MLU)); (3) A more general section, where parents are asked for some additional information, such as the number of hours a week each member of the family spends talking with the child, and in which language, the number of family members, and so on.

To date, 1107 questionnaires have been collected. As data for premature children and for children with successive ear infections during the first months were discarded (135), 972 subjects remained available for the purposes of our study. In order that the sample should be as representative as possible, data were collected in all three of the administrative territories that make up the Basque Country: the Comunidad Autónoma Vasca and the Comunidad Foral de Navarra, which are within Spain, and the Département des Pyrénnées Atlantiques in France. Moreover, data have been collected in predominantly Basque-speaking areas, but also in areas where the Basque-speaker frequency is very low. See Arratibel *et al.* (2005) and García *et al.* (2005) for more details. With regard to the educational level of the parents contained within the sample, 34% have completed secondary education and a further 56% have university qualifications.

Children's linguistic environment
- *Exposure to Basque language.* Parents are asked about the languages family members use in the presence of the child (number of hours per week). The degree to which each language is present in the immediate environment can be calculated from this information in terms of percentages for each language. Basque generally shares its domain with one Romance language (Spanish or French), although the presence of other European and non-European languages, although still very low, is becoming ever more frequently reported in the family environment of Basque children.
- *Parents' knowledge of Basque.* As is generally well known, all present-day, native Basque-speakers are bilinguals who are also competent in Spanish or French. However, not every adult living in the Basque Country is able to speak Basque. In order to examine the input in greater depth, parents were asked about their knowledge of Basque. Furthermore, they were asked about the use of this language when talking with their partners. Surprisingly, preliminary results of this study have shown that many Basque-speaking parents do not use Basque when talking to each other. This point is not explored further here (work in progress).

Presence of Basque at home

In terms of the presence of Basque at home, data were grouped as follows. Data for 947 children were studied with regard to this variable, given that 25 (out of 972 questionnaires) provided no information with regard to this point. Based on the degree to which Basque is present in their immediate environment, three groups were distinguished:

(1) Monolingual children (M): >90% Basque input;
(2) Bilingual children of Basque-dominant family environments (BB): 60–90% Basque input;
(3) Bilingual children from non-dominant Basque family environments, where Basque shares its space, in most cases, with a Romance language, Spanish or French (BR): <60% input.

The fact that the adapted questionnaire is written in Basque effectively excluded access to data for children brought up in families with a very low presence of Basque (input of 0–30%). The largest grouping in the

Table 4.2 Distribution of the sample by number of children from three kinds of linguistic environments

	Age (months)														
	16	17	18	19	20	21	22	23	24	25	26	27	28	29	30	Total
Monolingual	30	34	32	33	32	33	43	35	37	45	48	49	53	39	45	588
Bi-Basque	9	8	8	9	8	8	11	14	14	16	24	13	21	17	29	209
Bi-Romance	5	6	6	10	5	10	12	14	18	8	10	11	6	13	16	150
Total	44	48	46	52	45	51	66	63	69	69	82	73	80	69	90	947

Bi, bilingual.

sample is the monolingual one ($n = 588$, 62%), followed by the Basque-dominant bilingual group ($n = 209$, 22% of the sample) and by the third and smallest grouping, the non-dominant Basque group ($n = 150$, 16%). See Table 4.2 for their distribution into age groups.

Parents' knowledge of Basque

There were 31 forms that did not provide accurate answers on this point. Two groups are apparent within the remaining 941 forms, based on the answers given by parents about their knowledge of Basque:

(1) Children of Basque-speaking couples (BP) and
(2) Children of mixed couples (MP), where only one of the parents can speak Basque. In this group, data for couples where the mother is the Basque-speaker are combined with data for couples where the father is the Basque-speaker, due to the limited data for the latter kind ($n = 52$).

Most children in the study were born to Basque-speaking couples ($n = 744$, 79%), whereas only 197 (21%) of the sample correspond to mixed couples. See Table 4.3 for more details.

Lexical and grammatical development

Lexical development is measured in terms of the mean values of vocabulary items ticked out of the 657 items in the Basque version of the CDI. See the section 'Exposure to Basque language and linguistic development' for details.

Grammatical development is measured by taking two aspects into account. On the one hand, the mean length of utterance (MLU) is calculated in morphemes in the longitudinal study; however, the cross-sectional study collects only the three longest utterances produced by

Table 4.3 Distribution of the sample by number of children with regard to their parents' knowledge of Basque (BP/MP) and to their age in months

	Age (months)															
	16	17	18	19	20	21	22	23	24	25	26	27	28	29	30	Total
Basque-speaking couple (BP)	36	41	37	42	40	42	56	46	50	55	60	60	67	50	62	744
Mixed couple (MP)	9	7	8	10	5	7	10	17	19	12	21	14	11	19	28	197
Total	45	48	45	52	45	49	66	63	69	67	81	74	78	69	90	941

each child, therefore, rather than being an MLU, it is in this case a MaxLU. On the other hand, the production of three morphological suffixes in the nominal phrase is observed: absolutive plural -k, ergative case -k and dative case -(r)i. The following results sections deal with the results of longitudinal and cross-sectional studies, respectively.

Some Results from Longitudinal Studies

In this section, longitudinal data for the linguistic production of six Basque children are presented: three monolinguals (O,B,E) and three bilinguals (P,K,M).

MLU

Figure 4.1 shows MLU data for monolingual children, and Figure 4.2 MLU data for bilingual children. There is interindividual variation in

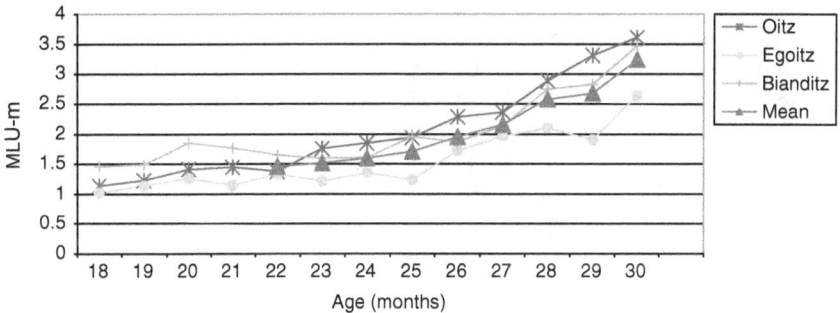

Figure 4.1 Longitudinal MLU-m values of three monolingual (M) children

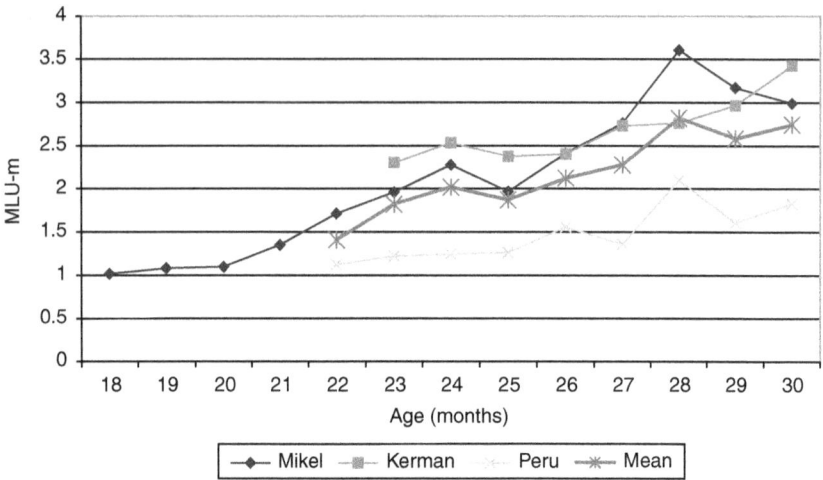

Figure 4.2 Longitudinal MLU-m values of three bilingual (BB) children

both groups, but the mean values are very similar in both cases, although it is surprising that mean values for BB (2.18) are slightly higher than for M (2.09). However, these values only refer to the period 22–30 months, as data for only one of the bilingual children were available at the earliest ages.

Grammatical suffixes

The first evidence of grammatical marking attested to in longitudinal studies is not always followed by its production in every subsequent context where it would be required. Even the regular production of such marking does not necessarily mean that all kinds of morphological marking will be present at that point. Although tentative, for the present study, the age at which the children produce each kind of grammatical marking at any frequency has been established as being the middle point between the first non-imitative production and the age where the suffix is produced adequately in 80% of the required contexts (Table 4.4 and Figure 4.3).

No visible differences are found between the two groups, although the monolingual group produces plural, ergative and dative marking somewhat earlier than the bilingual group. Variation is observed amongst individuals in each group, but this is not so noticeable between the groups themselves. First plural or first dative marking is subject to individual

Table 4.4 Age at which monolingual and bilingual children produce grammatical suffixes

	Plural-k			Ergative-k			Dative-ri		
	1st produced	>80% of required context	Sometimes	1st produced	>80% of required context	Sometimes	1st produced	>80% of required context	Sometimes
Monolingual children									
Oitz	2;00	2;03	2;02	2;00	2;06	2;03	2;00	2;00	2;00
Egoitz	2;01	2;02	2;02	2;01	2;02	2;02	1;11	2;03	2;02
Bianditz	1;06	1;06	1;06	1;06	1;10	1;08	1;09	1;09	1;09
Bilingual children									
Mikel	2;04	2;05	2;05	1;09	2;06	2;01	2;01	2;03	2;02
Kerman	1;11	1;11	1;11	1;11	2;09	2;04	2;00	2;00	2;00
Peru	2;04	2;05	2;05	2;05	2;09	2;07	2;07	2;07	2;07

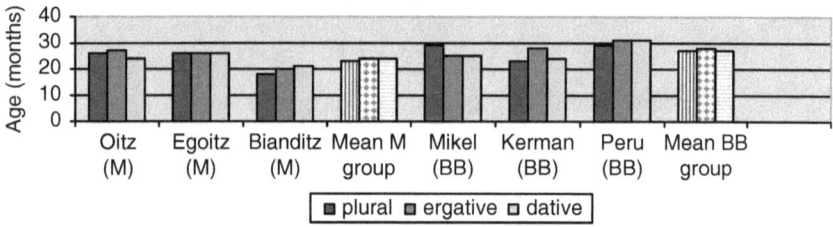

Figure 4.3 Age at which monolingual and bilingual children produce suffixes

variation, whereas ergative marking is the last kind of marking to be produced by both groups, and takes place at 26–28 months (Figure 4.4). However, the non-parametric Mann–Whitney test indicates that the differences observed for the plural are not statistically significant.

Summarising the previous section, as individual variation is attested to in both groups, longitudinal data for monolingual and Basque-dominant bilingual children are not easily distinguishable from each other. When measuring MLU values, they turn out to be very similar for both groups, and even a little higher for the bilinguals than for the monolingual children. With regard to grammatical development, the bilingual children behave very similarly to the monolinguals, although plural and dative marking are generalised a little later in the bilingual corpus than in the monolingual one. It is worth noting the fact that two homophonous markers, such as the plural absolutive and the ergative singular, are regularised at different ages, which is an indication that children

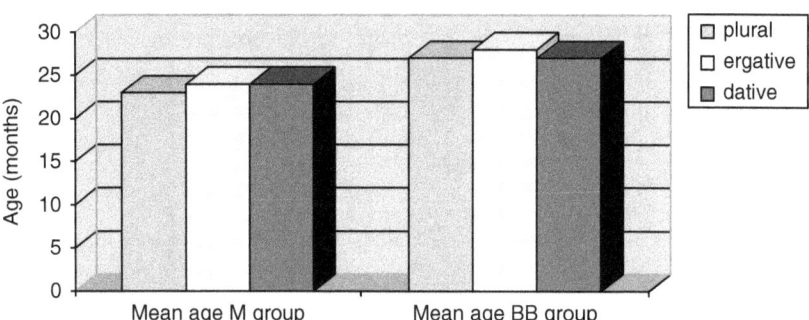

Figure 4.4 Mean age at which grammatical suffixes (*sometimes*) are produced in six longitudinal studies

analyse them differently.[5] Similar phenomena have also been observed in English (Guilfoyle & Noonan, 1992).

The absence of statistically significant differences between two such small groups may not reveal much about the influence of a given variable on the data. The cross-sectional study in the next section tries to compensate for the limited representativeness of the longitudinal data.

Some Results from Cross-Sectional Studies

In this section, the results of the cross-sectional study on lexical and grammatical development are analysed with regard to two variables related to the input: degree of exposure and parental knowledge of the language.

Exposure to Basque language and linguistic development

Exposure to Basque is analysed in terms of the degree of presence of this language at home. First, data concerning lexical development are presented, then data for grammatical development.

Exposure to Basque language and lexical development

In general, children from monolingual families produce a higher number of lexical items than children from bilingual families. However, in order to get a more precise picture, the sample has been divided into three groups, according to the degree to which Basque is present in the family input (Figure 4.5): monolingual (>90% Basque input), Basque-dominant bilingual (60–90% Basque input) and non-dominant Basque bilingual children (<60% Basque input).

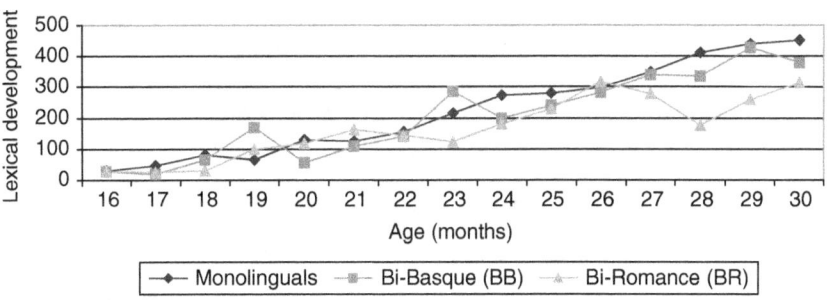

Figure 4.5 Lexical development of children from three kinds of linguistic environments

As an initial finding, the general effect of the input on lexical production does become statistically significant when dealing with three groups ($F = 7.21$; $p < 0.01$), although differences are only found between M and BR, that is, between monolinguals and bilinguals with less exposure to Basque.

Figure 4.5 indicates a very similar lexical development for all the groups, especially in the initial stages, with the only exception being at age 19 months, where the M group produce the lowest values of lexical knowledge ($F = 3.26$; $p < 0.05$). M and BB remain very close to each other during almost the whole study period, with M showing slightly higher values, especially after age 2 years. In contrast, values in the BR group tend to be lower, and the separation from the other two groups seems to become ever greater from 27 months onwards.

Differences among M, BB and BR turn out to be very significant statistically at 24 months ($F = 4.71$; $p < 0.018$), and again from 28 months onwards (28 months: $F = 8.87$; $p < 0.001$; 29 months: $F = 10.79$; $p < 0.001$; 30 months: $F = 5.74$; $p < 0.005$). In addition, intergroup comparison indicates that there are significant differences between BR and the other two groups from 28 months onwards, whereas M and BB groups show no significant differences.

In general, data from previous sections indicate that the degree of exposure to Basque does have an effect on the lexical production of the sample, although during the first months any one of the three groups can surpass either of the other two groups in terms of test scores recorded. At 23 months, but more consistently from 28 months onwards (mean 375 words), children from Basque-dominant environments, whether monolinguals or bilinguals, make use of a considerably wider vocabulary than children who grow up with less Basque input, whose lexicons may contain around 160 fewer words on average.

Exposure to Basque and grammatical development

Two kinds of grammatical elements are considered: MLU and three grammatical suffixes (plural (-*k*), ergative (-*k*) and dative (-*ri*)).

MLU

MLU has been measured in terms of the number of morphemes contained in the three longest sentences reported by the parents (MaxLU) in the CDI.

Figure 4.6 represents the development of three groups of children in terms of mean MLU-m values in each age group. Differences among monolinguals, Basque-dominant bilinguals and non-dominant Basque

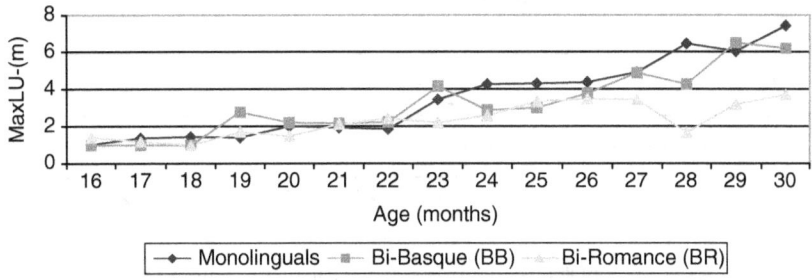

Figure 4.6 MaxLU-(m) averages for children from three kinds of linguistic environments

bilinguals become visible from 23 months onwards. Statistically, the effect of input appears to be significant in general terms ($p < 0.01$). Mean averages of M (3.76) and BB (3.77) groups are very similar, but the BR group produces a lower value (2.54).

Only very slight differences can be observed among the three groups before age 2 years, with the exception of 19 months ($F = 4.70$; $p < 0.05$). It is from 28 months onwards that differences become very significant (28 months: $F = 7.66$; $p < 0.01$; 29 months: $F = 3.61$; $p < 0.05$; 30 months: $F = 5.4$; $p < 0.01$). Moreover, the comparison between pairs of groups reveals significant differences between M and BR at age 2 years. At 28 months, the M produce significantly higher scores than the two bilingual groups, but after 29 months the BR give significantly lower mean values than both Basque-dominant groups (M and BB).

Summarising, it can be said that, with the specific exception of age 19 months, no important differences have been found between M and BB with regard to MLU-m values. In contrast, the BR group behaves differently with respect to the other two, showing lower values again. Although no data for MLU-w have been discussed in this section, due to limitations of space, a statistical analysis confirms the results obtained with MLU-m: the intergroup difference is also significant ($F = 8.58$; $p < 0.01$) in the same way as that observed for MLU-m.

Grammatical suffixes

In this section, the number of subjects in the sample who *sometimes* or *always* produce each suffix are expressed in percentages, in order to indicate the moment when the production of plural -*k*, ergative -*k* and dative -(*r*)*i* becomes generalised in each group of children. As children hardly ever combine words and/or morphemes before 22 months

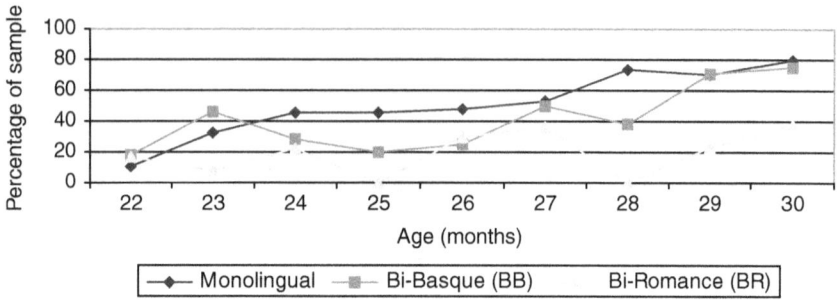

Figure 4.7 Percentage of the sample of each age group that (*sometimes, always*) produce plural marking

(MLU under 2), data for morphological production will only be considered from this age onwards.

Figures 4.7 to 4.9 represent data for the particular markings: plural, ergative and dative. In accordance with what has been observed in previous sections, the BR provide lower scores than the other groups in general, who, in contrast, behave quite similarly.

Significant and very significant differences are observed with regard to plural marking at 25 months ($\chi^2 = 7.38$; $p < 0.05$), 28 months ($\chi^2 = 17.05$; $p < 0.001$), 29 months ($\chi^2 = 9.86$; $p < 0.01$) and 30 months ($\chi^2 = 10.37$; $p < 0.01$).

There are some differences with regard to ergative case marking, initially at 23 months ($\chi^2 = 8.19$; $p < 0.05$). These disappear over the next two months but then reappear (26 months: $\chi^2 = 6.4$; $p < 0.05$) and

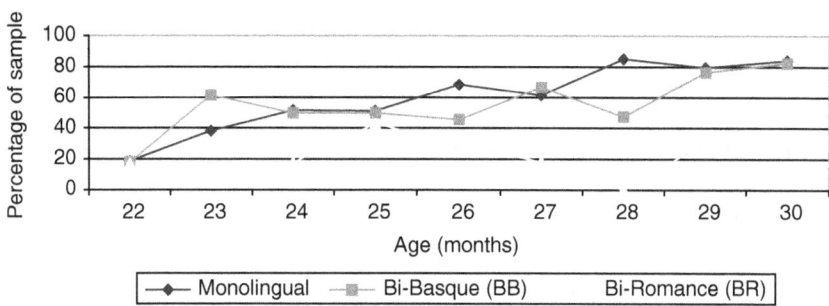

Figure 4.8 Percentage of the sample of each age group that (*sometimes, always*) produce ergative marking

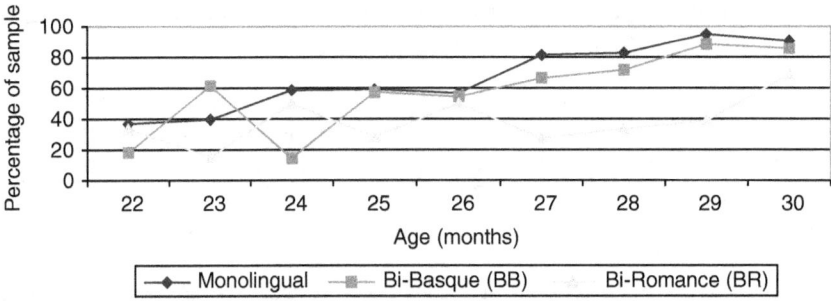

Figure 4.9 Percentage of the sample of each age group that (*sometimes, always*) produce dative marking

remain very significant during the later months (27 months: $\chi^2 = 7.46$; $p < 0.05$; 28 months: $\chi^2 = 24.0$; $p < 0.001$; 29 months: $\chi^2 = 11.43$; $p < 0.01$; 30 months: $\chi^2 = 22.49$; $p < 0.001$).

Dative case marking is also produced differently by the groups at various ages. M and BB groups show significantly higher rates at 27 months ($\chi^2 = 12.97$; $p < 0.001$), 28 months ($\chi^2 = 7.71$; $p < 0.005$) and 30 months ($\chi^2 = 22.09$; $p < 0.001$). Thus, the BB behave very similarly to the M, with the exception of data at 24 months, where only a few BB subjects produce dative marking ($\chi^2 = 7.98$; $p < 0.05$).

Summarising, the exposure to Basque affects the lexical development as much as the length of utterances and grammatical development. Such an influence is visible around age 2 years, but especially significant from 27–28 months onwards. In general, no differences are observed between the Basque-dominant groups of children, the M and BB, whereas the BR group shows lower scores and rates of production at the three levels measured: lexicon, length of utterance and grammatical suffixes. As a concluding remark, the degree to which Basque is present becomes a factor that distinguishes production data for groups with a high input (higher than 60%) from groups with a lower input, but not between monolinguals and bilinguals with high exposure to the language.

Parents' knowledge of Basque and children's linguistic development

The second variable to consider is whether the fact that only one or both parents know Basque has any influence on the linguistic knowledge of the children. Two groups have been distinguished: (1) children of

Basque-speaking parents (BP) and (2) children of mixed couples (MP), where only the father or the mother speaks Basque.

Parents' knowledge of Basque and children's lexical development

Generally, parental knowledge of the language has an effect on the vocabulary produced by their children (Figure 4.10). The mean vocabulary size of BP children is 242.87, whereas MP's children produce an average of 212.88 words. Such a difference is statistically significant ($t = 2.29; p < 0.05$).

There are no important differences between groups (BP and MP) before month 23.[6] BP children show a significantly greater vocabulary size compared to MP children at 24 months ($t = 2.15; p < 0.05$), and especially from 27 onwards ($t = 2.35; p < 0.05$). Although not very significant at 28 months ($t = 1.91; p < 0.1$), differences are significant in the oldest groups (29 months: $t = 3.44; p < 0.01$; 30 months: $t = 4.79; p < 0.001$).

Parents' knowledge of Basque and children's grammatical development

MLU. Parents' knowledge of a language appears to be a factor in the development of complexity in their children's language. Children of BPs, produce 3.81 morphemes per (longest) utterance on average, whereas children of mixed couples show a lower average in complexity, 2.69 morphemes. The general difference is very significant ($t = 5.60; p < 0.01$).

Figure 4.11 represents a very similar development in both groups until age 2 years. From 25 months on, considerably more complex utterances are observed in the group of children whose parents both speak Basque. Differences are only tentative at 25 months ($t = 1.72; p < 0.1$); they rapidly become significant (26 months: $t = 2.37; p < 0.05$;

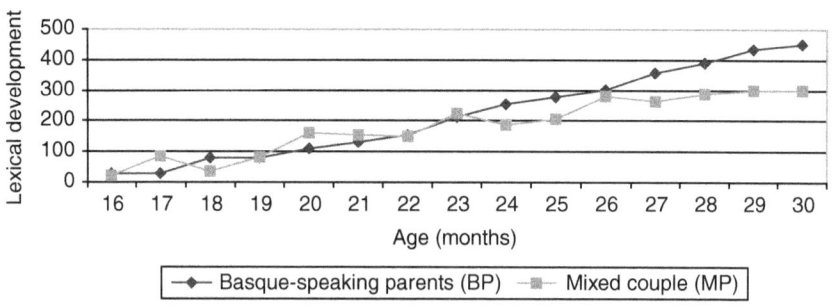

Figure 4.10 Children's lexical development and parental knowledge of Basque

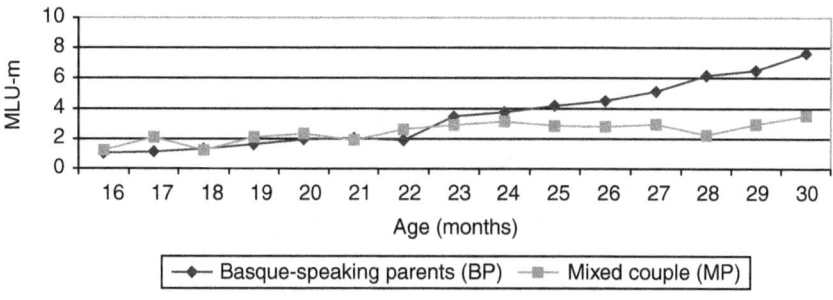

Figure 4.11 MLU-m development and parents' knowledge of Basque

27 months: $t = 2.48$; $p < 0.05$) and are very significant in the following months (28 months: $t = 3.70$; $p < 0.001$; 29 months: $t = 4.88$; $p < 0.001$; 30 months: $t = 4.96$; $p < 0.001$).

Grammatical suffixes. Figures 4.9–4.11 represent the percentages of children in each group and age group who *sometimes* or *always* produce the corresponding grammatical suffix. In general, children of Basque-speaking parents produce plural, ergative and dative marking at a higher rate than children of mixed couples (Figure 4.12). However, such differences are significant only when the groups are older. The fact that one or both parents can speak Basque has some statistical effect from 28 months onwards only (28 months, $\chi^2 = 8.80$; $p < 0.01$; 29 months, $\chi^2 = 8.04$; $p < 0.01$; 30 months, $\chi^2 = 16.52$; $p < 0.001$).

Figure 4.13 shows that ergative case production is also affected by the one/two Basque-speaking parents variable at 26 months ($\chi^2 = 5.93$; $p < 0.05$); its effect disappears at 27 months, but reappears at 28

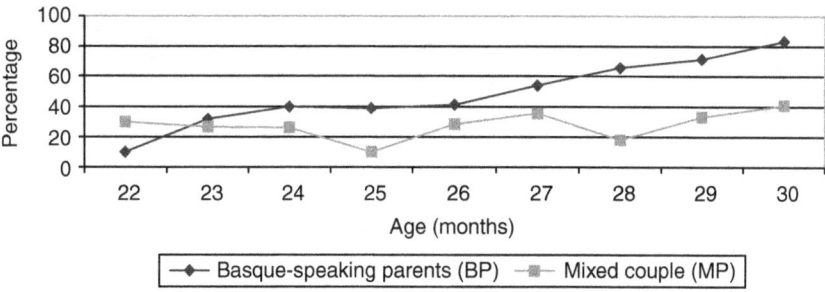

Figure 4.12 Children's production (*sometimes* or *always*) of plural marking and their parents' knowledge of Basque

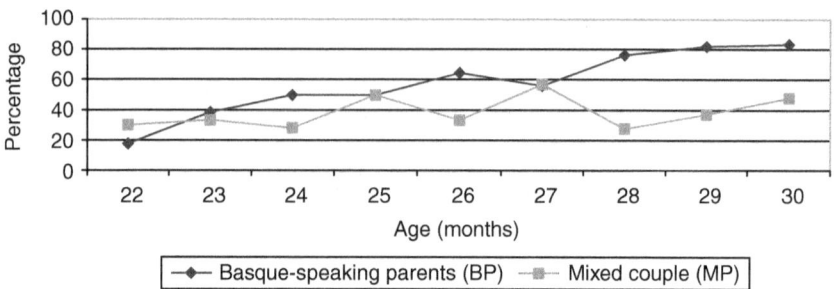

Figure 4.13 Children's production (*sometimes* or *always*) of ergative case and their parents' knowledge of Basque

months (28 months, $\chi^2 = 10.58; p < 0.01$; 29 months, $\chi^2 = 13.26; p < 0.001$; 30 months, $\chi^2 = 11.86; p < 0.01$).

Dative production by children of two Basque-speaking parents is statistically higher from 27 months onwards (Figure 4.14). At this stage, and during the following months, about 80% of the BP children produce the dative case, but less than 50% of the MP do so. Differences between both groups become significant during the later months (27 months, $\chi^2 = 6.80; p < 0.01$; 28 months, $\chi^2 = 10.72; p < 0.01$; 29 months, $\chi^2 = 11.88; p < 0.01$), with the exception of month 30. At this moment most children produce dative-case marking.

Summarising this section, the fact that one or both parents can speak Basque is a variable that affects linguistic knowledge, both at the lexical level and with regard to complexity or morphological production. Differences between BP and MP children are significant from 25 months

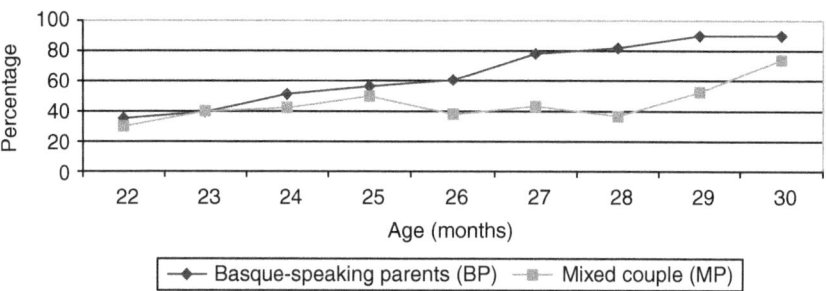

Figure 4.14 Children's production (*sometimes* or *always*) of dative case and their parents' knowledge of Basque

onwards for utterance complexity, and from 27 on for lexical and grammatical production.

Discussion

Longitudinal and cross-sectional data on early Basque indicate that monolingual and most bilingual children who acquire Basque as their mother language show very similar development in terms of vocabulary, MLU, and in terms of producing certain grammatical suffixes, such as plural -*k*, ergative -*k* and dative -(*r*)*i*.

It should be noted, however, that bilingual children in the longitudinal studies grew up in families where the presence of Basque is very high (about 70% of the linguistic input), as at least two members in the family use only Basque when talking together. In addition, in cases where only one of the parents addresses the child in Basque, the input is 'compensated for' by the regular presence of other Basque speakers at home (Mikel's case), or by the fact that parents talk together in Basque (Kerman's case).

In keeping with what has been found in longitudinal studies, the cross-sectional data reveal a very similar developmental pattern for children with a high level of Basque input (100–60%), which contrasts with a lower production of vocabulary, complexity and grammatical marking by children with less exposure to this language.

Moreover, the cross-sectional study provides very useful information with regard to three variables related to the input received by the youngest children. In addition to the degree to which Basque is present in their environment, the questionnaire used in the study includes questions about whether one or both parents can speak Basque, and about the frequency of use of Basque by the parents when talking to each other. These results confirm the predictions made in the Introduction section of this chapter.

(1) The degree to which Basque is present in the input has a clear influence on the lexical and grammatical development from 23–24 months onwards, and especially after 27–28 months. First differences are apparent at around age 2 years, when the mean vocabulary size is greater than 200 words and the production of two (or more) word utterances becomes generalised. Differences are still clearer at 27–28 months, the age when the mean vocabulary size surpasses the 300-word threshold and when the longest utterances contain on average more than 4 morphemes. Over a half of the sample produce morphology markers (plural, ergative, dative) at this stage. Thus, differences among groups seem to appear at the moment where

the critical mass is consolidating (Bates et al., 1988; Marchman & Bates, 1994).

In general, no significant differences have been found between the monolingual (M) and the Basque-dominant bilingual group (BB), either in the longitudinal or in the cross-sectional studies. In contrast, non-dominant Basque bilinguals (BR) in the cross-sectional study show a different developmental pattern, which is characterised by much lower scores on vocabulary size, complexity and morphological production.

(2) Data corroborate the second prediction. The fact that both parents can speak Basque has a positive effect on lexical development, on the complexity of utterances and on grammatical production as well, in the sense that these children obtain higher test scores in lexical and grammatical development than children of one-Basque-speaker couples. Differences are significant from 26 months onwards with regard to MLU-m, from 27 months on with regard to lexical production and the production of the morphological suffixes considered here. However, contrary to what may be expected, the frequency of use of Basque as a communicative language between the parents (*always/sometimes/never*), does not seem to have any marked effect on the children's linguistic development. The only statistical difference appears for the last age group (30 months). Two explanations may be proposed:
   (a) As the language used by the parents when talking together does not constitute real input for the child, this variable does not affect the linguistic development of the children
   or
   (b) This variable does have an influence on linguistic development, but its effect is not immediately apparent.

Methodological limitations of the cross-sectional study do not allow for any confirmation to be made as to whether the effect of the variables studied continues at later ages.

Conclusions

The degree of presence of each language in the family environment seems to have some influence on the linguistic development of the bilingual child. In the present work some differences have been observed among monolingual, Basque-dominant and Romance-dominant bilingual children, but these are not significant between the groups exposed to a consistent Basque input (more than 60%). Significant differences between Basque-dominant and non-dominant bilinguals become increasingly clear after 25–26 months.

Acknowledgements

We are very grateful to the children, their parents, the caregivers, and teachers who participated in this research. This project would not have been possible without them and the financial support of the following institutions: The Basque Government (PI2000-5, PI2004-16), The Ministry of Education, Science and Technology (BFF2003-05196), The Ministry of Education-EURESCO (BFF2002-10379-E) and the University of the Basque Country (9/UPV00033.130-13614/2001). Finally, we want to thank the editors of this volume for their patience and encouragement.

Notes

1. Slight differences are observed among the adaptations to different languages. See Jackson-Maldonado *et al.* (2003) for Mexican Spanish, López-Ornat *et al.* (2005) for Peninsular Spanish, Kern (2004) for French, or Arratibel *et al.* (2005) and Pérez Pereira *et al.* (2005) for Basque and Galician.
2. See Idiazabal (1991), Barreña (1995), Meisel (1994), Ezeizabarrena (1996), Elosegi (1998), Almgren and Barreña (2001), among others.
3. Many other research projects on early bilingualism have been based on similar spontaneous data. See, for instance, Bel (2001) for early Catalan-Spanish or Pérez-Vidal (1995) for early Catalan-English bilingualism.
4. KGNZ refers to *Komunikazio Garapena Neurtzeko Zerrenda* 'Inventory for Measuring Communicative Development'. Other members of this interdisciplinary research group are Margareta Almgren (UPV); Julia Barnes, Nekane Arratibel and Idoia Olano (U. Mondragon); Alazne Petuya and Amaia Colina of SEASKA.
5. See Ezeizabarrena and Larrañaga (1996) for some discussion of the delay in the regular production of both kinds of /-k/ suffixes.
6. The unexpected negative difference observed at month 17 is statistically significant ($t = -2.16; p < 0.5$).

References

Almgren, M. and Barreña, A. (2001) Bilingual acquisition and separation of linguistic codes: Ergativity in Basque versus accusativity in Spanish. In K.E. Nelson, A. Aksu-Koc and C.E. Johnson (eds) *Children's Language, Volume 11: Interactional Contribution to Language Development* (pp. 27–48). Mahwah, NJ: Lauwrence Erlbaum Associates.

Arratibel, N., Barreña, A., Pérez-Pereira, M. and Fernández, P. (2005) Comparaciones interlingüísticas euskara-gallego del desarrollo léxico y gramatical infantil. In M.A. Mayor, B. Zubiauz and E. Díez (eds) *Estudios sobre la Adquisición del Lenguaje* (pp. 983–996). Salamanca: Ediciones Universidad de Salamanca.

Barreña, A. (1995) *Gramatikaren jabekuntza-garapena eta haur euskaldunak* [Grammatical development and Basque children]. Bilbao: University of the Basque Country.
Barreña, A. (1997) Desarrollo diferenciado de sistemas gramaticales en un niño vasco-español bilingüe. In W. Glass and A.T. Pérez-Leroux (eds) *Contemporary Perspectives on the Acquisition of Spanish* (pp. 55–74). Somerville: Cascadilla Press.
Barreña, A. (2001) Grammar differentiation in early bilingual acquisition: Subordination structures in Spanish and Basque. In M. Almgren, A. Barreña, M.J. Ezeizabarrena, I. Idiazabal and B. McWhinney (eds) *Research on Child Language Acquisition* (pp. 78–94). Somerville: Cascadilla Press.
Bassano, D. (2000) Early development of nouns and verbs in French: Exploring the interface between lexicon and grammar. *Journal of Child Language* 27, 521–559.
Bates, E. and Goodman, J.C. (1997) On the inseparability of grammar and the lexicon: Evidence from acquisition, aphasia and real-time processing. *Language and Cognitive Processes* 12, 507–586.
Bates, E., Bretherton, I. and Snyder, L. (1988) *From First Words to Grammar: Individual Differences and Dissociable Mechanisms*. New York: Cambridge University Press.
Bates, E., Marchman, V., Thal, D., Genson, L., Dale, P., Reznick, J. S., Reilly, J. and Hartung, J. (1994) Developmental and stilistic variation in the composition of early vocabulary. *Journal of Child Language* 21, 85–123.
Bel, A. (2001) *Teoria lingüística i adquisició del llenguatge. Anàlisi comparada dels trets morfològics en català i en castellà*. Barcelona: Institut d'Estudis Catalans.
Caselli, M.C., Casadio, P. and Bates, E. (1999) A comparison of the transition from first words to grammar in English and Italian. *Journal of Child Language* 26, 69–111.
De Houwer, A. and Bornstein, M. (2005) Asymmetry in early bilingual lexical development: More evidence for dissociations between comprehension and production. Paper presented at the *X International Congress for the Study of Child Language*, Berlin.
De Houwer, A. (1995) Bilingual language acquisition. In P. Fletcher and B. MacWhinney (eds) *The Handbook of Child Language* (pp. 219–250). Cambridge, MA: Blackwell.
Deuchar, M. and Quay, S. (2000) *Bilingual Acquisition: Theoretical Implications of a Case Study*. Oxford: OUP.
Devescovi, A., Caselli, M.C., Marchione, D., Pasqualetti, P., Reilly, J. and Bates, E. (2005) A crosslinguistic study of the relationship between grammar and lexical development. *Journal of Child Language* 32, 759–786.
Elosegi, K. (1998) *Kasu eta preposizioen jabekuntza-garapena haur elebidun batengan*. Bilbao: Universidad del País Vasco.
Ezeizabarrena, M.J. (1996) *Adquisición de la morfología verbal en euskera y castellano por niños bilingües*. Bilbao: Universidad del País Vasco.
Ezeizabarrena, M.J. and Larrañaga, M.P. (1996) Ergativity in Basque. A problem for language acquisition? *Linguistics* 34–35, 966–991.
Fenson, L., Dale, P., Reznick, J.S., Thal, D., Bates, E., Hartung, J.P., Pethick, S. and Reilly, J. (1993) *MacArthur Communicative Development Inventories: User's Guide and Technical Manual*. Baltimore: Brookes.
García, I., Ezeizabarrena, M.J., Almgren, M. and Errarte, I. (2005) El desarrollo léxico infantil en euskera: Una nueva adaptación del Test MacArthur. In M.A. Mayor, B. Zubiauz and E. Díez (eds) *Estudios sobre la Adquisición del Lenguaje* (pp. 955–967). Salamanca: Ediciones Universidad de Salamanca.

Genesee, F., Nicoladis, E. and Paradis, J. (1995) Language differentiation in early bilingual development. *Journal of Child Language* 222, 611–631.

Guilfoyle, E. and Noonan, M. (1992) Functional categories and language acquisition. *The Canadian Journal of Linguistics* 37, 241–272.

Idiazabal, I. (ed.) (1991) *Adquisición del lenguaje en niños bilingües y monolingües – Hizkuntza jabekuntza haur elebidun eta elebakarretan*. San Sebastián: Universidad del País Vasco.

Jackson-Maldonado, D., Thal, D., Fenson, L., Marchman, V.A., Neuton, T. and Conboy, B. (2003) *MacArthur nventarios del desarrollo de habilidades comunicativas. User's Guide and Technical Manual*. Baltimore: Paul H. Brookes.

Jackson Maldonado, D. (2004) La evaluación de niños mexicanos con retraso inicial de lenguaje: Utilidad de reportes maternos y muestras espontáneas de lenguaje. Talk at the IV Congreso Internacional sobre la Adquisición de las Lenguas del Estado. Salamanca España.

Kern, S. (2004) French version of the MacArthur-Bates CDI words and sentences. Talk at the University of Mondragon in Eskoriatza, Basque Country: Spain.

Lanza, E. (1998) Cross-linguistic influence, input and the young bilingual child. *Bilingualism: Language and Cognition* 1 (3), 181–182.

Lleo, C., Kuchenbrandt, I., Kehoe, M. and Trujillo, C. (2003) Syllable final consonants in Spanish and German monolingual and bilingual acquisition. In N. Müller (ed.) *(In)vulnerable Domains in Multilingualism* (pp. 191–220). Amsterdam-Philadelphia: Benjamins.

López-Ornat, S., Gallego, C., Gallo, P., Karaousou, A., Mariscal, S. and Martínez, M. (eds) (2005) *MacArthur. Inventario de Desarrollo Comunicativo MacArthur*. Madrid: TEA.

Marchman, V. and Bates, E. (1994) Continuity in lexical and morphological development: A test of the critical mass hypothesis. *Journal of Child Language* 21, 339–366.

Meisel, J. (ed.) (1994) *La adquisición del vasco y del español en niños bilingües* (pp. 155–180). Frankfurt am Main: Vervuert-Iberoamericana.

Meisel, J. (2001) The simultaneous acquisition of two first languages: Early differentiation and subsequent development of grammars. In J. Cenoz and F. Genesee (eds) *Trends in Bilingual Acquisition* (pp. 11–41). Amsterdam: Benjamins.

Müller, N. and Hulk, H. (2000) Crosslinguistic influence in bilingual children: object omissions and root infinitives. In C. Howell *et al.* (eds) *BUCLD 24 Proceedings* (pp. 546–557). Somerville: Cascadilla Press.

Pérez Pereira, M., and García Soto, X.R. (2003) El diagnóstico del desarrollo comunicativo en la primera infancia: adaptación de las escalas MacArthur al gallego. *Psicothema* 15(3), 352–361.

Perez-Pereira, M., Jackson-Maldonado, D., Ezeizabarrena, M.J., Kern, S. (2005) The MacArthur-Bates CDI in some Romance languages and Basque: Language development and language differences. Poster presented at the X *Congress for the Study of Child Language*, Berlin.

Pérez Pereira, M., Almgren, M., Resches, M., Ezeizabarrena, M.J., Díaz, C. and García, I. (2006) Cross-linguistic comparisons between Basque and Galician. *Dubrovnic Meeting on the Adaptations of the MacArthur-Bates Test*, May 2006.

Pérez-Vidal, C. (1995) *La adquisición del Inglés de un niño bilingüe (Catalán/Inglés)*. Barcelona: Universidad de Barcelona.

Redlinger, W. and Park, T. (1980) Language mixing in young bilinguals. *Journal of Child Language* 7, 337–352.

Sebastián-Gallés, N. (2006) Native-language sensitivities: Evolution in the first year of life. *Trends in Cognitive Sciences* 10 (6), 239–240.

Serrat, E., Sanz-Torrent, M. and Bel, A. (2004) Aprendizaje léxico y desarrollo de la gramática: vocabulario verbal, aceleración morfológica y compejidad sintáctica. *Anuario de Psicología* 35 (2), 221–234.

Tabouret-Keller, A. (1969) La adquisición del lenguaje hablado en un niño criado en un medio bilingüe. In *Introducción a la Psicolingüística* (pp. 208–222). Buenos Aires: Proteo.

Volterra, V. and Taeschner, T. (1978) The acquisition of language by bilingual children. *Journal of Child Language* 5 (2), 311–326.

Chapter 5

Null and Overt Subjects in the Developing Grammars (L1 English/ L1 Spanish) of Two Bilingual Twins

JUANA M. LICERAS, RAQUEL FERNÁNDEZ FUERTES and ROCÍO PÉREZ-TATTAM

Introduction

Ever since Chomsky (1981) put parameters at the centre of learnability theory, parameters in general and the null subject parameter in particular have been one of the most studied topics in both linguistic theory and language acquisition research. The null subject parameter – a formalisation of Perlmutter's (1971) surface structure filter – is defined as a cluster of properties which determine two typological groups of languages: [+pro-drop] and [−pro-drop], depending on whether they allow:

- Null subjects
  (1) [ø] He encontrado el libro
      'I found the book'
- Free inversion in matrix sentences
  (2) [ø] Ha comido Juan
      'Juan ate'
- 'Long wh – movement' of the subject
  (3) El hombre$_i$ que me pregunto a quién [ø]$_i$ había visto
      'The man x such that I wonder who x saw'
- Empty resumptive pronouns in embedded clauses
  (4) Ésta es la chica$_i$ que me pregunto quién cree que [ø]$_i$ lo hizo
      'This is the girl that I wonder who thinks that she did it'
- Apparent violations of the *[that-t] filter
  (5) ¿Quién$_i$ crees que [ø]$_i$ se irá?
      'Who do you think (that) will leave'

According to Chomsky (1981), these constructions are possible in pro-drop languages because Agreement – a feature of Inflection – governs the empty category [ø]. The feature Agreement cannot govern an empty category in non pro-drop languages. The intuitive idea is that subjects can be dropped when there is overt agreement. Acquisition understood as parameter-setting implies that, by determining the characteristics of the features associated with a functional category in a particular language, children are able to set the properties of the corresponding parameter.

Null subjects in early child language as in (6) and (7) have occupied a special place in psycholinguistic research (Frazier & De Villiers, 1990; Guasti, 2002; Hyams, 1986) due to their null category status.

(6) Broke this   [Peter 2.0.1(Pierce, 1992: 116)]
(7) Veut lait   [Daniel 1.11.1 (Pierce, 1992: 109)]
    Wants milk
    'He/she wants milk'

Null subjects appear in early L1 acquisition data regardless of whether the adult language is a [−null subject] language (English or French in (6) and (7)), or a [+null subject] language (Spanish in (8)).

(8) Horita viene   [LV II:78–2.0 (González, 1970: 10)]
    Now is coming
    'He/she is coming now'

The presence of null subjects in early [+/−null subject] grammars has been accounted for mainly in two ways. In some accounts, child grammars were assumed to be different from adult grammars (competence account) (Hyams, 1986, 1996; Pierce, 1992; Rizzi, 1993/94; Weissenborn, 1992). In other accounts, child grammars were proposed to be similar to adult grammars, but children's production capability explained the superficial differences (performance account) (Bloom, 1970, 1990; Valian, 1990, 1991; Valian & Eisenberg, 1996).

In the case of [+null subject] languages such as Spanish, it was soon noticed that the presence of null subjects was not the main issue in relation to setting the null subject parameter, but the mastering of stylistic conventions that regulate the distribution of overt subjects in the [+null subject] adult grammar (Liceras, 1988, 1989). In recent literature on bilingualism and L2 acquisition, special attention has been paid to the distribution of overt subjects in [+null subject] languages, precisely because it is considered not to be the domain of syntax, but rather is regulated at the semantic/pragmatic interface (Montrul & Rodríguez-Louro, 2006;

Paradis & Navarro, 2003; Serratrice *et al.*, 2004). Overproduction of overt subject pronouns by English-Spanish, German-Italian and French-Italian bilinguals has been attributed to the propensity of cross-linguistic interference, which characterises the semantic/pragmatic interface. That is to say, in the case of an English-Spanish bilingual child, Spanish data are predicted to contain more overt subjects than monolingual Spanish data due to interference from the obligatory nature of subject pronouns in English, the [−null subject] language (Hulk & Müller, 2000; Paradis & Navarro, 2003).

In this chapter, we provide an analysis of null and overt subjects in the developing grammars of two English-Spanish bilingual twins (Fernández Fuertes *et al.*, 2002−2005; Spradlin *et al.*, 2003). In order to carry out our analysis, we recast recent minimalist accounts of the null subject parameter (Alexiadou & Anagnostopoulou, 1998; Speas, 1994) in terms of learnability. These accounts formulate the null subject parameter in terms of the Determiner (D) feature, which differentiates between the Spanish pronominal markers and the English pronominal subjects. More specifically, the presence (in Spanish) versus the absence (in English) of this feature implies that English has to create a specifier position to host the overt subject (*we* go), but Spanish has to merge the pronominal suffix with the verb (va-*mos*). We argue that this articulation of the null subject parameter provides new insights into the characteristics of child data from [+/− null subject] languages. It also offers a different perspective on the relationship between English subject pronouns and Spanish verbal agreement affixes, and allows us to formulate a markedness hypothesis that can be tested against empirical data. The relationship between markedness and parameter-setting has been defined in terms of establishing which of the two options of any given parameter represents the default or unmarked one. What we propose is that Alexiadou and Anagnostopoulou's (1998) formulation of the null subject parameter can be reinterpreted in the light of Roberts' (2001) markedness proposal. This proposal states that the marked option of the parameter will be realised by the language where the activation of an operation implies the creation of structure. Thus, we hypothesise that English represents the marked option of the parameter, and Spanish represents the default or unmarked option. We will refer to this view of markedness as the 'core-internal' view.

Another markedness proposal (Chomsky, 2001; Rivero, 1997) states that pure syntactic operations (those that belong to core grammar or the so-called computational component) are less marked than the operations that take place at the periphery (the phonological and the semantic/pragmatic interface levels). In this view (the 'core-external' view), creating the specifier position in English or merging the pronominal affix with the verb in Spanish are both operations of the computational component, and are therefore equally marked. However, because the distribution of overt subjects in [+null subject] languages is considered to be regulated at the semantic/pragmatic interface, this proposal would support the view that transfer from the syntactically obligatory use of English subjects may affect the use of overt subjects in the Spanish grammar of English-Spanish bilinguals. In addition, by determining whether the use of subjects in our Spanish data shows evidence of interference from English, we will offer new insights into the separation/ non-separation of the two systems in the bilingual mind (Genesee, 1989; Genesee et al., 1995; Köppe & Meisel, 1995; Volterra & Taeschner, 1978).

Finally, we address the competence/performance account controversy by investigating the comparative development of null, pronominal and lexical subjects in both English and Spanish. We focus on the trade-off between null and pronominal subjects, as well as the overall increase of overt subjects. We specifically investigate whether these phenomena occur only in our English data, or both in our English and Spanish data. In the former case, our data will provide evidence for a competence account (Hyams & Wexler, 1993), and in the latter, for a performance account (Valian, 1991; Valian & Eisenberg, 1996).

Null and Overt Subjects in English and Spanish: Minimalist Accounts

The syntactic status of agreement affixes and pronominal subjects

Following the so-called 'standard' Minimalist analysis (Chomsky, 1995), Alexiadou and Anagnostopoulou (1998) argue that the licensing of null noun phrases (NPs) not only depends on the nature of verbal agreement, but also on how the D feature of the verbal agreement affix is checked.

Alexiadou and Anagnostopoulou (1998) adopt Rohrbacher's (1992) generalisation, according to which 'strong morphemes have individual lexical entries and weak morphemes do not' (Speas, 1994: 185). This implies that, in languages with rich verbal agreement morphology like Spanish, each agreement morpheme represents a lexical entry. Therefore, [+null subject] languages have strong verbal agreement affixes with separate lexical entries. In other words, these verbal agreement affixes are in fact pronominal elements with semantic content. In Spanish, the D feature of the verbal agreement affix is checked by merging of the verb (X°-movement), as shown in (9).

(9)

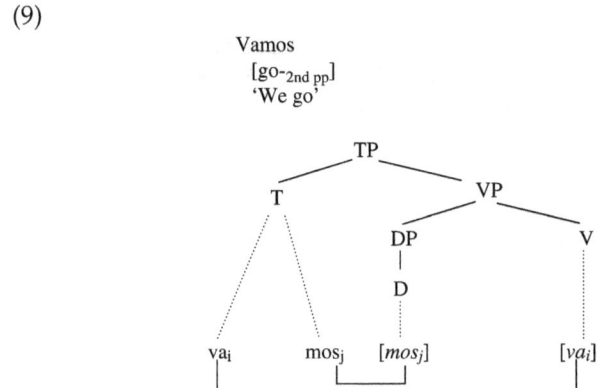

In contrast, weak verbal agreement affixes in [−null subject] languages cannot be characterised as pronominal elements. This implies that, in weak agreement languages like English, semantic features are associated with pronouns but not with affixes. In these languages, the lack of a D feature in the agreement affix requires the merging of an overt pronominal element in the specifier of the TP (XP-merge), as in (10). Thus, a null subject is not allowed.

(10)

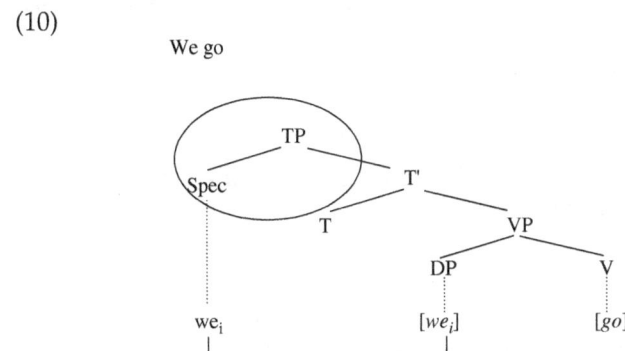

As for the overt subjects that occur in Spanish as well as other [+null subject] languages, they have semantic or pragmatic effects, such as signalling contrast or focusing on the subject, as shown in (11).

(11) Tú no te tiñes el pelo pero yo sí
You do not dye your hair but I yes
'You do not dye your hair but I do'

To account for the specific nature of Spanish strong subject pronouns, Kato (1999), following Ordóñez (1997), argues that Spanish-like subject pronouns appear in an adjunct position, as in (12).

(12)

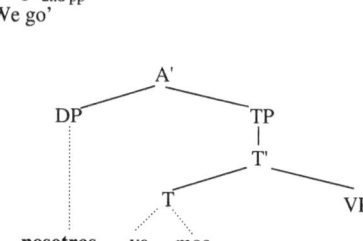

In Kato's proposal, strong pronouns include nominative pronouns in Spanish (*yo, tú, él,* ...), accusative pronouns in English (*me, him, her,* ...) and dative pronouns in French (*moi, toi, lui,* ...), but weak pronouns include free nominative pronouns in English (*I, you, he,* ...), nominative clitic pronouns in French (*je, tu, il,* ...) and, following Fernández-Soriano (1989), verbal agreement affixes in Spanish (-*o, -s, -Ø,* ...). Thus, overt pronominal subjects are weak pronouns in English but strong pronouns in Spanish.

The core/peripheral status of syntactic operations and the components of the grammar

Markedness proposals have been linked systematically to parameter-setting and learning difficulty. In Chomsky's (1981) idealised model of language acquisition, Universal Grammar (UG), an element of shared biological endowment, is supposed to be a characterisation of the child's pre-linguistic initial state, which is related to experience. The child approaches the task of learning a language equipped with UG and an associated theory of markedness. Chomsky suggests that 'UG determines a set of core grammars and that what is actually represented in the mind of an individual even under the idealization to a homogenous speech community would be a core grammar with a periphery of marked elements and constructions' (Chomsky, 1981: 8). What is needed to differentiate the domain of core grammar from the marked periphery is evidence from language acquisition, language processing, language deficit, and so on. Furthermore, it is also necessary to determine whether the core itself (now the computational component of the grammar) contains both default and marked operations (Liceras, 1986).

Roberts (2001) recasts Chomsky and Lasnik's (1977) and Chomsky's (1981) distinction between core (unmarked) and periphery (marked) aspects of the grammar within the so-called 'Functional Parametrization Hypothesis', according to which parametric variation among languages rests in the functional lexicon (Borer, 1984; Chomsky, 1991). In the case of Alexiadou and Anagnostopoulou's (1998) depiction of the null subject parameter, the actual property to be activated would be the categorial D feature of the pronominal agreement markers of Spanish versus the lack of the D feature in the case of English agreement markers, which in turn determine whether or not a null subject is allowed. Roberts (2001) also espouses the idea that all parameters have a default option that the child fixes without positive evidence, and a marked option that requires positive evidence to be fixed. This author further proposes that the child, who has both of these options available as part of his innate endowment, will first contemplate the default option. The second option will only be contemplated upon exposure to positive evidence. This is so because 'markedness [...] is a consequence of the computationally conservative nature of the parameter-setting device, the learner. This device has a built-in preference for relatively simple representations' (Roberts 2001: 103–104). Thus, as Martínez (2005) points out, if all movement operations are adjunctions (Kayne, 1994), they will create computationally complex structures (see (10)).

There are two different ways of interpreting Alexiadou and Anagnostopoulou's (1998) account of the null subject parameter with respect to markedness. One is to assume that the projection of a specifier in English is a marked operation. In contrast, the merging of the agreement marker with the verb in Spanish is not an adjunction operation and represents the default option of the parameter, in accordance with Roberts (2001). This implies that the rate of omission of agreement markers in Spanish will be smaller than that of subject pronouns in English. The other interpretation is to assume that both operations (the merging of the English pronoun by creating a specifier position and the merging of the Spanish agreement marker with the verb) have a similar status, because they are both core operations that belong to the computational component of the grammar. This means that there will be no differences as to the difficulty encountered by children when setting the plus or minus option of the null subject parameter. This second view of markedness is the one advocated by Rivero (1997), who maintains that core operations occur in the computational component of the grammar and are thus syntactic operations.

The distribution of Spanish subject pronouns, which occupy an adjunct topic or focus position (Fernández-Soriano, 1989; Kato, 1999; Ordóñez, 1997), is constrained at the semantic/pragmatic interface level and is therefore a peripheral operation. Thus, it is also considered a marked operation. In terms of learnability, the marked status of the semantic/pragmatic component provides justification for the proposed cross-linguistic interference that characterises the discourse-pragmatic area of the bilingual grammar (Hulk & Müller, 2000; Paradis & Navarro, 2003). This leads us to expect that there may be overproduction of pronominal subjects in the twins' Spanish data. In this respect, we assume that the directionality of interference is from English into Spanish – and not the other way round – because it is precisely in Spanish where the distribution of null and overt subjects is regulated at the comparatively more vulnerable (and more marked) semantic/pragmatic interface. In the case of English, it is the syntax that determines the obligatory presence of subjects, a component that is not supposed to be vulnerable.

Null and Overt Subjects in Early Child Language

A competence account

As indicated above, ever since Hyams (1986) addressed the issue of the null subject parameter in child language, the study of null subjects in early child language has received a great deal of attention (for example, Bel, 2001; Hyams, 1986, 1996; Rizzi, 1993/94; Valian, 1990, 1991, 1994; Wang et al., 1992; Weissenborn, 1992). One of the main issues investigated is whether non-adult null subjects represent a grammatical option that characterises the early child language, or whether they are the result of performance limitations.

Hyams and Wexler (1993) argue for a competence account of child null subjects on the basis of at least three pieces of evidence: (1) the strong asymmetries found in subject versus object omission in early child language; (2) the trade-off between null subjects and pronouns that characterises the development into more advanced stages and also differentiates child from adult speech; and (3) the use of many more lexical than pronominal subjects in the data of an English-speaking child, Adam (Brown, 1973).

A performance account

Valian (1991) and Valian and Eisenberg (1996) argue that children attempt to economise in production by performing as few computations as possible (Valian, 1991). One of the computations that they systematically avoid is the insertion of lexical items and syntactic features. Thus, these authors hypothesise that a performance-limitation explanation would predict that *all* children will increase their use of subjects over time, because all children's performance limitations will decrease over time. A competence-deficit explanation, on the other hand, would predict that only English-speaking children's subjects would increase.

Although it is a fact that English-speaking children increase their use of subjects over time, Valian's (1991) data indicate that Italian children's subjects as a whole did not increase over the one-year period that formed the basis of the observations, which would support a competence-deficit account. However, Valian and Eisenberg's (1996) examination of the development of subjects in another Romance language, Portuguese, reveal that the Portuguese-speaking children's development demonstrates an increase in the use of subjects similar to that found in English-speaking children. Therefore, these authors conclude that if subject use does increase among all children, regardless of language type, the performance account is validated.

In terms of the trade-off between null subjects and subject pronouns, data from Valian (1991) show that pronominal subjects in particular increase across development in English-speaking children. Hyams and Wexler (1993) have interpreted the increase as the consequence of a shift from a null subject grammar to a non-null subject grammar. They reason that the initial availability of the empty category *pro* substitutes for overt pronouns; as *pro* is phased out, use of overt pronouns increases. However, if children of null subject languages also increase their use of pronominal subjects, that reasoning is untenable (Valian & Eisenberg, 1996: 107).

The Study: The Development of the Null Subject Parameter in the Grammars of Two Bilingual (English/Spanish) Children

Methodology

We have analysed the spontaneous production of two bilingual children, Simon and Leo (Fernández *et al.*, 2002–2005; Spradlin *et al.*, 2003). They live with their parents in Spain. The father is a native speaker of Peninsular Spanish and the mother is a native speaker of American

English. The father always speaks to the children in Spanish and the mother always addresses them in English. The parents generally speak Spanish with each other, except on summers when they travel to the United States for approximately two months or when a monolingual English speaker is present. Therefore, we are dealing with bilingual English-Spanish first language acquisition in a monolingual Spanish social context, a type of bilingualism that is referred to in the literature as individual bilingualism (Bhatia & Ritchie, 2004).

During the first year, the mother was the primary caretaker of the twins. The father was present all day on weekends and less on weekdays. At age 1;10, the twins began attending day care for three hours a day on weekdays, where the language of the staff and other children was Spanish. Apart from the mother, additional contact with English was provided by occasional visits by the maternal grandparents and by the two-month visits to the United States every summer.

The data we have collected to this point cover the age range of 1;1–6;3. A total of 168 sessions have been recorded on videotape and DVD, of which 113 are in an English context (that is with an English interlocutor) and 55 in a Spanish context. The Spanish recordings were made at intervals of 2–3 weeks until age 3;00 (with some interruptions), and then they were made once a month. The English recordings were sometimes made more frequently, but the sessions are usually much shorter and recorded on consecutive days. The data that we have analysed for this study are described in Table 5.1.

The three stages were chosen *a priori* and they are justified in terms of both the age and the MLU (mean length utterance) differences. The MLU was calculated on the number of words per utterance (MLUw). Even though our data collection started earlier, we chose to begin our analysis at 2;04–2;06 (Stage 1) because the twins' language development lagged behind their singleton counterparts in accordance with what seems to be the case in this population (Dale *et al.*, 1998). We chose to include more English sessions because they were shorter in terms of time, which also resulted in the production of fewer utterances. The total number of utterances analysed per child, per stage and in total as well as the MLUw values are indicated in Tables 5.2 and 5.3.

In our data analysis we isolated all the instances of inflected and non-inflected verbal forms in main and subordinate clauses. The verbal forms were classified according to whether or not they occupied the structural position (inflected/non-inflected) that is required in the adult language. We also classified all the overt and the null subjects according to whether they were adult-like or not. Imperatives were not counted

Table 5.1 Data analysed in the study

	Sessions and age	Transcriptions	
		English	Spanish
Stage 1 (May–June 2001)	Age: 2;04–2;06	21	21
		22	22
		23	23
		24A	24A
Stage 2 (January–October 2002)	Age: 3;01–3;09	28	28
		34A	34A
		38E	38E
		39	—
Stage 3 (April–November 2003)	Age: 4;04–4;11	50B	50
		51	51
		52	—
		53	—
		54	54
		55	—
		56A	56B

together with the rest of the verbal forms because of the way in which null and overt subjects are realised with these forms. Relatives, wh- and control sentences were not included. Verb and subject repetitions were counted only once in the case of both emphatic and accidental repetitions. In the case of self-repairs, we only counted the last occurrence. Due to the

Table 5.2 Total number of utterances and MLUw (Spanish recordings)

	Simon	Leo	Total
Stage 1	510 [1.43]	529 [1.48]	1039
Stage 2	654 [3.77]	756 [3.35]	1410
Stage 3	1135 [4.28]	894 [3.88]	2029
Total	2299	2179	4478

The figures in brackets refer to the MLUw.

Table 5.3 Total number of utterances and MLUw (English recordings)

	Simon	Leo	Total
Stage 1	316 [1.31]	549 [1.16]	865
Stage 2	467 [3.45]	444 [3.11]	911
Stage 3	972 [4.17]	849 [4.48]	1821
Total	1755	1842	3597

The figures in brackets refer to the MLUw.

special nature of post-verbal subjects (Pierce, 1992) in early grammars, only preverbal subjects were included in our analysis.[1]

Research questions and hypotheses

Our first research question is whether markedness in the sense of Roberts (2001) (our 'core-internal' view) plays a role in parameter-setting. On this basis we formulate our first hypothesis:

Hypothesis #1. According to the 'core-internal' view, the English data will show more instances of omission of null subjects and, until a later age than the Spanish data, will show instances of omission of verbal agreement affixes. This is because merging the overt pronominal element in the specifier of TP (XP-merge), as shown previously for English in (10), is a more marked operation than merging the verbal agreement affixes on a head-to-head relationship (the $X°$-movement operation that accounts for the presence of null subjects in Spanish, as in (9)).

Our second research question addresses the issue of whether the comparison of null and overt subjects in a child [−null subject] versus a child [+null subject] grammar provides evidence for a competence or for a performance account of the data. We have formulated two hypotheses to address this question.

Hypothesis #2. If there is a similar ratio between the use of null subjects at the early stages and the use of subject pronouns at the older stages only in the English data, a competence explanation is favoured. If this happens in the case of both the English and the Spanish data, a performance explanation is more tenable. In fact, the Spanish grammar should show a lower increase in the use of subject pronouns, not only because they are not an obligatory option but also because they are regulated by semantic/pragmatic factors. According to the 'core-external' markedness proposal, these factors should be acquired later because their distribution belongs to the periphery of the grammar. However, if there is cross-linguistic interference from English, as predicted in Paradis and Navarro (2003) and Hulk and Müller (2000), these Spanish bilingual data will contain a higher percentage of subject pronouns than the monolingual data analysed in Paradis and Navarro (2003).

Hypothesis #3. If there is an overall increase in the use of overt subjects only in the English grammar, a competence explanation is favoured. If this happens in the case of both the English and the Spanish grammars, a competence explanation is untenable.

Data analysis

Table 5.4 shows the percentage of null subjects versus personal pronouns in English, and Table 5.5 shows the omission of verbal agreement markers in Spanish. These include all instances of infinitival forms (RIs) and participles used in context where the adult language requires an inflected [+personal] form, as in (13) and (14).[2]

(13) (a) Yo poner (Leo, 24ASP_02, 2;05)
 'I to put'
 (b) Tener [tiene] ojo como Elmo (Leo, 28SP_02, 3;00)
 'To have (he has) eye like Elmo'
(14) (a) Eso roto (Leo, 22SP, 2;05)
 'This broken'
 (b) Aquí visto (Simon, 24ASP_01, 2;05)
 'Here seen'
 (c) La bruja [ha] dado la manzana envenenada a Blancanieves (Simon, 34ASP_01, 3;05)
 'The witch (has) given the poisoned apple to Snow White'

It also includes all instances of third person singular indicative that referred to non third person subjects (bare forms) and all cases of first or second person whose referent was not first or second person as such (mismatches), as in (15).

(15) (a) Estos de aquí es animales (Leo, 28SP_02, 3;00)
 'These here is animals'
 (b) Yo cae (Leo, 50SP_01, 4;04)
 'I falls'
 (c) Yo ha [he] ido adentro (Simon, 51SP_01, 4;04)
 'I has [have] gone inside'

Table 5.4 Percentage of null subjects versus personal pronouns (Simon and Leo)

	Stage 1			Stage 2			Stage 3		
	Null	Pronoun	%	Null	Pronoun	%	Null	Pronoun	%
English	34	13	(72.34)	12	237	(4.82)	39	771	(4.81)
Spanish	173	15	(92.02)	701	84	(89.29)	698	135	(83.79)

Table 5.5 Omission of Spanish verbal agreement markers (Simon and Leo)

	Stage 1	Stage 2	Stage 3
RIs	2	3	1
[-Personal] (participle)	5	4	1
Bare form	1	5	25
Mismatches	1	4	10
Omission/total verb forms	9/210 (4.28%)	16/1062 (1.51%)	37/1036 (3.57%)

The figures in Table 5.4 show a clear trade-off between English null subjects and pronouns after Stage 1, as opposed to Spanish, where the null/pronominal subject ratio remains more or less constant throughout the three stages. In the case of English, the difference between Stages 1 and 2 is significant ($p = 0 < 0.05$), but it is not significant between Stages 2 and 3 ($p = 0.4988$). In the case of Spanish, the difference is not significant between Stages 1 and 2 ($p = 0.1337$), but it is significant between Stages 2 and 3 ($p = 0.0006$), and Stages 1 and 3 ($p = 0.001$). In other words, there is an effect of vocabulary learning in Spanish, but never a stage where personal pronouns override null subjects.

The figures in Table 5.5 show no evidence of an abrupt change regarding Spanish verbal agreement markers, even though there is a significant difference between Stages 1 and 2, and between Stages 2 and 3. In fact, what we see is a very small percentage of non-adult forms even at the very early stages, which we interpret as performance errors resulting from the mechanisms responsible for retrieving the agreement markers from the lexicon. Even within these very small percentages, there is a substantial decrease at Stage 2, which indicates that the abovementioned mechanisms are in the process of being automatised. We would like to suggest that the increase of non-adult forms at Stage 3 calls again for a performance explanation: The increase in the variety of verbal forms used by the twins puts a greater burden on the mechanisms responsible for retrieving the agreement markers from the lexicon.

A comparison between Tables 5.4 and 5.5 yields more interesting results. These data show that the synchronic and developmental patterns of omission and production of English weak pronouns and Spanish agreement morphemes are very different, because there are significantly more instances of omission of subjects (and until a later age) in the English data than instances of omission of verbal agreement affixes in the Spanish data.

Table 5.6 Percentage of 1st vs. 3rd person personal pronouns (singular)

	Stage 1			Stage 2			Stage 3		
	First	Third	%	First	Third	%	First	Third	%
English	7	4	(63.64%)	157	50	(75.85%)	430	178	(70.72%)
Spanish	10	2	(83.33%)	71	3	(95.95%)	79	21	(79%)

We interpret these results as evidence that English is the marked option with regard to Alexiadou and Anagnostopoulou's (1998) account of the null subject parameter.

The tendency shown by children to use first person pronouns at a higher rate than other personal pronouns is clearly depicted in Table 5.6 for English and Spanish. What is relevant here is the fact that the twins not only use many more pronouns in English than in Spanish for the third and the first person, but also use a higher percentage of first person pronouns in the case of Spanish. This suggests that if cross-linguistic influence from English were to be proposed as an explanation for the twins' use of subject pronouns in Spanish (Paradis & Navarro, 2003), it would be difficult to explain the very low number of third person pronouns in the Spanish data, as well as the substantially lower percentage of third person versus first person pronouns in all three stages, but mostly in the first two stages.

Table 5.7 shows the percentage of null versus overt subjects with inflected verbs. Overt subjects include all types of lexical subjects. We see a clear overall increase in the use of overt subjects in English after Stage 1, whereas in Spanish it remains more or less constant. The increase is significant for both languages between Stages 1 and 2, and Stages 1 and 3. However, it is more significant in English ($p = 0$) than in Spanish ($p = 0.0087$ and $p = 0.00045$, respectively). The fact that Spanish does not show abrupt changes between the first and second stages seems to indicate that the null subject parameter is set much earlier in Spanish than in English. There is no trade-off between null and overt subjects in Spanish, as we saw previously in Table 5.4 for null and personal pronoun subjects. These results support a competence account of the data and further corroborate, in contrast with Paradis and Navarro's (2003) findings, that transfer from English does not seem to influence the production of subject pronouns in Spanish in the case of these two bilingual children. In fact, their production of overt subjects is always below 30%, as Table 5.7 shows: the percentage of Spanish overt versus null pronouns is 16.02% for Stage 1, 26.37% for Stage 2, and 27.07% for Stage 3. The percentages of Spanish overt subjects are even lower than those reported in Bel (2003) for Spanish monolingual children.

Discussion and Conclusions

Our data show that, within the 'core-internal' view of markedness, English appears to be the marked option and Spanish the unmarked option of the null subject parameter, confirming our first hypothesis. In

Table 5.7 Percentage of null versus overt subjects with inflected verbs (Simon and Leo)

	Stage 1				Stage 2				Stage 3			
	Null	Overt	%		Null	Overt	%		Null	Overt	%	
English	34	16	(68)		12	266	(4.31)		39	837	(4.45)	
Spanish	173	33	(83.98)		701	251	(73.63)		698	259	(72.93)	

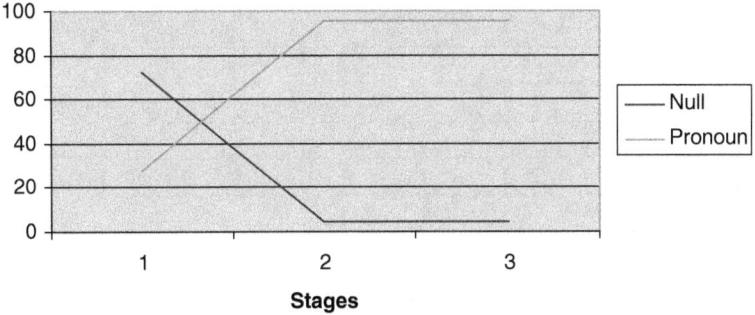

Figure 5.1 Null subject vs. personal pronouns (English)

addition, our results seem to provide evidence for the special role of bound versus free morphology that characterises first language acquisition as suggested in previous work (Vainikka & Young-Scholten, 1998; Zobl & Liceras, 1994). However, we would like to place a caveat to this assertion, as this is bound morphology that has a lexical status in the numeration (Spanish agreement markers). This type of morphology seems to play a spearheading role in first language acquisition.

With respect to our second hypothesis, we have found rather clear-cut evidence for a competence account of the data. Our results support Hyams and Wexler (1993) and provide evidence against Valian and Eisenberg (1996), in the sense that we obtained a trade-off between null subjects and pronouns in English but not in Spanish, as shown in Figures 5.1 and 5.2. In fact, as shown in Table 5.4 for Spanish, the percentage of subject pronouns versus null subjects in all three stages (7.98%,

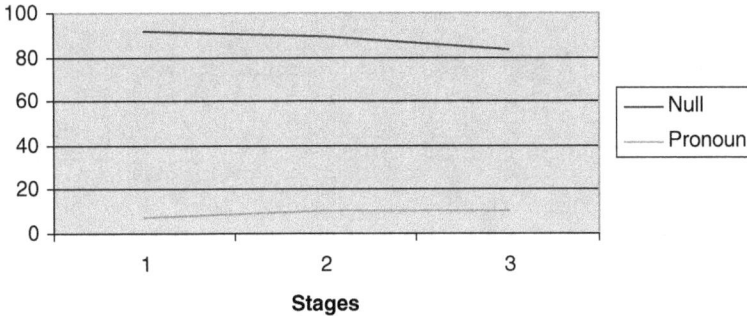

Figure 5.2 Null subject vs. personal pronouns (Spanish)

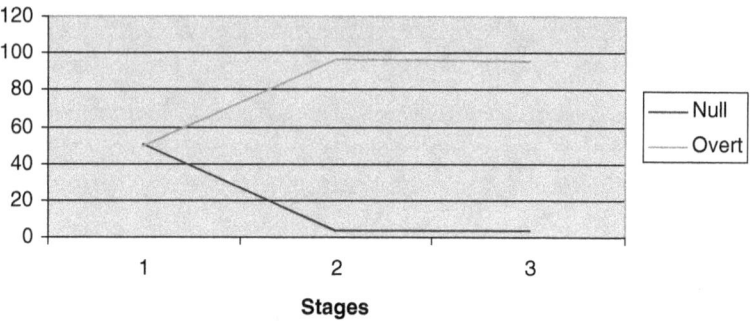

Figure 5.3 Null vs. overt subjects (English)

10.71% and 16.21%) is a strong indication that there is no cross-linguistic influence from English in the twins' Spanish grammar.

As for our third hypothesis, our data show an overall increase in the production of overt subjects in English but not in Spanish (compare Figures 5.3 and 5.4). This difference, which happens to be highly significant, provides evidence for a competence account of the data, because the Spanish data do not pattern with the L1 Portuguese data discussed in Valian and Eisenberg (1996), but with the Italian data discussed in Valian (1991) and Hyams and Wexler (1993).

To conclude, we would like to add that because our subjects were exposed to data compatible with the two options of the null subject parameter, we were able to investigate their development in the same 'population', as opposed to previous studies where the English and the Italian or Portuguese children represented two different populations. Our data

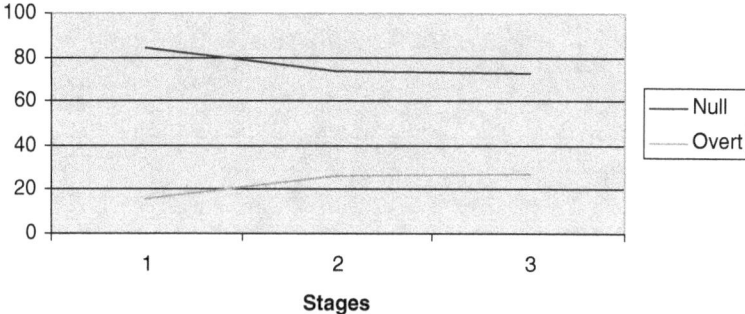

Figure 5.4 Null vs. overt subjects (Spanish)

show that, even though this is an obvious case where the children may entertain both options of the parameter on an equal footing until sufficient evidence leads them to favour one over the other (Valian, 1994) for each set of data, setting the marked value represented by English is more problematic than setting the Spanish value. In this respect, our results support Robert's (2001) 'core-internal' view of markedness, because it distinguishes two operations that take place within the computational component, rather than Rivero's (1997) 'core-external' view of markedness, according to which none of the operations that belong to the core is marked.

We should also point out that we obtained clear evidence that there are two separated systems in the bilingual mind. That is to say, although our subjects have two available grammars, there appears to be no transfer from either language with respect to the implementation of the two different options of the null subject parameter.

Acknowledgements

The general issues that we discuss here are related to the joint research program on language development and language contact at the Language Acquisition Labs of the University of Ottawa (Canada) and the University of Valladolid (Spain). We would like to thank E. Álvarez, M. Bermúdez, I. Parrado, M. K. Grimes, M. Llamazares, S. Muñiz, T. Spradlin and T. Vardomskaya for their help with the data collection and transcription. This research was funded by the Spanish Ministry of Science and Technology, Dirección General de Investigación Científica and FEDER (DGICYT #BFF2002-00442) and the Social Sciences and Humanities Research Council of Canada (SSHRC #410-2004-2034).

Notes

1. We have not included instances of postverbal subjects because: (1) they have a very different grammatical status in English and Spanish; (2) we did not find any postverbal subjects in the English affirmative sentences produced by the twins; and (3) in the case of Spanish, even if we had included them, neither the total of pronominal (Table 5.4) nor the total of overt subjects produced by the twins (Table 5.4 and Table 5.7, respectively) would have influenced the nature and significance of our results in any relevant way.
2. We have included infinitival and participial forms but not gerunds because there were no non-adult instances of the latter.

References

Alexiadou, A. and Anagnostopoulou, E. (1998) Parametrizing AGR: Word order, V-movement and EPP-checking. *Natural Language and Linguistic Theory* 16, 491–539.
Atkinson, M. (1992) *Children's Syntax: An Introduction to Principles and Parameters Theory.* Oxford: Blackwell.
Bhatia, T.J. and Ritchie, W.C. (2004) *The Handbook of Bilingualism.* Oxford: Blackwell.
Bel, A. (2001) *Teoria lingüística i adquisicio del llenguatge. Anàlisi comparada dels trets morfològics en català i en castellà.* Barcelona: Institut d'Estudis Catalans.
Bel, A. (2003) The syntax of subjects in the acquisition of Spanish and Catalan. *Probus* 15 (1), 1–26.
Bloom, L. (1970) *Language Development: Form and Function in Emerging Grammars.* Cambridge, MA: MIT Press.
Bloom, P. (1990) Subjectless sentences in child language. *Linguistic Inquiry* 21, 491–504.
Borer, H. (1984) *Parametric Syntax.* Dordrecht: Foris.
Brown, R. (1973) *A First Language: The Early Stages.* Cambridge, MA: Harvard University Press.
Chomsky, N. (1981) *Lectures on Government and Binding.* Dordrecht: Foris.
Chomsky, N. (1991) Some notes on economy of derivation and representation. In R. Freidin (ed.) *Principles and Parameters in Comparative Grammar* (pp. 417–454). Cambridge, MA: MIT Press.
Chomsky, N. (1995) *The Minimalist Program.* Cambridge, MA: MIT Press.
Chomsky, N. (2001) Derivation by phase. In J. Kenstowicz (ed.) *Ken Hale: A Life in Language* (pp. 1–52). Cambridge, MA: MIT Press.
Chomsky, N. and Lasnik, H. (1977) Filters and control. *Linguistic Inquiry* 8 (3), 425–504.
Dale, P.S., Simonoff, E., Bishop, D.V.M., Eley, T.C., Oliver, B., Price, T.S., Purcell, S., Stevenson, J. and Plomin, R. (1998) Genetic influence on language delay in two-year-old children. *Nature Neuroscience* 1 (4), 324–328.
Fernández Fuertes, R., Liceras, J.M. and Spradlin, K.T. (2002–2005) Bilingualism (English and Spanish) as a first language: A study of identical twins. Research project funded by the Spanish Ministry of Science and Technology, Dirección General de Investigación Científica, and FEDER.
Fernández-Soriano, O. (1989) Strong pronouns in null-subject languages and the avoid pronoun principle. In P. Branigan, J. Gaulding, M. Kubo and K. Murasugi (eds) *MIT Working Papers in Linguistics* 11, 228–239.
Frazier, L. and De Villiers, J. (1990) *Language Processing and Language Acquisition.* Dordrecht: Kluwer.
Genesee, F. (1989) Early bilingual development: One language or two? *Journal of Child Language* 6, 161–179.
Genesee, F., Nicoladis, E. and Paradis, J. (1995) Language differentiation in early bilingual development. *Journal of Child Language* 22, 611–631.
González, G. (1970) The acquisition of Spanish grammar by native Spanish speakers. PhD dissertation, University of Texas at Austin.
Guasti, M.T. (2002) *Language Acquisition: The Growth of Grammar.* Cambridge, MA: MIT Press.

Hulk, A. and Müller, N. (2000) Bilingual first language acquisition at the interface between syntax and pragmatics. *Bilingualism: Language and Cognition* 3 (3), 227–244.
Hyams, N. (1986) *Language Acquisition and the Theory of Parameters*. Dordrecht: Reidel.
Hyams, N. (1996) The underspecification of functional categories in early grammar. In H. Clahsen (ed.) *Generative Perspectives on Language Acquisition* (pp. 91–127). Amsterdam: John Benjamins.
Hyams, N. and Wexler, K. (1993) On the grammatical basis of null subjects in child languages. *Linguistic Inquiry* 24 (1), 421–459.
Kato, M.A. (1999) Strong and weak pronominals and the null subject parameter. *Probus* 11 (1), 1–38.
Kayne, R. (1994) *The Antisymmetry of Syntax*. Cambridge, MA: MIT Press.
Köppe, R. and Meisel, J. (1995) Code-switching in bilingual first language acquisition. In L. Milroy and P. Muysken (eds) *One Speaker, Two Languages*. Cambridge: Cambridge University Press.
Liceras, J.M. (1986) *Linguistic Theory and Second Language Acquisition: The Spanish Non-native Grammar of English Speakers*. Tübingen: Gunter Narr.
Liceras, J.M. (1988) Syntax and stylistics: More on the pro-drop parameter. In J. Pankhurst, M. Sharwood-Smith and P. van Buren (eds) *Learnability and Second Languages* (pp. 71–93). Dordrecht: Foris.
Liceras, J.M. (1989) On some properties of the pro-drop parameter: looking for missing subjects in non-native Spanish. In S. Gass and J. Schachter (eds) *Language Acquisition: A Linguistic Approach* (pp. 109–133). Cambridge: Cambridge University Press.
Martínez, C. (2005) El desplazamiento del verbo y la teoría de lo marcado: Adquisición del lenguaje y cambio diacrónico. MA thesis, University of Ottawa.
Montrul, S. and Rodríguez-Louro, C. (2006) Beyond the syntax of the null subject parameter: A look at the discourse-pragmatic distribution of null and overt subjects by L2 learners of Spanish. In V. Torrens and L. Escobar (eds) *The Acquisition of Syntax in Romance Languages* (pp. 401–418). Amsterdam: John Benjamins.
Ordóñez, F. (1997) Word order and clause structure in Spanish and other Romance languages. Dissertation, CUNY, New York.
Paradis, J. and Navarro, S. (2003) Subject realization and crosslinguistic interference in the bilingual acquisition of Spanish and English. *Journal of Child Language* 30, 1–23.
Perlmutter, D. (1971) *Deep and Surface Structure Constraints in Syntax*. New York: Holt, Rinehart and Winston.
Pierce, A. (1992) *Language Acquisition and Syntactic Theory: A Comparative Study of French and English Grammars*. Dordrecht: Kluwer.
Pollock, J.-Y. (1989) Verb movement, universal grammar, and the structure of IP. *Linguistic Inquiry* 20 (3), 365–425.
Rivero, M.L. (1997) Last resort and V-movement in the languages of the Balkans. In M.L. Rivero and A. Ralli (eds) *Comparative Syntax of Balkan Languages* (pp. 170–206). New York: Oxford University Press.
Rizzi, L. (1993/94) Some notes on linguistic theory and language development: The case of root infinitives. *Language Acquisition* 3, 371–394.
Roberts, I. (2001) Language change and learnability. In S. Bertolo (ed.) *Language Acquisition and Learnability* (pp. 81–125). Cambridge, MA: Cambridge University Press.

Rohrbacher, B. (1992) English AUX-NEG, Mainland Scandinavian NEG-AUX and the theory of V-to-I raising. *Proceedings of the 22nd Western Conference on Linguistics* (WECOL 92).

Serratrice, L., Sorace, A. and Paoli, S. (2004) Transfer at the syntax–pragmatics interface: Subjects and objects in Italian-English bilingual and monolingual acquisition. *Bilingualism: Language and Cognition* 7, 183–206.

Speas, M. (1994) Null arguments in a theory of economy of projection. *University of Massachusetts Occasional Papers in Linguistics* 17, 179–208.

Spradlin, K.T., Liceras, J.M. and Fernández Fuertes, R. (2003) Functional-lexical code-mixing patterns as evidence for language dominance in young bilingual children: A minimalist approach. In J.M. Liceras, H. Zobl, and H. Goodluck (eds) *L2 Links: Proceedings of the 2002 Generative Approaches to Second Language Acquisition (GASLA-6) Conference* (pp. 298–307). Somerville, MA: Cascadilla Press.

Vainikka, A. and Young-Scholten, M. (1998) Morphosyntactic triggers in adult SLA. In M-L. Beck (ed.) *Morphology and its Interfaces in Second-language Knowledge* (pp. 89–114). Amsterdam: John Benjamins.

Valian, V. (1990) Null subjects: A problem for parameter setting models of language acquisition. *Cognition* 35, 105–122.

Valian, V. (1991) Syntactic subjects in the early speech of American and Italian children. *Cognition* 40, 21–81.

Valian, V. (1994) Children's postulation of null subjects: Parameter setting and language acquisition. In B. Lust, G. Hermon and J. Kornfilt (eds) *Syntactic Theory and First Language Acquisition: Cross-linguistic Perspectives. Vol. 2: Binding, Dependencies, and Learnability* (pp. 273–286). Hillsdale, NJ: Erlbaum.

Valian, V. and Eisenberg, Z. (1996) The development of syntactic subjects in Portuguese-speaking children. *Journal of Child Language* 23, 103–128.

Volterra, V. and Taeschner, T. (1978) The acquisition and development of language by bilingual children. *Journal of Child Language* 5, 311–326.

Wang, Q., Lillo-Martin, D., Best, C.T. and Levitt, A. (1992) Null subject versus null object: some evidence from the acquisition of Chinese and English. *Language Acquisition* 2, 221–254.

Weissenborn, J. (1992) Null subjects in early grammars: implications for parameter-setting theories. In J. Weissenborn, H. Goodluck, and T. Roeper (eds) *Theoretical Issues in Language Acquisition*. Hillsdale, NJ: Lawrence Erlbaum.

Zobl, H. and Liceras, J.M. (1994) Functional categories and acquisition orders. *Language Learning* 44, 159–180.

Chapter 6
Contributions from Bilingual Specific Language Impairment in Catalan and Spanish to the Understanding of Typical and Pathological Language Acquisition

MÒNICA SANZ-TORRENT, IRIS BADIA and MIQUEL SERRA

Introduction: Bilingual Language Acquisition

Native language acquisition is a requirement for all children; however, the situation where this involves more than one language is often neglected by both the authorities and researchers. It is therefore important to study bilingual acquisition in order to understand the particular processes it involves.

Given the presence of two official languages in Catalonia, all children are faced with a compulsory bilingual acquisition. These special learning conditions may be regarded as a difficulty for all children: in some cases they might cause unsuccessful learning, while in others – in children with developmental difficulties – they might be a risk. According to the simplistic notion that bilingualism may be an added difficulty in language acquisition, a greater number of children with language difficulties in bilingual communities than in monolingual would be predicted. In our case, what would be expected is a greater impairment prevalence index than the one reported, for example, by Leonard (1998), at around 7%. However, this is not so. According to the data reported by Serra (2002), who follows stricter criteria, the prevalence index in Catalonia is 0.3%. Current available data coming from language difficulties centres in public schools yields an even smaller percentage.[1] However, these data do not account for the total number of cases.

Simple reasoning would conclude that bilingual acquisition should be *twice* as difficult. However, as we have seen in other chapters of this book, this is a miscalculation: a second language is not *two times* a first one (De Houwer, 2005; Meisel, 2001). It is our intention to provide evidence that will modify this opinion: language acquisition is not more difficult for children with Specific Language Impairment (SLI) merely because of being bilingual or living in a bilingual context.

In this chapter, we will first clarify when it is considered – and when it is not – that a child suffers from SLI. While explaining the core of the difficulties (e.g. the diversity of profiles), we will present different perspectives and explanations, including our own. Then we will examine the specificity of the situation of being bilingual and what consequences this situation causes. We will base our work both on our own as well as on other available data. However, the main part of this contribution will deal with our own ideas and data. After synthesising it, we will present some suggestions as to how our very special situation can facilitate a better comprehension of this difficulty.

Language Acquisition in Children with SLI

Among many different difficulties in understanding language acquisition, the construct of Specific Language Impairment has emerged quite recently, but it has come a long way since the first publications dealing with it (Ajuriaguerra & Inhelder, 1976). In addition to different clinical schools – French (*Troubles du langage, Dysphasie, Audimudité*); English (*Language Impairment, Delay or Disturbance*) (this pathological concept has different approaches medical, psychological and, more recently, linguistic) that follow diverse theories. It has been relatively simple to clarify that a Specific Language Impairment is independent of clinical evident symptoms, such as mental deficiency or deafness. However, defining the critical symptoms of this impaired development has not been so easy. There is no general agreement as regards both profile and quantification of the symptoms. Nevertheless, there is an agreement that is widely accepted: the main components affected are morphology and syntax.[2] Despite being considered orthogonal (independent), phonology is frequently associated with other components. In addition, there is a recognised phenomenon that can have implications: the individual differences among children with SLI are considerable when compared to those with typical development (TD), thus impeding an easy characterisation of the SLI group.

Despite the controversy and difficulty in defining the aforementioned construct, roughly speaking, the SLI is defined as a delay in language acquisition and development that is not associated with other factors, such as hearing impairment, psychopathological problems, socio-emotional adjustment difficulties, evident neurological impairment or brain damage, or severe phonological and/or articulatory impairment. It is specifically defined as a delay of at least one year (large criteria) in language with regard to the subject's chronological or mental age (Leonard, 1998; Stark & Tallal, 1981; Watkins, 1994). A greater prevalence has also been observed among subjects with a family clinical history of language learning impairment (Bishop & Leonard, 2000). Finally, it is necessary to add that not only must we deal with the aforementioned controversy regarding the definition of this pathological concept, but early-age SLI diagnosis is also difficult to apply. This is due to the fact that these children show the same profiles as children with Language Delay (LD) and cannot be clearly distinguished from them until they reach the age of 4, which hinders precocious identification. That is why the evolution of the language profile over time, even with intervention, is one of the best criteria for the identification of SLI children. They become competent with the basic structures of language, but some difficulties persist: inflection and agreement, lexical grammatical confusions and omissions.

Some data about SLI across languages

When we study children with SLI in different languages, we observe that these children show a number of features in their language that can be caused by two different factors. On the one hand, we notice a set of features common to all the impaired children, regardless of the language, which means that they are caused by the general learning difficulties brought about by the impairment. We also see a series of features related to the typology of the language; that is, they are specific to a given language and cannot be generalised to all children with SLI.

Regarding the common features of children with SLI, studies show slow development of lexicon in these children when compared to children with a typical development of language. They also show how these children start combining words later and, generally, their level of understanding is higher than their level of language production.

For the study of SLI in different languages, the largest amount of data available is in English, as is the literature in relation to lexical development, which points out that children with SLI present special difficulties with verbs (Fletcher & Peters, 1984). In this line of research, Watkins, *et al.*

(1993) claim that children with SLI use a smaller variety of verbs than their MLU controls. Moreover, experimental studies carried out by Rice *et al.* (1990) confirm that the referents related to actions and facts present the highest difficulty level for these children. As far as morphology is concerned, the verbal morphology in the linguistic profile of these children has been widely studied – especially in samples in English – and it is currently considered one of the most vulnerable aspects that these children present. As for specific data, studies show the absence of production of the *-ed* past tense suffix and the *-s* inflection, as well as verb agreement errors (Rice & Oetting, 1993). In English, the verb form of the past tense is acquired later than in Spanish and it appears to cause significant difficulties in English-speaking children with SLI (Leonard, 1998). This is not so much the case with Spanish-speaking children with SLI (Bedore & Leonard, 2001; Restrepo, 2003; Sanz-Torrent, 2004). Moreover, these English-speaking children also show an overuse of non-inflected verb forms (Fletcher & Peters, 1984; Rice *et al.*, 1995; Conti-Ramsden & Jones, 1997).

SLI in Romance languages

In Italian, the limited use of function words, such as articles and clitics, in children with Impairment is cited as a relevant feature when compared to those with a typical development of language. Specifically, studies show significant differences in the use of these two types of grammatical morphemes between children with impairment and children with an approximate MLU (Cipriani *et al.*, 1991; Leonard *et al.*, 1992). The most common error the studies show is the omission of the article or clitic, rather than its substitution. Cipriani *et al.* (1991) found that children with SLI have fewer difficulties with the use of prepositions than with articles or clitics. Likewise, Leonard *et al.* (1992) compared the use of articles in an Italian-speaking group of children with SLI with an English-speaking one and find similar percentages of use and omission of articles in both languages. However, the Italian-speaking children with SLI differ from the English-speaking ones in grammatical inflections. In Italian, children with SLI present difficulties related to inflection substitution, rather than to the use of non-inflected forms, as happens in English. Nevertheless, Italian-speaking children with SLI do not seem to show special difficulties in this aspect when compared with their respective MLU controls. However, Cipriani *et al.* (1995) point out that children with SLI with severe difficulties omit more lexical verbs than their MLU controls.

In French, it is relevant to refer to some data that differ from that shown in languages that are typologically alike. In this language, the percentages of the use of articles in required contexts by children with SLI is as high as those shown by MLU controls, while they are higher than those shown in an Italian-speaking group of children with SLI (Le Normand *et al.*, 1993). As regards verb morphology, the results show that, in this language, children with SLI omit copulative forms and auxiliary verbs more frequently than their age controls and those two years younger in a significant way. The use of the infinitive instead of an inflected verb form, however, occurs in a very low percentage (Methé & Crago, 1996). Some aspects of the use of function words in French-speaking SLI children are very similar to the data reported in English. Thus, it is observed that SLI children use fewer nominative case pronouns than their MLU control children.

Spanish, for its part, shares many features with Italian – such as noun, verb and adjective inflection, the use of clitics, and the elision of the subject – and it also shares the same canonical order. Therefore, it is foreseeable that common features will be observed in the children with SLI speaking these languages. Thus, a study by Restrepo (1995) with Spanish-speaking children with SLI shows that they omit grammatical morphemes more frequently than age control children and they also show a higher occurrence of incorrect morphemes. The most frequent type of error appears in the use of articles: they do not show gender agreement with the noun. Likewise, verb inflections do not sometimes agree with the subject in number. Nonetheless, the tense is correct and, unlike in the case of English SLI children, non-finite forms rarely appear instead of finite forms.

Bedore and Leonard (2001) point out agreement errors in relation to verb marks, along with other non-verbal morphological errors. In this line of study, Sanz-Torrent (2002) point out the presence of fewer verbs in their utterances as a differentiating feature of children with SLI compared to their age controls. In addition, these verbs show little associated morphology and more verb errors and omissions; in particular, copulative verbs are omitted. All in all, studies in Spanish conclude that children with SLI present difficulties in grammatical morphology (Anderson, 2001).

SLI and Bilingualism

The identification and classification of a population of children that present clinical symptoms of communication and language disability or impairment has long been a challenge for researchers, clinicians and educators (Bishop, 1997; Leonard, 1998). Although the challenge of identifying those children is cumbersome, it is also interesting to explore the possible specific failures that take place in this situation of bilingual language processing and learning.

Some data about bilingual children with SLI

Cross-linguistic studies with monolingual language-impaired children have defined the features of these children's language in different tongues. However, these studies do not tackle the question of whether these features are altered when a subject acquires two languages, that is, in a bilingual situation (Paradis *et al.*, 2003).

Thus, regarding SLI in a bilingual situation, there are few studies that compare these children's linguistic features in bilingual and monolingual situations. Moreover, apart from the impairment itself, we find that there is a lack of precision in the term 'bilingualism', which has been used indiscriminately to refer to different situations of acquisition of two languages. Specifically, the acquisition of two languages can be either successive or simultaneous. Bilingualism refers to the acquisition of two languages simultaneously, and the successive acquisition is referred to as second language acquisition (Genesee *et al.*, 2004).

For data about bilingualism in SLI, Paradis *et al.* (2003) study a group of French-English bilingual impaired children compared with two groups of monolingual French and English impaired children. The goal of the study was to determine whether bilingual children with SLI were similar to monolingual children with SLI, in each of the languages. The authors examined the use of tense-bearing and non-tense-bearing morphemes according to the hypothesis of the Optional Infinitive Extended period. The results showed that both the bilingual and monolingual children presented a higher accuracy with non-tense-bearing morphemes than with the tense-bearing ones, as predicted by the hypothesis adopted. In addition, the bilingual children obtained a similar average accuracy in the tense-bearing morphemes to that of the monolingual children. This means that bilingual children do not have more difficulties in the use of grammatical morphemes than do monolingual children. The bilingual children showed similar results to those of the monolingual children with respect to the grammatical morphology examined in each of the languages. Therefore, it appears that the Specific Language Impairment is not a hindrance to learning two languages, at least as far as grammatical morphology is concerned. Also, some other answers can be inferred from these studies: bilingual children with SLI show difficulties in both languages, although they show more in the less dominant language; SLI bilingual children acquire language as slowly as their monolingual peers with this disorder. Following this line of thought, in a study with English-Spanish bilingual children, Gutiérrez-Clellen and colleagues (2000) concluded that bilingual children with SLI make the same kind of grammar errors as monolingual SLI children. In a study currently being carried out, Gutiérrez-Clellen and Erikson (in press) do not find different code-switching patterns. However, Restrepo (2003) reported a child with a high code-mixing frequency: the article 'the' followed by nouns in Spanish. These authors explain these divergences in relation to pragmatic aspects and the kind of context (additive or subtractive).

The Present Study

We have seen that very little research exists on SLI children with either simultaneous or successive bilingualism. Even less research deals with two typologically similar languages, like Catalan and Spanish, which could make it more difficult to differentiate them. Many questions arise in relation to this disorder and the implications of dealing with two languages. With this study, we will only be able to answer some of these questions.[3] We will mainly focus on answering whether SLI presents the same profile of difficulties in a bilingual situation as it does in a monolingual situation, and whether one of the clear indexes of relation between two languages – code-switching – appears more or less frequently when compared to children with typical acquisition.

Goals

Specifically, in this chapter we examine incidence in bilingual SLI children with two close languages: Catalan and Spanish.

(1) We have observed that monolingual children with SLI present special difficulties regarding relational words, words with morphology and/or words that are not phonetically salient. The first goal of this study is to examine the profile of the grammatical difficulties of bilingual children with SLI when compared to the controls. In order to do this, we will examine omission and production errors that occur in verbs, prepositions, pronouns and articles. We expect to find a differentiated profile of difficulties when compared with that shown by children with typical acquisition, age and MLU controls.

(2) It has been assumed that the children who acquire two languages simultaneously undergo an initial stage where the two languages are not differentiated (Unitary Language System Hypothesis).[4] This is based on the fact that most bilingual children mix linguistic

elements from both languages and, from this point of view, this is a reflection of the two of them being confused. However, these code mixings do not necessarily imply a lack of differentiation between the languages. They can also occur during the development of linguistic competence in order to fill in gaps (Gap-Filling Hypothesis). Given the bilingual and language-impaired condition of the SLI children in our study, as our second goal, we examine whether these children produce a higher number of mixings (as well as a different code-mixing pattern) than children with typical development, due to their lower linguistic competence.

These data will be discussed taking into account the literature on monolingual children with SLI, such as the cross-linguistic studies collected by Leonard (1998). Likewise, the data will be compared to the early available literature on bilingual children with SLI, specifically to English-French bilinguals (Paradis *et al.*, 2003; Paradis, 2007) and Spanish-English bilingual children (Restrepo & Gutiérrez-Clellen, 2004). The similarities between Catalan and Spanish cause certain particularities in code-switching, which can help us clarify the weight of the different language components both in children with SLI as well as in children with a typical development.

Methodology

Sample

The data presented here belong to a longitudinal project that followed a group of six SLI children under therapy from 3 to 6 years of age and their age controls and MLU-w controls. This study is based on three annual interviews and the results offered here provide average data on these children's development.

The subjects belong to a sample that was very strictly selected, following the usual criterion at 3.6 years of age (no clinical or emotional signs, no history of ear inflammation, and non-verbal IQ over 80). After a year's treatment, a subgroup from this first sample[5] was diagnosed as SLI due to slow progress and sustained difficulties. Table 6.1 presents the children from the study according to the group they belong to, age and gender.

Linguistic features and context

The languages our SLI children have to learn have two special features. The first and structural feature is that Catalan and Spanish are very similar languages. They have many lexical items and rules in common. Besides being very similar, both languages are also well known by all the possible interlocutors (there is no problem in borrowing and shifting

Table 6.1 Subject data

N	Gender	Age T1	Age T2	Age T3	Group
1	Male	4;01	5;01	6;02	SLI
2	Male	3;05	4;07	5;07	SLI
3	Male	3;10	4;09	5;08	SLI
4	Female	3;10	4;10	5;10	SLI
5	Male	3;07	4;10	5;09	SLI
6	Male	3;07	4;08	5;07	SLI
1	Male	4;03	5;03	6;03	Age control
2	Male	3;07	4;07	5;07	Age control
3	Male	4;00	4;10	5;10	Age control
4	Female	3;06	4;09	5;06	Age control
5	Male	3;09	4;10	6;01	Age control
6	Male	3;07	4;09	5;09	Age control
1	Male	2;03	2;07	–	MLUw control
2	Female	1;11	3;01	–	MLUw control
3	Male	2;05	2;11	–	MLUw control
4	Female	2;08	3;00	–	MLUw control
5	Male	2;08	3;08	–	MLUw control
6	Male	2;02	3;09	–	MLUw control

when one of the languages presents trouble). The second feature refers to the socio-linguistic situation, which, although not simple, is quite stable: Catalan is used in school and Spanish in the playground, with a highly variable presence at home. Most of the subjects in this contribution have Spanish as the family language, and Catalan is present in school and re-education. Personal communication in class or therapy, however, is bilingual. Therefore, what we have is a distinctive population of successive early bilingualism.

An important methodological clarification should be made here, to the effect that each language was analysed separately and with different grammatical codes. However, we decided to apply the same analysis in order to analyse the equivalent categories in both languages.

Our data were obtained from a guided conversation – with obligatory questions – about family, school, and preferred games. The interviews lasted from 30 to 45 minutes and took place in both languages, but mainly in Catalan. The interviewer was a speech therapist unfamiliar to the subjects. Only intelligible sentences were analysed. Minor utterances, stereotypes and unintelligible imitations were excluded. The interviews were transcribed and coded in CHAT format and analysed with CLAN Programs. Statistical analysis was performed (Mann–Whitney U non-parametric tests) for the grammar categories and the types of code-switching.

Results

Profile of difficulties of children with SLI in Catalan and Spanish

Grammatical difficulties in Spanish appear to lie, in particular, in determiners, pronouns and prepositions, both for bilingual Spanish-English and monolingual Spanish children. We will examine these data (in Catalan and Spanish) for six bilingual children.

In Figure 6.1 we can observe the comparisons of production errors in the verb and omission errors in obligatory contexts between the SLI group and the control groups. The SLI group omits the verb more frequently, and also makes more verb morphology errors. The profile differs significantly from that shown by the age control group.

We present the following examples from the categories studied to complement the graphs:

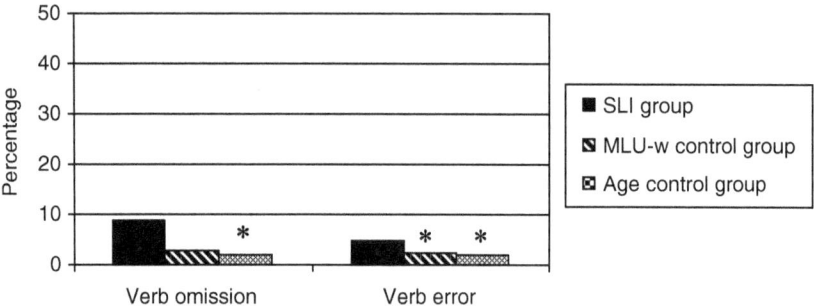

Figure 6.1 Verb omission and error percentage (The verb omission percentage has been calculated based upon the total number of required verbs, and the error percentage upon the total number of uttered verbs. The asterisks mark the significant differences $p < 0.05$ Inter-groups; SLI vs. controls)

(1) *SLI: aquello (*es*) pan, xxx que se menja. 'that (*is*) bread, xxx that is eatable'
    [spoken in Spanish]
    (Copulative verb omission)
(2) *SLI: quatre, després *tinc* [*tindré*] cinc. 'four, later I have [I'll have] five'
    [spoken in Catalan]
    (Verb tense error, present for future)

In examining the inaccurate production or omission of determiners (Figure 6.2), a difficulty in the use of this particle may clearly be seen: it is frequently omitted by the SLI group, especially in relation to the age control group. We can see how the percentage of omitted determiners in contexts where they are required lies at around 25%. However, only 3% of the determiners produced present gender or number errors and the values do not differ from the control groups. The following (3) and (4) are examples.

(3) *SLI: per tot (*el*) poble. 'for all (*the*) village'
    [spoken in Catalan]
    (article omission)
(4) *SLI: Perquè a obrir a [*la*] porta a [*la*] claus a [*la*] porta. 'because to open at a [*the*] door a [*the*] keys at a [*the*] door'
    [spoken in Catalan]
    (use of schwa particle instead of article)

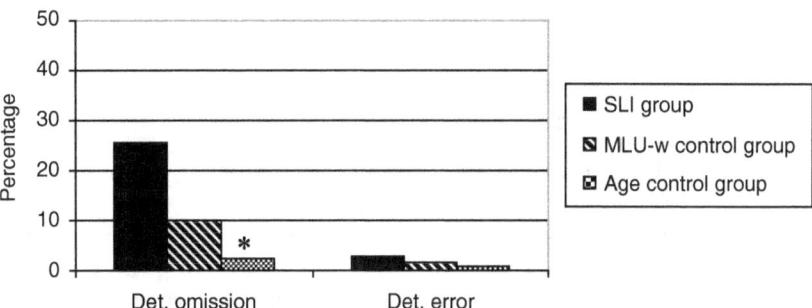

Figure 6.2 Determiner omission and error percentage (The determiner omission percentage has been calculated based upon the total number of required determiners, and the error percentage upon the total number of uttered determiners. The asterisk marks the significant differences $p < 0.05$ inter-groups; SLI vs. controls)

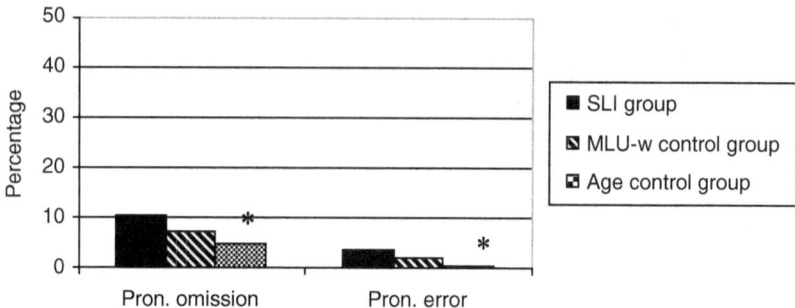

Figure 6.3 Pronoun omission and error percentage (The pronoun omission percentage has been calculated based upon the total number of required pronouns, and the error percentage upon the total number of uttered determiners. The asterisks mark the significant differences $p < 0.05$ inter-groups; SLI vs. controls)

Figure 6.3 represents the errors the children make in the different types of pronouns (mostly weak, personal and demonstrative). We can observe how the SLI children present a higher percentage of pronoun production and omission errors (in person, number or gender) when compared to the age controls. Notwithstanding, no significant differences can be observed in relation to the youngest group of children. The following are examples.

(5) *SLI: que no podia tirar (*la*). 'that no could to throw (*it*)'.
 [spoken in Spanish]
 (weak pronoun omission)
(6) *SLI: me *la* [*les*] menja [menjo]. 'I *it* [*them*] eats [eat]'
 [spoken in Catalan]
 (weak pronoun error)

In Figure 6.4 we can observe how the omission of prepositions is one of the most frequent errors made by children with SLI: they omit 30.5% of the prepositions when they are required. These data are remarkably divergent from the data presented by the control age and MLU-w groups. However, no group displays significant incorrect preposition production errors. The following are examples.

(7) *SLI: sí, (*amb*) (el) flotador i bragues. 'Yes, (*with*) (the) lifebelt and panties'
 [spoken in Catalan]
 (preposition omission)

Bilingual Specific Language Impairment 147

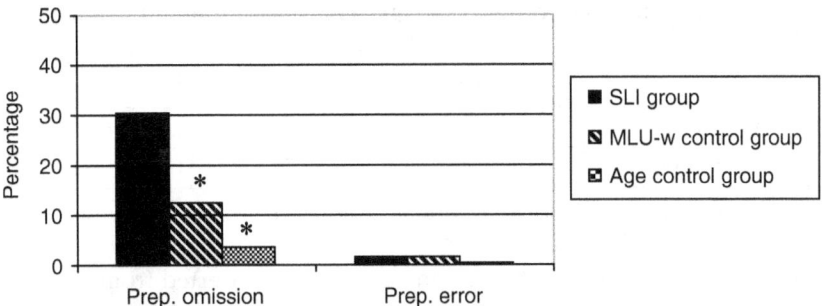

Figure 6.4 Preposition omission and error percentage (The preposition omission percentage has been calculated based upon the total number of required prepositions and the error percentage upon the total number of uttered prepositions. The asterisks mark the significant differences $p < 0.05$ inter-groups; SLI vs. controls)

(8) *SLI: una caixa a [de] llet. 'a box a [of] milk'
    [spoken in Catalan]
    (use of schwa particle instead of preposition).

Code-mixing data

In this chapter, we are especially interested in examining at data related to code-switching. We start from the notion that if the bilingual context is a handicap for children with SLI, these data should set a divergent pattern, both from same-age children and from younger children. We will work on the insertion of words from the other language within the utterance (intra-utterance code-mixing), which occurs with these children in the situation of a spontaneous and controlled conversation with their speech therapist (Table 6.2).

Table 6.2 Intra-utterance code mixing percentage

	SLI group	*MLU-w control group*	*Age control group*
Code-mixing, words	0.93	0.55	1.15
Code-mixing, utterances	2	1.07	2.9

The intra-utterance code-mixing words percentage has been calculated based upon the total number of words, and the intra-utterance code-mixing utterances percentage has been calculated based upon the total number of utterances.

Table 6.3 Intra-utterance code-mixing percentage according to language

	SLI group	MLU-w control group	Age control group
Catalan insertion	17	21	18
Spanish insertion	83	79	82

The percentages have been calculated based upon the total number of insertions.

In Table 6.2 we can see the percentage of words inserted from the other language during the conversation in relation to the total number of words produced. The number of inserted words is relatively small: approximately 1% of the whole word production. All the groups present similar percentages, and no differences among them are observable. If we take a closer look, we see that 2% of the total number of utterances by SLI children contain code-mixing. The values from the control groups do not differ either: the youngest age group lies at around 1% and the age control group at around 3%.

Catalan is the majority language of the sample studied, which means that most insertions occur in the other language, Spanish. Table 6.3 displays how the linguistic behaviour of both SLI children and controls is similar.

(9) *SLI: la mare està *echant* [tirant/echando] sal al nen xx al culet. 'the mother is *throwing* salt to the boy xx at the bottom'
[spoken in Catalan]
(Insertion of a Spanish word, but with Catalan morphology).

(10) *SLI: cuando llegue a primero *faré* [haré] los siete. 'when I'd *be* in first, I'll be seven'
[spoken in Spanish]
(Insertion of a Catalan word).

In the following graphs, we will examine the type of code-mixing carried out by the children (Figures 6.5 and 6.6).

We were interested in observing to what extent there were insertions characterised by the phonology of the other language. We observe that the groups do not diverge with regard to the production of words with the phonology of the other language.

(11) *SLI: aquí per *llimpiar* [limpiar] els gots. 'here to *clean* the glasses'
[spoken in Catalan]
(Insertion of a Spanish word in a Catalan context but with Catalan phonology: /λ/ for /l/).

Bilingual Specific Language Impairment 149

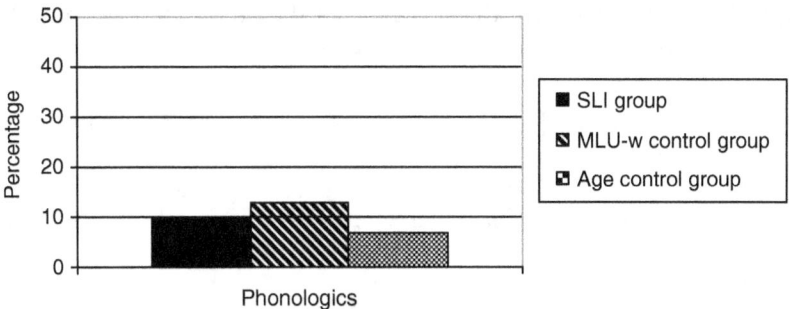

Figure 6.5 Phonological intra-utterance code mixing percentage (The percentage has been calculated based upon the total number of insertions)

(12) *SLI: *jugo* [in Spanish] al golf. 'I *play* at golf'
 [spoken in Spanish]
 (Catalan word with Spanish phonology: /x/ for /z/ and /o/ for /u/).
(13) *SLI: *havia* un llop que volia destrossar les cases. '*there was* a wolf who wanted to demolish the houses'
 [spoken in Catalan]
 (Spanish phonology: /a/ for /ə/).

In Figure 6.6, we can observe code-mixing with errors. We considered there was an error when the word inserted caused an agrammatical sentence or the word was incorrect. In this case, we observe that SLI children produce 20% of the insertions with some sort of grammatical violation,

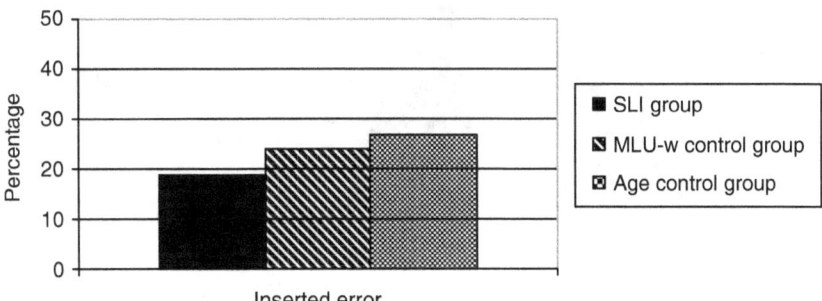

Figure 6.6 Intra-utterance code mixing with error percentage (The percentage has been calculated based upon the total number of insertions)

but it does not differ from the percentages shown by the age control or MLU-w groups, which lie around the same value.

(14) *SLI: i *le* vaig *dar* [li vaig donar] una patada. 'and I *gave him* a kick'
[spoken in Catalan]
(Insertion of Spanish words)
(15) *SLI: y se metió *a* [en] la bañera. [spoken in Spanish] 'and he went *in* the bathtub'
(Insertion of Catalan word)
(16) *SLI: *pedir-li* [pedirlo, demanar-lo] als reis. '*to ask it* the kings'
[spoken in Catalan]
(Insertion of Spanish word)
(17) *SLI: jugando *a* [en] la clase. 'playing *in* the class'
[spoken in Spanish]
(Insertion Catalan word)
(18) *SLI: i la porta se *vaig caer* [caure]. 'and the door *went to fall*'
[spoken in Catalan]
(Insertion of Spanish word and inflection error).

We classified all the code-mixing utterances according to their grammatical category. In Figure 6.7 we only highlight two of the words that were produced in a different way from the age control group. We observe that the SLI children are different from the age controls in the fact that they produce proportionally more verbs in the other language

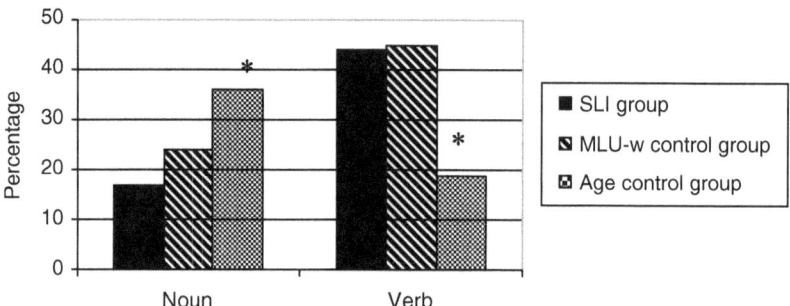

Figure 6.7 Intra-utterance code-mixing percentage according to grammatical category (The percentage has been calculated upon the total number of insertions. The asterisks mark the significant differences $p < 0.05$ Inter-groups; SLI vs. controls)

… and fewer nouns. The MLU control group is no different from the SLI group in this aspect.

Here are some noun insertion examples:

(19) *SLI: i la nena la posarem a l'altra *cama* [llit]. 'and the girl we'll place her to the other *bed'*
[spoken in Catalan]
(Insertion of a Spanish word)

(20) *AGE: que has de posar a l'*abuel* [avi/abuelo]. 'that you have to place the *grandfather'*
[spoken in Catalan]
(Insertion of a Spanish word but with Catalan morphology or Catalan syllabic structure)

(21) *MLU: ara tiro *cargoles* [cargols]. 'now, I throw *snails'*
[spoken in Catalan]
(Spanish morphology in Catalan word)

The following are some verb insertion examples:

(22) *SLI: vaig a *ver* [veure] a piloteta. 'I'm going *to see* a (the) small ball'
[spoken in Catalan]
(Insertion of a Spanish word)

(23) *SLI: *tene* [te/tiene] unes joguines. 'She *has* some toys'
[spoken in Catalan]
(Insertion of a Spanish word but with Catalan language root)

(24) *SLI: llavors quan *estoy* [estic] dormint. 'then, when I *am* sleeping'
[spoken in Catalan]
(Insertion of a Spanish word)

(25) *MLU: està *rot* [roto/trencat]. 'It is *broken'*
[spoken in Catalan]
(Insertion of a Spanish word with Catalan morphology).

Regularisations with rules of the other language

Finally, in Figure 6.8 we can observe verb regularisation errors due to the application of either the morphology or the lexicon of the other language.

Regularisations give us a notion about in which phase these children's language development lies, where some of these errors are considered progression errors. Here are some examples of this type of errors:

(26) *ADU: com li van destrossar la casa? 'How did they demolish the house?'

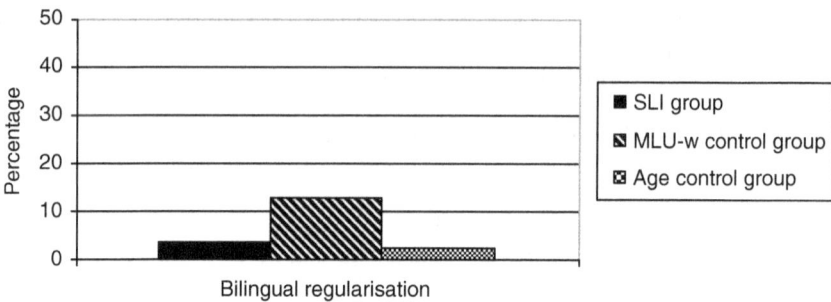

Figure 6.8 Regularised intra-utterance code mixing percentage (The percentage has been calculated based upon the total number of insertions)

      *SLI: *suplant* [bufant/soplando]. *'blowing'*
      [spoken in Catalan]
      (Spanish verb root, Catalan morphology)
(27) *SLI: ... ha trucat el timbre, ha *oit* [sentit/oído] el pare... '... He has touched the bell and has *listened* the father...'
      [spoken in Catalan]
      (Spanish verb root insertion, Catalan morphology)
(28) *SLI: ... i la seva mare, no *hablis* [parlis/hables] amb desconeguts. '... and her mother, don't *speak* with strangers'
      [spoken in Catalan]
      (Spanish verb root insertion, Catalan morphology)
(29) *AGE: se ha *ficado* [ficat/metido] en la bañera para rentarse. 'He has *went* in the bathtub to clean himself'
      [spoken in Spanish]
      (Spanish morphology applied to Catalan word)

We can observe how the SLI group shows the same percentage of this type – around 3.7% of total code-mixing utterances – as the age controls. The youngest control group carried out more regularisations, around 13%, although the differences were not significant.

Conclusions

First, we intended to determine the grammatical profile of SLI children. We aimed to compare it to the data relative to the impairment in other languages and in a monolingual situation. The data here presented show simplification and difficulty patterns in the language production of children with SLI at preschool age. *Simplicity* can particularly be observed in the data relative to word omission errors, mostly prepositions and determiners. The *difficulty* pattern can be observed especially in verb and pronoun production errors. Other studies have shown how the evolution of the simplicity profile practically disappears over time, whereas the difficulty pattern lasts longer (Sanz-Torrent, 2004). If we look at error frequency, two inverse patterns can be observed: if we follow a frequency order from greatest to smallest, we observe that prepositions, determiners, pronouns and verbs are the most omitted elements. However, if we examine error percentage from greatest to smallest, we observe that the order is reversed: the element with most errors is the verb, then pronouns, determiners and prepositions. This fact is related to the formal features of every element, but also to the phase of evolution the children are in, because this percentage relation matches those shown by MLU-w control children, although with much lower values. However, it clearly does not match the age control group values. This leads us to think that children with SLI, depending on the language feature, show an acquisition delay more prominently than do the youngest control children.

Cross-linguistic comparisons are difficult to carry out due to the different contexts of the languages to be compared and the use of different methodologies (watching spontaneous talk, experimental tasks, data treatment, and so on). However, if we observe the data from a global perspective, we see how it reveals that the words reported as 'especially difficult' in Romance languages for monolingual children have also been considered so for bilingual Catalan-spanish children. For instance, we have seen that determiners are one of the most troublesome categories both in Catalan and Spanish (especially their omission) for children with SLI of preschool age. This also occurs – with very high values – in SLI monolingual Italian children (Leonard *et al.*, 1992), and does not differ from the behaviour of their English-speaking peers. The same results also occur in French monolinguals, with no difference from the youngest children, but with much lower values (Le Normand *et al.*, 1993). Likewise, it is also highlighted as one of the most important errors in a study with Spanish-speaking children (Restrepo, 1995), and also in a study with Catalan and Spanish children between 6 and 9 years (Bosch & Serra, 1997). We have also seen that pronouns and verbs are the categories with the most production errors. Data coming from Italian monolinguals (with ages similar to those of the study) show that this particle is even more difficult, as it is only used correctly in 25% of the required contexts. It has also been an error highlighted in Spanish (Bedore & Leonard, 2001; Bosch & Serra, 1997). Our data from bilingual children match that for the use of clitic pronouns in Spanish by children with SLI (Gutiérrez-Clellen et al., 2000).

Literature has paid less attention to prepositions as a source of error. A study by Cipriani et al. (1991) claims that not so many difficulties appear in Italian in this area as they do with articles and clitics. However, in our study, we have witnessed that this has been the most omitted word, although hardly any production errors occurred. The verb, however, has received attention, due to its key role in the grammaticalisation process. The verb is the element where the greatest similarity in the type of errors occurs; that is, omission and error values are similar and differ significantly from those and the control group. The percentages of verb errors in our bilingual sample are similar to the percentages reported in an experimental situation for Spanish (Bedore & Leonard, 2001), and also to the values obtained from a sample of older Catalan and Spanish children (Bosch & Serra, 1997). In a smaller sample of younger children, there was a higher occurrence of production errors than of verb omission (Sanz-Torrent, 2002). Nevertheless, by increasing the sample, verb errors increased to around 7% and omission to around 8% (Sanz-Torrent, 2004). These difficulties have also been reported in other languages. For example, associated morphology has been regarded as a troublesome area in Italian – especially for the third person plural – but, in English, the omission of auxiliaries and difficulties with verb inflections have been commonly highlighted (Leonard, 1998; Rice & Oetting, 1993). A study on older children with SLI in French (Methé & Crago, 1996) showed that they significantly omitted copulative forms and auxiliaries.

Therefore, in this approximate comparison of languages, especially between Romance languages and between monolingual and bilingual children, there appears to be no special trait that can be attributed to the situation of learning two languages simultaneously.

The second main goal of our study was to analyse one of the indexes that might suggest specific difficulties due to the bilingual situation: the overuse of insertions of words from one language into utterances in the other language. Data show very small code-mixing percentages in the whole vocabulary and in the total number of utterances and, most importantly, equal patterns in the three groups compared.

No significant differences have appeared in comparison with the results of the control groups. Neither have they appeared in the global values of insertions, nor due to the kind of code used, nor to the kind of insertions: according to the phonological component, according to the grammatical accuracy or inaccuracy that it bears. We have seen how both groups, on most occasions, produce grammatical code mixings and how verb regularisations occur, most of them in the dominant language. This occurs especially in the youngest children, and equally between the SLI and the age control groups. However, the only significant difference between the groups studied has been that both children with SLI and MLU-w control children produce a higher percentage of verb insertions rather than of nouns. This is a result that contrasts with the one obtained from the age control group. It seems then that verb insertions, with more grammatical implications, decrease over age, and the number of insertions with nouns that bear more lexical repercussions increases. That is to say, it may be necessary to use the known code at the beginning, especially in complex words, like verbs; however, as acquisition improves, as does the control of morphological resources, insertions may only consist of and be saturated with nominals. This has fewer morphosyntactic implications.

The data available for bilingual English-Spanish children (Restrepo & Gutiérrez-Clellen, 2004) and French-English children (Genesee et al., 1995; Paradis, 2007) also do not point out significant differences or special problems caused by dealing with two languages. These data support the conclusion that the learning of both languages is not challenged by the SLI and that both languages present similar deficits (Paradis et al., 2003; Genesee et al., 2004).

Therefore, we can confirm that the use of code-mixing does not show a deficit by the child, but it is the result of the implicit process of learning two languages simultaneously. There exists an idea that a bilingual situation would further challenge the production, as would the fact that children with language delay or impairment have to deal with learning two languages. This idea, however, is not confirmed by the data available, at least from the point of view of code-mixing and in typologically near languages such as Spanish and Catalan.

Our data confirm that there is minimal influence on the development of the language impairment by the bilingual context, as indicated by the scarce data available on the subject (Paradis, 2007). Exposing an SLI or a language delayed child to a dual language input in the first years is not a negative factor for him/her. Nevertheless, as is the case for every child, the exposure to language must be continuous, sufficiently rich and functional in order to ensure a well organised acquisition.

Acknowledgements

The authors would like to thank the following organizations for their collaboration: Centre Recursos per a Deficients Auditius (CREDA) de la Generalitat de Catalunya and the group Adquisició de Llengües des de la Catalunya Multilingüe (ALLENCAM). This publication has been carried out, partly, thanks to the BSO-2003-02200 grant from the Ministerio de Educación y Ciencia (MEC) and the FPU-AP-2002-2508 grant from the MEC.

Notes

1. Children with SLI treated by the CREDA = 1645 (course 2003–2004); 1734 (course 2004–2005). Total number of kindergarten pupils from the public sector (2003–2004) = 119,706. Total number of elementary school pupils from the public sector (2003–2004) = 218,796.
2. The differences among languages will be dealt with later on.
3. Is it much more *difficult* for them, as it intuitively may seem? Is the learning *different* because of the scope of the task? Is there a different profile of errors that reveals any particularity in their processing or is there just a low level of competence similar to TD? Is there a different *timing* of acquisition? Does simultaneous or successive bilingualism lead to different profiles in SLI children? Is it possible for them, as many others not impaired, to become fluent, even if they do not master a full and independently coordinated doubled system?
4. The differentiation will occur once functional categories emerge, usually during the third year.
5. Of the 20 subjects that composed the first sample, only seven (here, six for the study) were considered SLI. The rest, with a good evolution, were diagnosed as language delayed.

References

Ajuriaguerra, J. and Inhelder, B. (1976) The development and prognosis of dysphasia in children. In D.M. Morehead and A.E. Morehead (eds) *Typical and Deficient Child Language*. Baltimore: University Park Press.

Anderson, R.T. (2001) Learning an invented inflectional morpheme in Spanish by children with typical language skills and with SLI. *International Journal of Language & Communication Disorders* 36 (1), 1–19.

Bedore, L. and Leonard, L. (2001) Grammatical morphology deficits in Spanish-speaking children with specific language impairment. *Journal of Speech, Language, and Hearing Research* 44, 905–924.

Bishop, D.M.V. and L.B. Leonard (eds) (2000) *Speech and Language Impairments in Children: Causes, Characteristics, Intervention and Outcome*. Hove, UK: Psychology Press.

Bishop, D.M.V. (1997) *Uncommon Understanding*. London: Psychology Press.

Bosch, L. and Serra, M. (1997) Grammatical morphology deficits of Spanish-speaking children with specific language impairment. In A. Baker, M. Beers, G. Bol, J. de Jong and G. Leemans (eds) *Child Language Disorders in a Cross Linguistic Perspective*. Amsterdam: University of Amsterdam, Institute for General Linguistics.

Cipriani, P., Chilosi, A. and Bottari, P. (1995) Language acquisition and language recovery in developmental dysphasia and acquired childhood aphasia. In K.E. Nelson and Z. Réger (eds) *Children's Language* 8, 245–273. Hillsdale, NJ: Lawrence Erlbaum.

Cipriani, P., Chilosi, A., Bottari, P., Pfanner, L., Poli, P. and Sarno, S. (1991) L'uso della morfologia grammaticale nella disfasia congenita. *Giornale Italiano di Psicologia* 18, 765–779.
Conti-Ramsden, G. and Jones, M. (1997) Verb use in specific language impairment. *Journal of Speech, Language and Hearing Research* 40, 1298–1313.
De Houwer, A. (2005) Early bilingual acquisition: Focus on morphosyntax and the separate development hypothesis. In J.F. Kroll and A.M.B. De Groot (eds) *Handbook of Bilingualism* (pp. 30–48). New York: Oxford University Press.
Fletcher, P. and Peters, J. (1984) Characterizing language impairment in children: An exploratory study. *Language Testing* 1, 33–49.
Genesee, F., Nicoladis, E. and Paradis, J. (1995) Language differentiation in early bilingual development. *Journal of Child Language* 22, 611–631.
Genesee, F., Paradis, J. and Crago, M. (2004) *Dual Language Development & Disorders. A Handbook on Bilingualism & Second Language Learning*. Baltimore: Paul H. Brookes Publishing.
Gutiérrez-Clellen, V.F., Restrepo, M.A., Bedore, L., Peña, L. and Anderson, R. (2000) Language sample analysis: Methodological considerations. *Language, Speech and Hearing Services in the Schools* 31, 88–98.
Gutiérrez-Clellen, V.F. and Erickson, A.B. (in press) *Codeswitching in SLI Children*. Unpublished manuscript.
Le Normand, M.T., Leonard, L. and McGregor, K. (1993) A cross-linguistic study of article use by children with specific language impairment. *European Journal of Disorders of Communication* 28, 153–163.
Leonard, L. (1998) *Specific Language Impairment*. London: MIT Press.
Leonard, L., Bortolini, U., Caselli, M.C., McGregor, K. and Sabbadini, L. (1992) Morphological deficits in children with specific language impairment: The status of features in the underlying grammar. *Language Acquisition* 2, 151–179.
Leonard, L., Sabbadini, L., Volterra, V. and Leonard, J. (1988) Some influences of the grammar of English- and Italian-speaking with SLI. *Applied Psycholinguistics* 9, 39–57.
Meisel, J. (2001) The simultaneous acquisition of two first languages. Early differentiation and subsequent development of grammars. In J. Cenoz and F. Genesee (eds) *Trends in Bilingual Acquisition* (pp. 11–41). Amsterdam: Benjamins.
Methé, S. and Crago, M. (1996) Verb morphology in French children with language impairment. Paper presented at the Symposium on Research in Child Language Disorders, University of Wisconsin, Madison.
Paradis, J., Crago, M., Genesee F. and Rice, M. (2003) French-English bilingual children with SLI: How do they compare with their monolingual peers? *Journal of Speech, Language and Hearing Research* 46, 1–15.
Paradis, J. (2007) Bilingual children with specific language impairment: Theoretical and applied issues. *Applied Psycholinguistics* 28, 551–564.
Restrepo, M.A. (1995) Identifiers of Spanish-speaking children with language impairment who are learning English as a second language. Doctoral dissertation, University of Arizona.
Restrepo, M.A. (2003) Spanish language skills in bilingual children with specific language impairment. In S. Montrul and F. Ordoñez (eds) *Linguistic Theory and Language Development in Hispanic Languages. Papers from the 5th Hispanic*

Linguistics Symposium and the 2001 Acquisition of Spanish and Portuguese Conference (pp. 365–374). Somerville, MA: Cascadilla Press.

Restrepo, M.A. and Gutiérrez-Clellen, V.F. (2004) Grammatical impairments in Spanish–English bilingual children. In B.A. Goldstein (ed.) *Bilingual Language Development and Disorders in Spanish–English Speakers* (pp. 213–234). Baltimore: Paul H. Brookes Publishing.

Rice, M. and Oetting, J. (1993) Morphological deficits in children with SLI: Evolution of number marking and agreement. *Journal of Speech and Hearing Research* 36, 1249–1257.

Rice, M.L., Buhr, J.C. and Nemeth, M.J. (1990) Fast mapping word-learning abilities of language-delayed preschoolers. *Journal of Speech and Hearing Disorders* 55, 33–42.

Rice, M., Wexler, K. and Cleave, P. (1995) Specific language impairment as a period of extended optional infinitive. *Journal of Speech and Hearing Research* 38, 850–863.

Sanz-Torrent, M. (2002) Los verbos en niños con trastorno del lenguaje. *Revista de Logopedia, Foniatria y Audiologia* XXII(2), 100–110.

Sanz-Torrent, M. (2004) El trastorn específic del Llenguatge: aspectes lèxics, semàntics i morfo-sintàctics en l'adquisició del verb. Doctoral dissertation, Universitat de Barcelona.

Serra, M. (2002) Trastornos del lenguaje: Preguntas pendientes en investigación e intervención. *Revista de logopedia, Foniatría y Audiología* XXII (2), 63–76.

Stark, R.E. and Tallal, P. (1981) Selection of children with specific language deficits. *Journal of Speech and Hearing Disorders* 46, 114–122.

Watkins, R. (1994) Specific language impairments in children: An introduction. In A.R. Watkins and M.L. Rice (eds) *Specific Language Impairments in Children*. Baltimore: Brookes Publishing.

Watkins, R., Rice, M.L. and Moltz, C. (1993) Verb use by language-impaired and typically developing children. *First Language* 13, 133–143.

Chapter 7
The Simultaneous Development of Narratives in English and Spanish

ESTHER ÁLVAREZ

Introduction

Bilingual First Language Acquisition (BFLA) has become an area of investigation within the field of bilingualism. A child is considered a case of BFLA if two conditions are met: the child has been exposed to two languages from birth, and has had regular exposure to them until the time of the investigation (De Houwer, 1990). The crucial question that arises in this pattern of language acquisition is how the two languages develop. Recent studies in this area have demonstrated that bilingual children are able to make a pragmatically differentiated use of their two languages as early as one year and nine or ten months of age (Nicoladis & Genesee, 1996), and that their two grammars develop separately as soon as they emerge (De Houwer, 1990). Notwithstanding the fact that there is broad agreement on the issue of language separation, researchers in this field may examine their data while exploring two hypotheses (Meisel, 2001): (1) the two languages develop autonomously, resembling monolingual language acquisition (Autonomous Development Hypothesis), and (2) one of the languages acts as a developmental guide for the other language (Interdependent Development Hypothesis), thus suggesting some degree of cross-linguistic influence.

Examining this question, some studies have looked at the emergence of the core grammar of different language pairs: French-German (Meisel, 1990), French- or Italian-German or Dutch (Müller & Hulk, 2001), Basque-Spanish (Meisel & Ezeizabarrena, 1996), German-English (Döpke, 1999), Catalan-English (Juan-Garau & Pérez-Vidal, 2000), among others. However, fewer BFLA studies have addressed the issue of the development of the two languages at the later stages of acquisition (Lanza,

2001, and Álvarez, 2003a, constitute some examples). Studies in monolingual language acquisition have shown that after the emergence of the core grammar, which takes place between the ages of four and six years, approximately, children still have ahead of them the difficult task of learning how to employ their grammars in the construction of discourse (Hickmann, 2003). The study of narratives provides a good opportunity to trace the language development of bilingual children at later ages and to deepen our understanding of the pattern of interaction between the two languages.

Narrative Discourse

Three domains are central in the organisation of a narrative text: reference to person, time and space. In each domain, children have to learn some universal principles of text organisation using the grammatical and lexical means that their particular language offers. Bilingual children are faced with the task of making use of the language-specific ways in which their two languages encode universal principles.

Reference to Person, Time and Space in English and Spanish[1]

Reference to person

In a narrative text, characters have to be introduced and then referred to at subsequent moments in the story. This opposition of characters mentioned for the first time and those that have already been mentioned previously in the text is the linguistic reflection of the universal cognitive distinction that speakers/hearers make between new information and given or old information. Different languages, therefore, differ in the way they encode this distinction and they usually have in their systems forms that cover a continuum from totally new or inaccessible information to information with the highest degree of accessibility. A narrator has to continually assess the degree of accessibility of each referent and encode it with forms that give the listener the required amount of information: the maintenance of the same character across two or more clauses (a high accessibility status) demands less linguistic material (null subjects and pronouns), whereas the first mention of a character or the switch from one character to another (a low accessibility status) demands more linguistic material (full noun phrases).

In the present chapter only reference maintenance will be examined, as it is the function for which English and Spanish employ similar grammatical means, but with a difference in its use. In both languages, the most suitable forms include pronouns and the null subject. However, the former are obligatory in English (a) and optional in Spanish (b), whereas the latter is the preferred form in Spanish (c) and only possible in English in coordinate clauses (d):

(a) *A boy was looking at his frog. Then **he** went to sleep.*
(b) *Un niño miraba a su rana. Luego (**él**) se fue a dormir.* (A boy looked at his frog. Then (*he*) went to sleep.)
(c) *Un niño miraba a su rana. Luego **0** se fue a dormir.* (A boy looked at his frog. Then **0** went to sleep.)
(d) *A boy said good-night to his frog and **0** went to sleep.*

The use of a full noun phrase for reference maintenance represents overexplicitation, that is, an excess of information, as the referent is still active in the listener's mind (e):

(e) ***The boy*** *climbed a tree.* ***The boy*** *looked in a hole in the tree.*

Reference to time

Another aspect that is crucial to the organisation of narrative discourse is the temporal relationship between the situations and events of the story, which have to be presented as forming part of the plot-advancing foreground or the supportive, evaluative background of the narrative (Labov, 1972). The relationship between situations and whether they belong to the foreground or background of the narrative is effected by such linguistic markers as aspect (both grammatical and lexical) and connectives such as *meanwhile, and, then*.

One of the main differences in the tense-aspect systems in English and in Spanish is that the distinction of perfective/imperfective is obligatory in the past tense in Spanish. The distinction between the two aspects is the distinction between complete/incomplete, but a clause with imperfective aspect in combination with another clause with perfective aspect will also express a certain degree of simultaneity between foreground and background actions (f). In English, this distinction is expressed by overlapping perfective and progressive aspects (g). The progressive is also part of the aspectual system of Spanish, but it is seldom used to express this distinction of co-existence.

(f) *El niño se **cayó** del árbol, mientras las abejas **perseguían** al perro.* (The boy **fell**-PERFECTIVE from the tree, while the bees **chased**-IMPERFECTIVE the dog.)
(g) *The boy **fell off** the tree, while all the bees **were chasing** the dog.*

Reference to space

Reference to space is another discourse organiser that contributes to narrative cohesion. In order to mark spatial relations, the child has to learn how to indicate static location (h), and movement from one point to another (i):

(h)　*The frog was in a jar.*
(i)　*The deer took the child to the edge of a cliff.*

The lexical devices that have to be acquired for these purposes include motion/posture verbs, prepositions, particles and certain adjectives and adverbials. In narrative discourse, Berman and Slobin (1994) report how typological differences affect what spatial information is included, both at the local level of successive clauses and at the global level of the text. They show how young children are sensitive to the specific way in which their language selects the spatial information to be included and to the distribution of such information between the verb and the other constituents in the clause; that is, they are sensitive to the lexicalisation pattern of their native language (Talmy, 1985). This author has classified languages according to the way they conflate the semantic entities of a motion event. Spanish encodes motion and its path in the verb and indicates the manner of the movement separately, generally with a gerund complement (j), but English conflates motion and manner in the main verb and specifies path separately by means of a particle (k):

(j)　*El niño* **salió corriendo.** (The boy **went-out running**.)
(k)　*The boy* **ran out**.

Slobin (1996) has further examined Spanish and English lexicalisation patterns by considering motion events in narratives. Motion events are often stretched across clauses and the path is often described in much detail as taking place between a source and a goal. The amount of detail in the description of movement varies greatly from Spanish to English. Spanish uses a much smaller set of movement verbs, includes fewer ground elements in clauses, and tends to elaborate on static descriptions leaving paths to be inferred (l). English, on the other hand, elaborates the path and accumulates particles and prepositional phrases around one verb of movement (m):

(l)　... *y el niño cayó* **donde había un lago.** (... and the boy fell **where there was a lake**.)
(m)　*The boy fell* **off the cliff into a pond**.

Research Questions

In order to contribute further evidence to the question of language separation, the present study focuses on the acquisition process that takes place after the core grammar of the two languages has been established. It considers the development of the ability to use linguistic forms to produce a cohesive narrative text in each of the bilingual subject's two languages. The English-Spanish language pair is considered as their grammars differ in their aspectual systems and in the encoding of change of location, but at the same time they also use similar, if not identical, means to maintain reference. The two research questions that will guide the study are the following:

- What is the developmental language acquisition pattern of a narrative discourse in the two languages as regards referential maintenance, time grounding and explicitation of movement?
- Are the developments parallel in both languages or does the subject's choice of grammatical and lexical means suggest transfer of the conventions of one language to the other?

The Present Study

The subject

The subject of this study, Jan, is the first-born child in a bilingual family (English-Spanish). He is a case of BFLA following the pattern One Parent–One Language (Romaine, 1995): his mother speaks to him in Spanish and his father in American-English. The family lives in Barcelona, the capital city of Catalunya (an autonomous bilingual Spanish-Catalan community in Spain). At the age of 3;1 Jan started attending a British English school where Catalan and Spanish children follow an English immersion programme. In Barcelona, there are a number of immersion schools, where children are taught in a second language at the start and their native languages are then introduced gradually into school tuition. In the particular school that Jan has attended, most children come from Spanish- or Catalan-speaking families and the school is their first contact with English; therefore, children play and interact with each other in Spanish or Catalan outside the classroom. The English teachers are English native speakers who, for the most part, speak or understand Spanish and/or Catalan. The English teachers address the children exclusively in English and children are expected to reciprocate. By the end of their schooling, children who attend these immersion schools are Spanish-Catalan bilinguals and have a very high command of the English language. The children like Jan, who have English at home, are truly trilingual.

The present study will focus on the two languages that the subject has been exposed to on a daily basis since birth, namely English and Spanish; therefore, Catalan will not be considered.

Material and data collection

The picture book story *Frog, Where are you?* (Mayer, 1969) was chosen because it has repeatedly proven to be suitable in eliciting narratives. It contains 24 pictures (Appendix 1) in which a boy and his dog have a pet frog that escapes one night from the jar where it was kept. Their attempts at finding the frog in different places are unsuccessful, until the end of the story when they finally find their frog.

The recordings were carried out at school at the ages of 6;11, 7;11, 8;11, 9;11 and finally 10;11. Jan's English teacher gave him time to look at the pictures and then gave him the cue *Once upon a time ...* in order to indicate to the child that she expected a story. The teacher was sitting next to the child looking at the pictures at the same time as the child and, after the first cue, she did not intervene. A week later, the Spanish teacher followed the same procedure giving Jan the cue *Érase una vez ...* The next recordings continued at one-year intervals.

The transcriptions of the tapes were carried out following the CHILDES system (MacWhinney, 1991). The utterances were divided, selecting the clause as the basic unit of analysis.

Results and Discussion

Reference to person

Jan's accuracy rate when maintaining reference in Spanish (Table 7.1) is already relatively high at the beginning of the recordings at age 6;11. In 71.4% of the cases he uses the correct form, mostly the null form, whereas in 28.6% of the clauses he uses a full NP, which is not incorrect, but represents overexplicitation. The very few instances of pronouns are either relative pronouns (1) or a personal pronoun for emphasis (2), all of them suitable:

(1) ... *y las abejas,* **que** *estaban en el panal, persiguieron al perro.* (7;11) (... and the bees, **who** were in the honeycomb, chased the dog.)
(2) ... *y el niño intentó escaparse de él* [el búho]. *Él* [el niño] *pensaba que se había montado en un árbol.* (9;11) (... and the boy tried to escape from him [the owl]. **He** [the boy] thought that [he] had climbed a tree.)

Table 7.1 Reference maintenance*

		\multicolumn{5}{c}{Age}
		6;11	7;11	8;11	9;11	10;11
(1) Pronouns	English	50.0	65.2	50.0	44.4	50.0
	Spanish	–	7.7	–	8.7	7.1
(2) Null forms	English	–	13.1	25.0	33.3	31.3
	Spanish	71.4	61.5	76.9	73.9	85.8
(3) Definite NPs	English	50.0	21.7	25.0	22.3	18.7
	Spanish	28.6	30.8	23.1	17.4	7.1

*Percentages in relation to all maintenance forms.

Progressively, the use of null forms increases in Spanish with the corresponding decrease of full NPs to almost total adequacy at 10;11. There are some non-canonical forms left at that stage, but, in fact, these are used appropriately in order to avoid ambiguity. For example, in sentence (3) the intervening clause with an inanimate object makes the repetition of the full NP desirable:

(3) *Estaban* [el perro y el niño] *en una casa muy agradable. Era* **la noche. El perro y el niño** *se durmieron.* (9;11) ([the dog and the boy] were in a very nice house. It was **night time. The dog and the boy** went to sleep.)

Thus, development in this area in Spanish is largely based on an increase in the use of the prototypical null form. The development is also characterised by variation in the possible forms, by the inclusion of appropriate use of pronouns, and by the fact that the full forms become less redundant because of the particular context in which they are used. At 9;11 there is very good command of the system and at 10;11 reference maintenance is almost adult-like with respect to the forms.

In English, Jan starts off with a lower degree of accuracy with respect to maintenance forms (50%). He does not make the distinction between pronominal and nominal reference to mark different discourse functions: in order to maintain reference he uses either the relevant pronominal form (50%) or the redundant full nominal (50%). There is a developmental leap at 7;11, when he is much more aware of the discourse function of these two forms (65.2% pronouns vs. 21.7% definite NPs), and he also starts using other forms correctly, such as null forms (13.1%) in coordinate clauses:

(4) ... *and the boy opened the window and* **0** *shouted.* (7;11)

At the onset of the recordings, at age 6;11, Jan is already able to construct an endophorically cohesive oral text out of a set of pictures: he relies on the previous linguistic context when anchoring coreferential devices. The developmental progression that takes place is in the adequacy of information status marking across clauses, a process that is practically complete in the last recording at 10;11. In order to achieve this universal aspect of discourse cohesion, Jan has had to come to terms with the language-specific aspects of his two language systems. The results for the acquisition of referring expressions have shown that there is an interplay between universal and language-specific aspects, but that development is characterised by intra- rather than inter-language resolution. For example, reference maintenance improves in both languages by a reduction in the number of overexplicit forms. In Spanish, as would be expected, Jan relies more heavily on verb morphology and so the use of null forms increases. In English, greater adequacy is achieved not by an increase in the use of pronouns, which would be the characteristic forms, but by an increase of null forms. However, unlike in Spanish, the null form is exclusively used to maintain reference across coordinate clauses, which is the only context allowed by the language system.

Reference to time

The contrast perfective–imperfective to mark the foreground vs. background discourse contrast is not used in the Spanish narratives until age 8;11. Before that age, the imperfective is used frequently, although unrelated to other forms, in order to state existence, possession or location and other functions.

At age 7;11, there is perfective–imperfective contrast, but it does not mark the background vs. foreground opposition: the 'being' (imperfective) in the beehive necessarily has to finish when the 'chasing' (perfective) starts:

(5) ... *y las abejas, que* **estaban** *en el panal,* **persiguieron** *al perro.* (7;11)
     (... and the bees, who **were**-IMPERFECTIVE in the honeycomb, **chased**-PERFECTIVE the dog.)

At the ages of 6;11 and 7;11, the foreground is set off from the background using other means, namely, the contrast perfective–progressive, which has already been reported in Berman and Slobin (1994) as an early way to express the background–foreground distinction in Spanish monolingual young children:

(6) ... *y el niño* **ponió** (should be 'puso') *la nariz en un agujero, y el perro* **estaba intentando** *coger el abejar.* (6;11) (... and the boy **put** the nose in a hole, and the dog **was trying** to take the beehive)

It is at the age of 8;11 when the use of the imperfective for durative actions reaches a high degree of maturity. The contrast imperfective–perfective is used for a foregrounded perfective action that happens against an imperfective backgrounded action, and the backgrounded action is reported as such, not only by the use of imperfective, but also by the use of a temporal conjunction.

(7) ... *pero* **salió** *un búho y le* **empujó** *y se* **cayó** *al suelo, y* **mientras tanto** *todas las abejas le* **perseguían** *al perro.* (8;11) (... but an owl **came out**-PERFECTIVE and **pushed**-PERFECTIVE him and [he = the boy] **fell down**-PERFECTIVE to the floor, and **meanwhile** all the bees **chased**. IMPERFECTIVE the dog.)

The two contrasts, perfective with progressive or with imperfective, are acceptable possibilities in Spanish and, in fact, sometimes are interchangeable, although adults seem to favour the second contrast in this story as reported in Berman and Slobin (1994). In the next two stories at 9;11 and 10;11, both forms coexist and the progressive is sometimes used when the background is a particularly short moment, as in example (8) below. In most cases, the idea of background activity is reinforced by the use of *cuando* or *mientras* (when or while).

(8) *Miraron por un agujero bajo tierra, por el sitio donde viven las abejas.* **Cuando** *el niño* **estaba mirando** *por el agujero bajo tierra, un hámster le* **dió** *en la nariz.* (9;11) ([They] looked in a hole underground, in the place where the bees live. **When** the boy **was looking** in the hole underground, a hamster **hit** him on the nose.)

In English, at age 6;11, the contrast perfective–progressive is an incipient attempt at establishing the background, but the perfective and imperfective actions are not yet related lexically to indicate simultaneity in the way that will be done in later stories: the connector 'and' merely lists the actions in these clauses:

(9) ... *and then he* [= the boy] *went to sleep, the frog came out of the container* **and** *the dog* **was sleeping** XXX.[2] (6;11)

It is not until the age of 9;11 that the use of the progressive with narrative functions really takes off. The same implicit relation between a backgrounded situation and a foregrounded event commented on at age 6;11 is now overtly stated by the use of the temporal conjunction:

(10) *The frog wanted to escape, and* **when** *the dog and the boy* **were sleeping***, the frog* **went out** *of his pot.* (9;11)

At the age of 10;11, another development is the explicit marking of two durative actions which are simultaneous by using a combination of inceptive aspect (*started shouting*), an adverb of simultaneity, and the progressive aspect:

(11) The boy **started shouting** inside the tree and an owl came out and pushed him down. **At the meanwhile** the dog **was being chased** by some bees. (10;11)

There is no evidence that the complexity of tense/aspect system in one of the languages influences the development of the system in the other language. There are no signs of a reduction in the extensive Spanish aspectual system, and forms that are absent from the English morphological paradigm are frequent in the Spanish narratives (imperfective, perfective and imperfective contrast instead of the progressive form). On the other hand, it is also the case that there is no attempt in English at compensating for the lack of those distinctions made in Spanish. Jan seems to be guided in his development of temporal relations by the two languages separately and he makes the pertinent adjustments within each system as he becomes aware with age of the forms to mark the distinctions that each language encodes.

Reference to space

The difference in the lexicalisation patterns of motion events in the two languages is examined in this section. Tables 7.2 and 7.3 show the variety of motion verbs and of their particles and prepositions.

There are more different lexical items in Spanish than in English (19 vs. 15 different verbs). However, Berman and Slobin's (1994) results of monolingual children and adults telling the same story show 27 movement verbs used by 12 Spanish speakers compared to 47 verbs used by 12 English speakers. This difference reflects the English typological characteristic of expressing movement and manner in the same verb, which results in a massive variety of such verbs in English. Compared to English monolingual children, Jan's variation in terms of verbs of movement is very limited.

The difference between Jan's English verbs and those used by monolinguals in the above study is even more striking when we compare the 123 combinations of English verbs + satellites that have been attested in the 12 English monolingual stories. Even allowing for the fact that the monolingual group consists of 12 diverse people in each age group and that adults are included, it can safely be concluded that Jan's two languages do not show a parallel development as regards the variety of verbs of movement: his Spanish stories are close to those of Spanish monolinguals, whereas his English stories are not. Moreover, more than a third of Jan's verbs of

Table 7.2 English motion verbs and their prepositions and particles*

Age	Types	Tokens	Verbs	Prepositions and particles
6;11	10	22	climb+, come+, fall, go+, jump+, leave, push, put+, run, throw	on, out, away, in, over, up, down
7;11	9	18	chase, splash, take+, (throw+)	against, for, into
8;11	6	14	escape, (fall+, run+)	off, on top of, after, to
9;11	6	13	get+	–
10;11	8	13	(escape+, push+)	from
Total		80	15	15

*In the columns under the headings 'verbs' and 'prepositions and particles', those added each year are to be found after the first list at age 6;11. Verbs with a plus sign indicate that the verb has been used with a ground element. The parentheses show verbs that have already been used in previous years, but without a ground element at that time.

movement are deictic verbs (*come* and *go*) in his English narratives, although a development with age is also evident.

Figures 7.1 and 7.2 show which semantic components of the motion event are encoded in the verb itself. The expression of direction constitutes the greatest difference between the two languages. In the English stories, there is only one verb containing inherent (downward) direction: *fall*. In Spanish, the occurrences of verbs indicating direction, for example, *subir, salir, caer,* (*go up, go out* and *fall* respectively) outnumber those in

Table 7.3 Spanish motion verbs and their prepositions

Age	Types	Tokens	Verbs	Prepositions
6;11	10	20	andar, caerse+, correr, escaparse, irse, montarse+, ponerse+, salir+, subir+, tirar	a, en, de
7;11	10	14	escalar, llevarse, perseguir+, resbalarse+, (tirar+)	–
8;11	9	17	empujar, hacer caer,	–
9;11	12	18	cargarse, (escaparse+), levantarse, quitar del camino	–
10;11	8	15	–	desde
Total		84	19	4

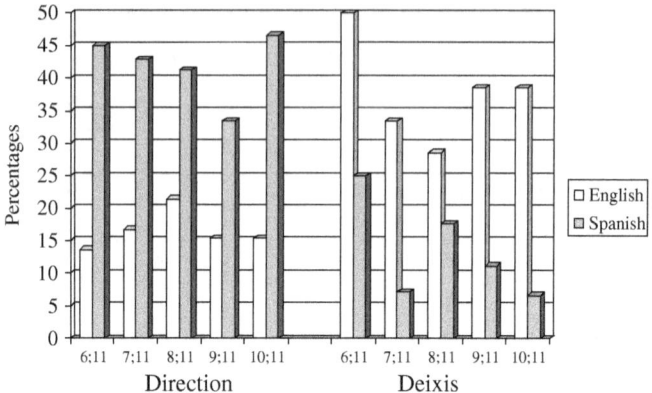

Figure 7.1 Verbs of movement: conflation of semantic components

English (35 instances in Spanish representing 41.7% of motion verbs vs. 13 instances in English representing 16.3%). Deictic verbs in English are very frequent (31 instances), especially in the earlier narratives (11 instances). Most cases (18 times) correspond to the verb *go*, which combines with a higher number of particles than any other motion verb. The number of these verbs decreases to half from the first to the last narrative. In Spanish, except for the first narrative (5 instances), deictic verbs are not as common.

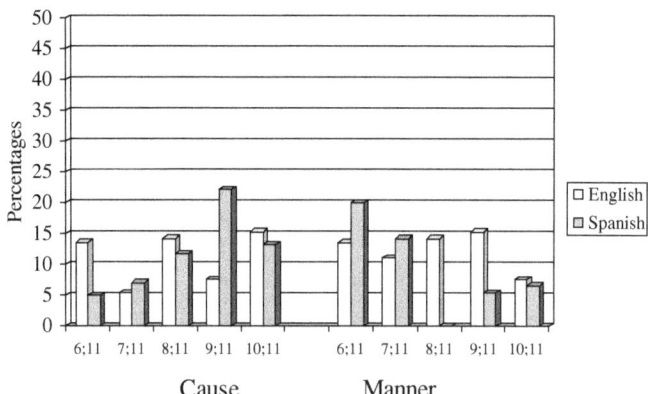

Figure 7.2 Verbs of movement: conflation of semantic components

There are basically two causative verbs in English (9 instances), *push* and *throw*. They first appear at 6;11 without further locative specification. As of 7;11 both verbs appear with a particle (*push down*) or with the specification of the goal (12). In Spanish there is more variety in causative verbs (5 types and 10 instances), which sometimes are used in the presence or absence of a prepositional phrase indicating goal (13 and 14). Thus, there is no such clear developmental pattern as in English:

(12) *The deer threw the boy **in the water**.* (7;11)
(13) ... *y después el cuervo* [meaning '*ciervo*'] *le **tiró** al niño **al agua**.* (7;11) (... and then the crow [should be 'deer'] **threw** the boy **in the water**.)
(14) *El ciervo le **tiró**.* (9;11) (The deer **threw** him.)

Verbs expressing manner are infrequent in both languages and it is only expressed separately from the verb in the Spanish data on four occasions:

(15) *El ciervo se lo **llevó corriendo**.* (8;11) (The deer **carried.away** him [= the boy] **running**.)
(16) ***Salieron** sus hijos **disparados** de unas plantas.* (9;11) (Their children **came.out shooting** [= shot out] from behind some plants.)

The information that is encoded outside the verb itself in both languages corresponds most often to the expression of ground elements, that is, the source of the movement (17) or the goal where the movement finishes (18):

(17) ... *y la rana se escapó **delpote** de cristal.* (9;11) (... and the frog escaped **from the glass pot**.)
(18) *The boy fell **in the floor** because the owl hit him.* (8;11)

Table 7.4 shows the percentages for motion verbs that specify either the source or the goal. Although the percentages are generally higher in Spanish, there is no evidence in Jan's stories of a greatly differentiated use in both his languages of the number of ground adjuncts specifying

Table 7.4 Percentage of motion verbs specifying source or goal

	Age				
	6;11	**7;11**	**8;11**	**9;11**	**10;11**
English	31.8	27.7	50.0	38.5	23.1
Spanish	45.0	35.7	29.4	33.3	33.3

the beginning or the end of the movement specified in the verb. Slobin (1996) finds that, at age 3 years, monolingual English and Spanish children include the same number of ground elements in their clauses. However, as of age 4, English-speaking children start including more of these landmarks in their narratives. At age 9;11 the percentages seem to coincide again (62% English and 61% Spanish) and the biggest difference is found in adults (82% English vs. 63% Spanish). This means that nine-year-old Spanish children perform like adults in this respect, but English-speaking children have still some development ahead. Jan's mention of sources and/or goals with movement verbs is noticeably lower than both English and Spanish monolinguals. Moreover, clauses that contain a ground-mark seem to decrease with age and, consequently, the narratives at 10;11 contain the fewest mentions of source or goal, contrary to results of monolingual data.

Encoding movement may be an area in the acquisition process where, due to the stark opposition in terms of lexicalisation patterns, this bilingual child is still actively sorting out the different ways in which his two languages narrate a motion event. There is no mixing in that, for example, direction is expressed in the verb in Spanish (only 16.3% of English motion verbs include direction in the verb, but 41.7% of Spanish verbs do so), and particles express direction in English (38.7% English verbs express direction with a particle, but only 1.2% have an adverbial expression denoting direction in Spanish). In this sense, there is no interference of one language on the other, but Jan's use of a restricted number of verbs of movement and particles in English and a reduced number of ground adjuncts in both languages results in a description of change of location that is limited.

Choi and Bowerman (1991) show how the language-specific lexicalisation patterns of motion events in English and Korean influence the moment when children first start talking about spontaneous and caused motion. They conclude that the production of locative expressions does not depend solely on cognitive complexity, but that the specific language being acquired is also a determinant factor. The consequences of this finding for bilingual children are not as yet fully understood.

The fact that the difference between Jan's stories and monolingual English-speaking children is more marked than with Spanish-speaking monolinguals also raises the question of how much input is necessary for the child to learn how to encode movement. Despite the fact that his exposure to English is more restricted than to Spanish, the amount and type of English input seems to have been adequate enough for the development of, at least, the other two areas of this study, namely reference maintenance and time grounding. In the next section a tentative explanation is offered, but clearly this is an area that needs more careful investigation.

Conclusions

In order to draw the conclusions for the first research question, a developmental picture of the narrative abilities of the subject over a five-year period is presented below. Starting with the age of 6;11, the English story evidences a poor command of the regulation of information status as regards the knowledge shared by the listener, because reference to those characters already introduced is, in 50% of the cases, carried out with a full NP, resulting in redundant information. There is a rudimentary attempt at marking the opposition of foreground and background using grammatical aspect (perfective vs. progressive). However, the link between the clauses, which in later years underlines their discourse-internal relationship, is not yet present, as the clauses are mostly coordinated. The English story at this age is that which, in the whole sample, displays the most change of location verbs, although 50% of these are the deictic verbs *come* and *go*. This interest in describing movement scenes, even with impoverished lexical resources, is also evident in the fact that it is in this story that Jan gives most attention to goals and sources, an attention that in later years diminishes.

The Spanish story at this same age is more mature than the English one in many respects. First, the regulation of the status of information as a function of communicative focus is already well managed; there is a relatively good command of the amount of material that the listener needs when reference to characters is maintained (only 14% of full NPs in subject position for reference maintenance are redundant). Regarding temporality, Jan attempts the foregrounding and backgrounding of information using the same forms in the two languages, a contrast of perfective and progressive. This accounts for a high percentage of progressive forms in Spanish, which is not conventional adult usage. However, an influence from English may be disregarded as the same phenomenon has been encountered in Spanish monolingual children telling this same story at this age. Jan is stretching a form of early acquisition, the progressive for ongoing activity, to cover a new discourse function, that is, that of backgrounding information with respect to the plot-advancing perfective. As regards reference to space, verbs expressing direction are by far the most numerous group and, contrary to the general tendency in both languages, verbs expressing manner are slightly more frequent in Spanish than in English. Finally, as in the case of English, the Spanish story at 6;11 has more explicit sources and especially goals for verbs of movement than later stories.

The age of 7;11 sees a surge in the use of pronouns in English, which improves redundancy for reference maintenance.

The advances at age 8;1 in Spanish are in the domain of temporality, where Jan is now fully able to background and foreground information using grammatical and lexical means at the same time: an imperfective and a perfective clause joined together by an adverb of simultaneity (*mientras tanto* = meanwhile), stressing the aspectual relations established by the grammatical means. As regards reference to space, in English the percentage of deictic verbs is still decreasing and verbs expressing the cause of movement or the manner or direction become more frequent. However, a decreasing interest in referring to space is also manifest in the stories in both languages, the story at 8;11 being the one with the fewest ground points.

At the age of 9;11, the backgrounding and foregrounding of events is now successfully realised in the two languages in combination with an array of grammatical and lexical means. On the other hand, the great effort at organising the plot, which is evident at this age, may represent a considerable burden on the child's attention capacity and, consequently, reference to verbs of movement, which has proved to be the weakest part in Jan's narratives, suffers noticeably.

At age 10;11, there are no more redundant maintenance forms in either language. The distinction between background and foreground is now fully marked with the newly acquired connector to express simultaneity of foregrounded events and backgrounded durative activities in English. For changes of location, the age of 10;11 is one where the number of goals and sources mentioned explicitly in the same clause as the verb is very reduced, particularly in English. The percentage of deictic verbs is still high and manner verbs, so typical of the rhetorical style of the English language, are now down to 8%, the lowest percentage in all the stories.

Turning now to the second research question, a series of conclusions can be drawn. In two of the areas studied, development has advanced regularly and followed a similar course towards adult usage in the two language, but the developmental change in the expression of movement in the narrative constitutes the striking exception. In this area of the investigation, the subject displays in his youngest story greater effort in the narration of change of location events than in the rest of the stories, and this effect is more marked in English. It should be said, however, that this phenomenon does not extend to the entire management of reference to space. In studies of the same subject carried out elsewhere (Álvarez, 2003b), verbs of position and the specification of locations proceed in an upward developmental trend in both languages. Therefore, it is clearly the motion events, so differently lexicalised in the two languages, that confront a bilingual child with conflicting information and, in this case, the child seems to opt for a 'third' in-between style, characterised by a frequent use of 'all-purpose' movement verbs, such as deictic verbs, and by a lack of attention to change of location. The fact that simultaneous bilinguals use different strategies from their monolingual peers has already been noted by other authors (see for example Lanza, 2001). She notes that, for the last two decades the emphasis in bilingual studies has been on showing that bilingual children keep their two languages apart in their acquisition process, and therefore these studies have stressed the similarities between bilingual and monolingual acquisition. However, as Grosjean (1985) has strongly argued, the bilingual child is not the sum of two monolinguals in one person and therefore there is also a need to describe how they differ. In the case of the present study, the difference in the lexicalisation patterns of the two languages seems to be hindering predicted development, more so in English.

The obvious question at this point is why contradictory cues have not posed as much of a problem for Jan in the other two areas studied, namely reference to person and time. A possible explanation is that the effect of the guidance that the two languages have offered Jan in the schematisation of an event has been related to how closed the system is. This would explain why temporal descriptions fits the aspectual system of each language, as this category has a closed number of forms and functions. On the other hand, the acquisition of an adequate number of manner verbs in English or sufficient combinations of verbs and particles or prepositional phrases is an open class system and one that puts no restraints on the way the story might be told. The child is not forced to make a choice and it therefore becomes a question of vocabulary acquisition, which may or may not develop in the future with further exposure to the language.

The results of the present study are presented with the caveat often stated in bilingual research that each bilingual child is a unique case and generalisation of findings from one particular child is unadvisable. Other bilingual children with characteristics similar to Jan's need to be studied to compare results with those presented above. Moreover, comparison with longitudinal data from English and Spanish monolinguals carrying out the same task at the same ages as Jan would also shed more light on the degree of language specificity in bilingual development.

Notes

1. The examples in this section come from the corpus used for the present study.
2. Unfortunately, the rest of the sentence is unintelligible from the tape.
3. Talmy (1985) relates deictic Direction closely to Path. However, Choi and Bowerman (1991) consider that deixis is lexicalised differently than other kinds of Path and therefore consider it a separate category. In the present study, we expect a high number of deictic verbs and so they have been coded separately in order to have different frequency counts for deixis and for paths.
4. Motion verbs that deal with pursuit and escape (*escape, chase*, and so on) are particularly frequent in this story and they have been counted separately.

References

Álvarez, E. (2003a) Character introduction in two languages: Its development in the stories of a Spanish-English bilingual child age 6;11–10;11. *Bilingualism: Language and Cognition* 6, 1–17.

Álvarez, E. (2003b) Telling stories in two languages: The development of reference to space between the ages of 7 and 11. In F. Ordóñez and S. Montrul (eds) *Linguistic Theory and Language Development in Hispanic Languages* (pp. 336–349). Sommerville, MA: Cascadilla Press.

Berman, R. and Slobin, D. (1994) *Relating Events in Narrative: A Crosslinguistic Developmental Study*. Hillsdale, NJ: Lawrence Erlbaum Associates.

Choi, S. and Bowerman, M. (1991) Learning to express motion events in English and Korean: The influence of language-specific lexicalization patterns. *Cognition* 41, 83–121.

De Houwer, A. (1990) *The Acquisition of Two Languages from Birth: A Case Study*. Cambridge: Cambridge University Press.

Döpke, S. (1999) Crosslinguistic influence on the placement of negation and modal particles in simultaneous bilingualism. *Language Science* 21, 143–175.

Grosjean, F. (1985) The bilingual as a competent but specific speaker-hearer. *Journal of Multilingual and Multicultural Development* 6, 467–477.

Hickmann, M. (2003) *Children's Discourse. Person, Space and Time Across Languages*. Cambridge: Cambridge University Press.

Juan-Garau, M. and Pérez-Vidal, C. (2000) Syntactic development and subject optionality. *Bilingualism: Language and Cognition. Special Edition on Syntactic Development* 3, 173–191.

Labov, W. (1972) *Language in the Inner City. Studies in the Black English Vernacular*. Philadelphia: University of Pennsylvania Press.

Lanza, E. (2001) Temporality and language contact in narratives by children bilingual in Norwegian and English. In L. Verhoeven and S. Strömqvist (eds) *Narrative Development in a Multilingual Context* (pp. 15–50). Amsterdam: John Benjamins.

MacWhinney, B. (1991) *The CHILDES Project. Tools for Analyzing Talk*. Hillsdale, NJ: Lawrence Erlbaum Associates.
Mayer, M. (1969) *Frog, Where Are You?* New York: Dial Books for Young Readers.
Meisel, J. (1990) Grammatical development in the simultaneous acquisition of two first languages. In J. Meisel (ed.) *Two First Languages. Early Grammatical Development in Bilingual Children* (pp. 6–20). Dordrecht: FORIS Publications.
Meisel, J. (2001) The simultaneous acquisition of two first languages: Early differentiation and subsequent development of grammars. In J. Cenoz and F. Genesee (eds) *Trends in Bilingual Acquisition* (pp. 11–41). Amsterdam: John Benjamins.
Meisel, J. and Ezeizabarrena, M.J. (1996) Subject–verb and object–verb agreement in early Basque. In H. Clahsen (ed.) *Generative Perspectives on Language Acquisition: Empirical Findings, Theoretical Considerations, and Crosslinguistic Comparisons* (pp. 201–239). Amsterdam: John Benjamins.
Müller, N. and Hulk, A. (2001) Crosslinguistic influence in bilingual acquisition: Italian and French as recipient languages. *Bilingualism: Language and Cognition* 4, 1–21.
Nicoladis, E. and Genesee, F. (1996) A longitudinal study of pragmatic differentiation in young bilingual children. *Language Learning* 46, 439–464.
Romaine, S. (1995) *Bilingualism*. Oxford: Blackwell Publishers Ltd.
Slobin, D. (1996) Two ways to travel: Verbs of motion in English and Spanish. In M. Shibatani and S.A. Thompson (eds) *Grammatical Constructions: Their Form and Meaning* (pp. 195–219). Oxford: Clarendon Press.
Talmy, L. (1985) Lexicalization patterns: Semantic structure in lexical forms. In T. Shopen (ed.) *Language Typology and Syntactic Description, Vol. III. Grammatical Categories and the Lexicon* (pp. 57–149). Cambridge: Cambridge University Press.

Appendix

The pictures: *Frog, where are you?*

Picture 1

Picture 2

Picture 3

Picture 4

Picture 5

Picture 6

Development of Narratives in English and Spanish 179

Picture 7

Picture 8

Picture 9

Picture 10

Picture 11

Picture 12

Picture 13

Picture 14

Picture 15

Picture 16

Picture 17

Picture 18

Development of Narratives in English and Spanish

Picture 19   Picture 20

Picture 21   Picture 22

Picture 23   Picture 24

Part 2
Bilingual and Multilingual Acquisition at Later Ages and in Instructional Settings

Chapter 8
Classroom Bilingualism at an Early Age: Towards a More Natural EFL Context

ANA LLINARES GARCÍA

Introduction

Bilingualism and bilingual education

The term bilingualism has been used in very different ways; it has been defined as the native-like control of two languages, mostly referring to individual bilingualism (Bloomfield, 1933), but also as the mere alternate use of a language by one individual, mainly in the context of educational programmes (Mackey, 1968). In this chapter, we see a further example of the polysemy of the word in its application to 'bilingual' schools in the Spanish context. This term is used to refer to private schools that follow the British curriculum, in which learners are taught in English for most of the day, as explained below, as well as to those schools (state or private) that offer two or three subjects in the target language,[1] and even to those private schools that offer a few more hours of exposure to the foreign language than those required by the Spanish curriculum.

Early bilingual education in Spain

In the mainstream education system, most Spanish children attend school from the ages of three to five (preschool education), although compulsory schooling begins at six. They usually learn English from the age of three, with different degrees of immersion depending on the type of school. State-funded schools are encouraged to teach English to preschool children, provided that they have enough English specialists to do so. They are allowed to teach up to an hour-and-a-half per week (distributed in at least two sessions). At the other end of the spectrum, as far as the number of hours of instruction is concerned, there are private schools that follow a British curriculum, where the pupils are taught in English for almost the whole school day. The teaching of English at preschool level in state, private and schools with mixed funding has been introduced in Spain fairly recently, and there is an urgent need for both linguistic and pedagogic research.

Key factors in second/foreign language acquisition: context and age

A number of authors claim that the acquisition of a second language in childhood is more efficient in natural contexts (at home, in the playground, or in other settings where children also learn their mother tongue naturally). The classroom is seen as an artificial context where children find it more difficult to learn the L2 than adults, as the latter seem to take more advantage of formal learning (Foster-Cohen, 1999). In contrast, other studies consider the classroom an effective second language learning setting for young learners.

In line with some studies that show that the classroom can become a natural learning scenario for first language young learners (e.g. Geekie & Raban, 1994), I would like to contend that this is also the case for the learning of second and foreign languages. Geekie and Raban (1994) observe the importance of organising the structure of classroom discourse in order to facilitate five-year-old children's acquisition of the skills associated with literacy learning. In their study, they examine patterns in the interactions of children with their teachers in the classroom that are also found in the interaction between mothers and children, and propose that the teacher link the classroom content to the children's experience.

This view is confirmed by Wong-Fillmore (1991), who points out that classroom contexts can work well if learners feel the need to learn the L2, as happens in a natural context. Indeed, research has already shown that, in order to encourage young learners' production in a foreign language (FL), it is necessary to respond to children's desire to communicate in this language and to promote interesting activities that create contexts to achieve this (Tabors & Snow, 1994).

However, as Cenoz indicates, it is important to distinguish between foreign and second language contexts. 'Learners in foreign language contexts have very limited exposure to the language and typically have non-native teachers and no communicative need to use the target language outside the classroom' (Cenoz, 2003: 78). Thus, in foreign language contexts, certain conditions are necessary to stimulate children's motivation to learn the foreign language and, in particular, to feel the need to use it for communicative purposes.

I would like to propose that a significant condition could be the opportunity of using *discourse initiations*, defined by Llinares García (2007) as the communicative functions used by the child to initiate an interaction. Indeed, in natural contexts outside the classroom, children's language use is not restricted to responding to the adults' questions. Therefore, it would appear that in order to make classroom interactions mirror the conditions of natural contexts, children should be given the opportunity of using discourse initiations.

Another key factor in second/foreign language acquisition concerns the age at which foreign language learning should start in relation to proficiency levels. Cummins (1980) has argued that the greater cognitive maturity of older learners allows them to master features of the L2 such as syntax, morphology and vocabulary, which are more literacy-related. On the other hand, older learners do not seem to show an advantage in less cognitively demanding areas such as oral fluency. These results contrast with those from other studies, such as that of Ervin-Tripp (1974), which reveals a better performance of 7- to 9-year-olds when compared to 4- to 6-year-olds in areas such as comprehension and imitation, when given a short-term exposure.

In the Spanish EFL context, it is important to mention the two main projects on the age factor and foreign language acquisition in Catalonia (Muñoz, 2006) and the Basque Country (García Mayo, 2003). The findings reported by Muñoz (2003, 2006) seem to prove a higher level for all areas of competence achieved by late starters compared with early starters.[2] One of the reasons suggested by Muñoz for the lower oral performance of young learners in an elicited interview task is 'the very low level of proficiency of the ES1 group, a characteristic which prevented them from adopting an active role in the interview...' (Muñoz, 2003: 176). However, the descriptors used to identify each of the stages were based either on formal features or interaction strategies, just as Cummins was referring to aspects of grammar. I would like to suggest that another possible line of research that adds a further dimension to the study of FL oral performance is to analyse the learners' production on the basis of the communicative functions performed in the foreign language, and the type of activities that motivate such communicative production, depending on the age group and proficiency level. We might then find that younger learners do not perform so differently from late starters.

Functional approaches to language learning

For the analysis of the communicative functions realised by young learners, it is necessary to refer to Halliday's (1975) pioneering work on the functional development of the language of the child (later developed by Painter, 1999). Halliday (1975) identified seven main functions in the protolanguage of the child: heuristic, informative, personal, regulatory, instrumental, interactional and imaginative. In his theory, most of these functions are then merged in two macrofunctions: mathetic (heuristic, informative and personal) and pragmatic (regulatory and instrumental), which respectively correspond to the ideational and interpersonal functions in the language of the adult, in Halliday's (1994) terminology. The mathetic function represents the use of language to interpret reality and the pragmatic function corresponds to the language used to interact with others. With the analysis of the language development of their respective children in a natural setting, Halliday and Painter demonstrate that children use the language because they want to do things with it (talk about their personal world, ask people to perform actions, ask for information, and so on). This view of first language development approaches Vygotsky's (1978) stance that language can only function as a characteristic of individual cognition when it happens in communication with the others. According to Vygotsky, the 'tutor' (parent, teacher, ...) should praise successful communication and encourage enthusiasm.

When analysing classroom discourse a number of studies have used a similar categorisation of functions to Halliday's and Painter's functional classification of the language of the child in natural contexts. In a first language classroom context, Cazden (1988) distinguished three main functions in the language used by the learners: the language of the curriculum, the language of personal identity and the language of social relations.[3] Similarly, in a second language classroom context, Cathcart (1986) observed Spanish-speaking kindergarten children's functional production in English and classified their acts into 'control acts', 'information acts', 'social routine' and 'play with language'.[4] Finally, in a foreign language classroom context, Llinares García (2004, 2006, 2007) analysed the language used by children in different types of EFL preschool classrooms in Spain (with higher or lower immersion in the L2) and compared it with native children's functional production in the same type of classroom context. The results of this study showed that, even in low-immersion contexts, children may use the foreign language to convey the same functions as those realised by native speakers in the same context, if teachers develop appropriate tasks to facilitate children's use of these functions.

Preschool classroom activities: *Show and tell* and *task work*

Two of the most common activities[5] carried out in the preschool class are *show and tell* and *task work*. *Show and tell* sessions, where children have to bring a personal belonging and talk about it in front of the class, represent a very common type of early morning activity at the preschool and early primary levels. However, according to Christie (2002), who classifies these sessions into *the morning news genre*, they have proved not to be very recommendable for the desired linguistic development of children in first language contexts, as they seem to be very restrictive (i.e. not leading to much linguistic production) because of the excessive control by the teacher. *Task work* sessions are those where children are involved in performing some kind of fixed activity. I have followed Long (1985) in his definition of task as 'a piece of work undertaken for oneself or for others, freely or for some reward', and therefore have considered as such any group-work activity where children were involved in completing a piece of work.

Aim of the Study

Drawing from previous studies that have focused on the description of the language used by children and teachers in different types of EFL contexts (Llinares García, 2004, 2006, 2007; Romero Trillo & Llinares García, 2001), the aim of this chapter is to observe five-year-old preschool children's functional use of the foreign language in a bilingual school in the city of Madrid that follows a British curriculum. The study will specifically look at the children's functional production in two types of activities: *show and tell* sessions and *task work* sessions. In order to find out which type of classroom activities generates a more 'natural' functional production in the foreign language, the children's L2 production in four *show and tell* sessions will be compared with that of four *task work* sessions. Thus, the aim of this study is twofold. In the first place it seeks to determine whether the children's use of the foreign language in certain types of classroom activities approaches their use of the L1 in natural contexts, as shown by their capacity to respond to adults' questions but primarily to use functions of initiation (also called discourse initiations), such as giving information, asking for information, making requests, and so on. In the second place, the study focuses on two specific functions: the degree of use of the personal function (the most frequent function in the language of young children, according to Beveridge & Brierley, 1982), following Halliday's categories, and children's responses to 'free questions' as opposed to 'bound questions' (Romero Trillo & Llinares García, 2001). The latter are not functions for initiation but are also commonly used by children in the L1 in natural contexts. Free questions are those that are formulated to ask for unknown information and bound questions are those where the speaker knows the answer (for example, when teacher is checking the pupils' knowledge). These respectively correspond to 'referential' and 'display' questions in Long and Sato's (1983) terminology.

The research questions addressed are the following:

(1) What kind of activity leads to a more 'natural' FL functional production in a high-immersion preschool bilingual context? In other words, which activities encourage learners to produce a higher number of functions of initiation (or discourse initiations), such as the ones that children use in the process of learning their mother tongue (Halliday, 1975, 2003)?
(2) What kind of function of initiation is promoted in the different types of activities?
(3) What is the role of the teacher in the children's functional production in the L2?
(4) What percentage of learners' responses to 'free' and 'bound' questions can be found in the data?

Methodology

Data

The data used for this study[6] were collected in two different preschool groups from a 'bilingual school', where the children are immersed in the foreign language for the whole school day, except for one hour of Spanish. The groups (A and B) had different teachers, both of them native speakers of English.[7] All the children in both classes were Spanish, except for one child in group B who was bilingual (English/Spanish). Although the micro-society of this school uses English as if it were the L1, it can be considered a foreign language context, as the language of the external environment is the children's L1.

Four sessions from each group were videorecorded and transcribed. Both teachers followed the same curriculum and performed the same type of activities. All the sessions in both groups were based on *show and tell* and *task work* activities, which were recorded and studied. The number of words analysed was 16,531 (in a total of eight sessions).

Analysis

Functional production was measured in terms of the type of communicative functions performed by the children in the L2, with a special focus on those functions used for discourse initiations, called 'functions of initiation' (Llinares García, 2007), as opposed to those functions used as a response to the teacher's initiation. The functional categorisation of the data, which uses the utterance as the unit of analysis, follows the taxonomy described by Llinares García (2004, 2006), based on Halliday's (1975) functional analysis of the language of the child. Each utterance that was an initiating utterance was coded according to the main functions described below, which are illustrated with examples from the corpus:[8]

Heuristic (H): The mathetic function of language used to request information.

Example 1:

CH: *But why there's a five?*

Informative (Inf): The mathetic function of language used to give information about people, things and actions.

Example 2:

CH: *And here's a button.*

Personal (P): The mathetic function used to express the uniqueness of the speaker and his/her perception of things and events.

Example 3:

CH: ((plays with yoyo)) *It's very hard.*

Instrumental (I): The pragmatic function that language serves to satisfy the child's needs.

Example 4:

CH: *Can I go to the toilet?*

Regulatory (R): The pragmatic function used to control the behaviour of others.

Example 5:

CH: *You have to put a little finger.*

The data were processed using *Wordsmith Tools*.

Table 8.1 Distribution of teachers' and children's functions in the ST and TW sessions (percentages)

	Teacher		Children	
	Group A	*Group B*	*Group A*	*Group B*
ST session 1 (S1)	74	79	26	20
ST session 2 (S2)	83	71	16	28
TW session 1 (S1)	89	87	10	12
TW session 2 (S2)	92	90	07	09

ST, *show and tell*; TW, *task work*.

Results of the Analysis

Table 8.1 shows the number of functions produced by teachers and children respectively in both *show and tell* (ST) and *task work* (TW) sessions (S1 and S2) in each group. As expected, in both groups the teachers produce a higher frequency of functions than the children in both types of sessions. However, it is interesting to point out that the teachers talk more in the TW sessions (t-test: $p = 0.01$), whereas the children do most of the talk in the foreign language in the ST sessions (t-test: $p = 0.01$). This result was found for both groups.

Figure 8.1 shows the number of children's functions of initiation in both sessions and for both groups. The percentage is high in the ST sessions and low in the TW sessions (t-test: $p = 0.01$).

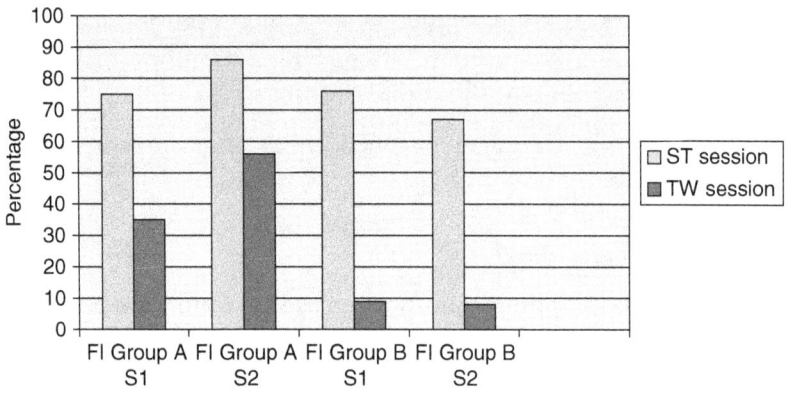

Figure 8.1 Distribution of children's functions of initiation (FI) in the ST and TW sessions (percentages)

Table 8.2 Distribution of children's functions of initiation in the ST and TW sessions (percentages)

	Regulatory	Instrumental	Heuristic	Informative	Personal
ST Group A S1	11	05	04	35	42
ST Group A S2	05	06	12	37	37
ST Group B S1	35	09	05	26	23
ST Group B S2	16	16	09	22	34
TW Group A S1	17	17	34	13	17
TW Group A S2	17	11	38	14	17
TW Group B S1	0	12	75	12	0
TW Group B S2	40	20	20	0	20

The specific types of functions of initiation realised by the children are presented in Table 8.2. Personal and informative functions in both groups show the highest percentage in the ST sessions, and the lowest in the TW sessions (t-test: $p = 0.03$ for the personal function and t-test: $p = 0.00$ for the informative function). In fact, the personal and informative functions together constitute at least 50% of the functional realisations of the children in the ST sessions (in two of the sessions 74% and 77%, respectively). On the other hand, the heuristic function (the use of language to ask for information) is the most frequent function in both groups in the TW sessions. In spite of the fact that the t-test does not show significant differences between the two types of sessions ($p = 0.72$), the heuristic function is the most frequent in three of the four TW sessions. This result is not surprising as children performing a task usually need to ask their teacher questions in order to achieve their goal effectively. Excerpts 1 and 2 below respectively show the use of the personal function (P) in a ST session and the use of the heuristic function (H) in a TW session:[9]

In excerpt 1 we can observe the importance of the teacher's realisation of the personal function (TP), as it seems to encourage the children to continue using it.

Excerpt 1 (show and tell session, Group A):

TCH: What do you want to show us, Nacho?
CH1: Is a ⟨L1 bicho L1⟩. **I see the film in ⟨L1 Continente L1⟩. (P)**
TCH: Is that where you went to see it?
CH1: Yes. **And I saw more ones. (P) And I saw one of terror. (P)**
TCH: Uhh, one of terror. **I don't like to see films of terror. (TP)**
CH1: **I saw Alien. (P)** ((Spanish pronunciation))
TCH: You saw Alien! You're too small to see Alien. That's a very scary film. **I can't watch that, otherwise I'll have nightmares when I sleep. (TP)**
CH2: **My brother, my brother see see that that film (P) and he and he like it (P) and he also see it a lot of time (P) and and he don't have any ⟨L1 miedo L1⟩. (P)**

Excerpt 2 (task work session, Group B):

CH: Mrs. X, **which is this word? (H)**
TCH: Well, look at the board. **What page does it say? (H)**
CH: Two.
TCH: Page two.

Figure 8.2 shows an interesting correlation between the teachers' and the children's use of the personal function, which is more frequent in the ST sessions:

Finally, excerpt 2 shows the realisations of the heuristic function by a pupil and the teacher in a *task work* session. The question used by the

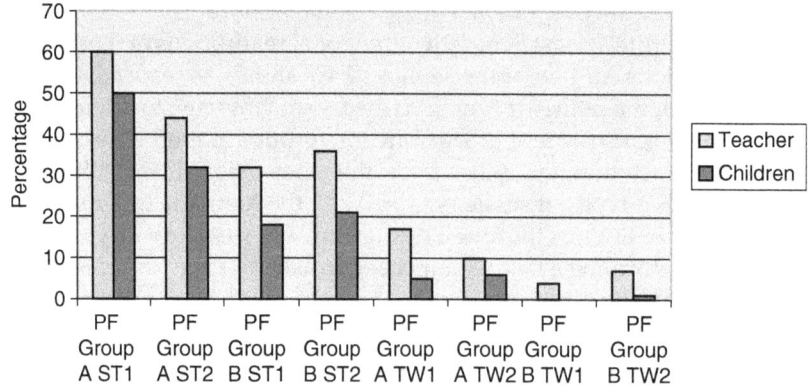

Figure 8.2 Distribution of children's and teachers' realisation of the personal function in the ST and TW sessions (percentages)

Classroom Bilingualism at an Early Age

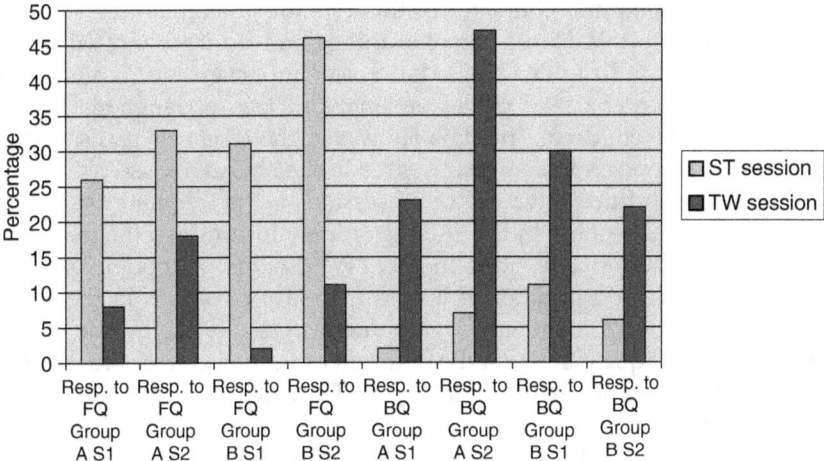

Figure 8.3 Types of questions, free (FQ) or bound (BQ) responded by the children in the ST and TW sessions (percentages)

pupil is free, whereas the teacher asks a bound question with the intention of checking if the child can find the answer to his/her previous free question. In the present study, the different types of questions used by the teacher in each session were measured. Figure 8.3 shows that children's responses to free questions are more common in the ST sessions in both groups, whereas TW sessions contain a high frequency of children's responses to bound questions.

Discussion of Results

The analysis has shown a higher percentage of functions of initiation on the part of the learners in *show and tell* sessions. They also concentrate on two functions: the personal and the informative. The results of this study contradict Christie's (2002) view of ST sessions as being too teacher-focused in L1 classroom contexts. Although the teachers do most of the talk in both types of sessions, as can be expected in a classroom context, the data presented in Table 8.1 show that, in ST sessions, the children do between 16% and 28% of the talk, as opposed to TW sessions where they realise between 9% and 12% of the total oral production in the class.

Another interesting result of the analysis is that ST sessions seem to encourage the use of the foreign language to convey such functions as the personal, one of the most frequent in those sessions. This feature also shows the natural character of this type of session as five-year-old children need to talk about personal things and do it very often in the L1 (Beveridge & Brierley, 1982). It is also important to highlight the relation between the use of the personal function of language by the teacher and the children. The data show that the teacher's realisation of this function appears to a similar degree in the children's use.

Finally, an additional feature of ST sessions is the frequent use of free questions by the teacher in the ST session and, in contrast, the more frequent use of bound questions in the TW sessions. Although parental talk contains a good number of bound (display) questions in the initial stages of children's language development (Kess, 1992), by the age of five most of the questions that the children are exposed to are free (referential). The frequent use of the latter in ST sessions constitutes a further example of the natural character of this type of session.

When evaluating these results, it is important to keep in mind the type of learning context under analysis. This study has been carried out in a high-immersion context and ST sessions would probably not be effective in low-immersion contexts where children's proficiency in the foreign language is lower. In fact, in a recent experimental study carried out in a low-immersion preschool context, Llinares García (2007) shows that the use of specific games and role plays designed for each communicative function (heuristic, personal, regulatory, and so on) was highly effective in generating children's functions of initiation in the foreign language. Therefore, different contexts call of different types of activities, and this is an area of study that clearly needs further research, especially in view of the increasing variety of FL teaching and learning situations in Spain.

Conclusions

The analysis presented above has shown that *show and tell* sessions seem to constitute a more appropriate context than *task work* sessions to promote the use of the foreign language to convey the functions of language used in natural contexts. It would appear that very young learners can indeed realise a variety of functions in their L2 oral performance and use this language to initiate interactions, provided that the classroom activities allow for language uses similar to those happening in natural language learning contexts. The present study demonstrates that *show and tell* sessions are more useful than *task work* sessions for young learners' functional production in high-immersion EFL contexts. The opportunity to select and describe objects of their choice seems to encourage children to use the foreign language for communicative purposes and to use discourse initiations in the target language, as they do in their mother tongue.

Learning a foreign language implies learning how to do things with it (Halliday, 1975). If children are given the opportunity of using the foreign language from a very early age and they learn it similarly to the way they learn the L1, they will probably be ready to use it more naturally in the future.

Acknowledgements

I would like to thank Rachel Whittaker and Jesús Romero for their helpful comments during the revision of this chapter. Special thanks go to Cármen Pérez-Vidal and María Juan-Garau for their thorough editorial comments, which helped me polish the final draft.

Notes

1. See, for instance, Pérez Vidal and Escobar Urmeneta (2001) and Pérez Vidal (2005) on *Content and Language Integrated Learning*.
2. Similarly, García Mayo (2003) did not find statistically better results in earlier starters involved in grammaticality-judgement tasks.
3. The first two functions can be related to the mathetic function and the third can be mapped to the pragmatic function. The relevance given by Cazden to the mathetic function coincides with the results obtained by Llinares García (2004), where the personal function of language is the most common in the language of five-year-old children, both in first and foreign language contexts.
4. These functions correspond, respectively, to Halliday's regulatory, interactional, informative and imaginative functions.
5. Although the terms task and activity are used almost interchangeably in SLA theory, I have used 'activity' with a more general meaning, considering that 'task' usually refers to a specific type of activity.
6. The data used for the present study are part of the UAMLESC (Universidad Autónoma de Madrid Learner English Spoken Corpus), which has been collected since 1998 in different types of schools, with different degrees of immersion in the L2, following the same subjects from the age of five. At the time of writing, data are being collected from ten-year-old children (at the primary school level). This project has been financed by the Comunidad Autónoma de Madrid (06/0027/2001) and is currently being funded by the Ministry of Science and Technology in Spain (BFF2003-08381).
7. The reason for using two groups was to control the influence of the 'teacher variable' on the children's functional performance.
8. Halliday's interactional and imaginative functions have not been included in the analysis, as they were rarely used in the type of activities that have been studied.
9. The realisation of the main function (personal or heuristic) is highlighted in bold and the symbol corresponding to each function is presented in brackets.

References

Beveridge, M. and Brierley, C. (1982) Classroom constructs: An interpretative approach to young children's language. In M. Beveridge (ed.) *Children Thinking Through Language*. London: Edward Arnold.
Bloomfield, L. (1933) *Language*. New York: Holt.
Cathcart, R. (1986) Situational differences and the sampling of young children's school language. In R. Day (ed.) *Talking to Learn: Conversation in Second Language Acquisition*. Rowley, MA: Newbury House.
Cazden, C. (1988) *Classroom Discourse: The Language of Teaching and Learning*. Portsmouth, NH: Heinemann.
Cenoz, J. (2003) The influence of age on the acquisition of English: General proficiency, attitudes and code-mixing. In M.P. García Mayo and M.L. García Lecumberri (eds) *Age and the Acquisition of English as a Foreign Language*. London: Multilingual Matters.
Christie, F. (2002) *Classroom Discourse Analysis*. London: Continuum.
Cummins, J. (1980) The cross-lingual dimensions of language proficiency: Implications for bilingual education and the optimal age issue. *TESOL Quarterly* 14 (2), 175–187.
Ervin-Tripp, S.M. (1974) Is second language learning like the first? *TESOL Quarterly* 8, 111–127.
Foster-Cohen, S. (1999) *An Introduction to Child Language Development*. London: Longman.
García Mayo, M.P. (2003) Age, length and grammaticality judgement. In M.P. García Mayo and M.L. García Lecumberri (eds) *Age and the Acquisition of English as a Foreign Language*. Clevedon: Multilingual Matters.
Geekie, P. and Raban, B. (1994) Language learning at home and school. In C. Gallaway and B.J. Richards (eds) *Input and Interaction in Language Acquisition*. Cambridge: Cambridge University Press.
Halliday, M.A.K. (1975) *Learning How to Mean: Explorations in the Functions of Language*. London: Edward Arnold.
Halliday, M.A.K. (1994) *An Introduction to Functional Grammar*. London: Edward Arnold.
Halliday, M.A.K. (2003) *The Language of Early Childhood*. London: Continuum.
Kess, J.F. (1992) *Psycholinguistics*. Amsterdam: John Benjamins.
Llinares García, A. (2004) La interacción lingüística en el aula de segundas lenguas en edades tempranas: Análisis de un corpus desde una perspectiva funcional. In *Premios Nacionales de Investigación Educativa 2002*. Madrid: Ministerio de Educación y Ciencia.
Llinares García, A. (2006) A pragmatic analysis of children's interlanguage in EFL preschool contexts. *Intercultural Pragmatics* 3 (2), 171–193.
Llinares García, A. (2007) Young learners' functional use of the L2 in a low-immersion EFL context. *ELT Journal* 61, 39–45.
Long, M. (1985) Input and second language theory. In S.M. Gass and C. Madden (eds) *Input in Second Language Acquisition*. Rowley, MA: Newbury House.
Long, M. and Sato, C. (1983) Classroom foreigner talk discourse: Forms and functions of teachers' questions. In H. Seliger and M. Long (eds) *Classroom-Oriented Research in Second Language Acquisition*. Rowley, MA: Newbury House.

Mackey, W.F. (1968) The description of bilingualism. In J.A. Fishman (ed.) *Readings in the Sociology of Language*. The Hague: Mouton de Gruyter.

Muñoz, C. (2003) Variation in oral skills development. In M.P. García Mayo and M.L. García Lecumberri (eds) *Age and the Acquisition of English as a Foreign Language*. London: Multilingual Matters.

Muñoz, C. (2006) *Age and the Rate of Foreign Language Learning*. London: Multilingual Matters.

Painter, C. (1999) *Learning through Language in Early Childhood*. London: Cassell.

Pérez Vidal, C. and Escobar Urmeneta, C. (2001) Spain. In M. Grenfell (ed.) *Modern Languages Across the Curriculum*. London: Routledge.

Pérez Vidal, C. (2005) *Content and Language Integrated Learning in Europe. Teaching Materials for the Secondary Classroom*. Barcelona: UPF-European Commission.

Romero Trillo, J. and Llinares García, A. (2001) Communicative constraints in native/non native pre-school settings. *International Journal of Corpus Linguistics* 6 (1), 27–46.

Tabors, P.O. and Snow, C.E. (1994) English as a second language in pre-school programs. In F. Genesee (ed.) *Educating Second Language Children*. Cambridge: Cambridge University Press.

Vygotsky, L.S. (1978) *Mind in Society: The Development of Higher Psychological Processes*. Cambridge, MA: Harvard University Press.

Wong-Fillmore, L. (1991) Second language learning in children: A model of language learning in social context. In E. Bialystok (ed.) *Language Processing in Bilingual Children*. Cambridge: Cambridge University Press.

Chapter 9
First Language Influence on Second Language Acquisition: The Case of Immigrant L1 Soninke, Tagalog and Chinese Children Learning Catalan

ELISABET SERRAT, LLUÏSA GRÀCIA and LAIA PERPIÑÁ

Introduction

Second language acquisition is a typical phenomenon in contemporary society. There are more than 6000 languages around the world, languages that speakers use to communicate in their economic, social or political relationships. As a direct consequence of that, people are constantly learning languages that are different from their own. This situation is also found in Spain and in Catalonia, where around 300 languages are spoken nowadays as a direct result of the arrival of people from other countries. This situation is new in the region, as most of these immigrants come from countries that are culturally and linguistically distant from our culture and our language.

The immigrants arriving in Catalonia find a society in which they can interact mainly in Spanish or in Catalan. Children from immigrant families go to an educational system that promotes teaching mainly in Catalan. This means that these children are immersed in a process of acquisition of Catalan from the beginning of their education, a language that is not usually present in their family or social environment.

There are several issues that affect the second language acquisition process. In this chapter, however, we focus on the influence that the speaker's native language, or L1, has on the acquisition process of a second language, or L2. The study that we have carried out deals with the acquisition of Catalan by speakers of three of the most used languages in immigrant communities in Catalonia: Chinese, spoken mainly in

China; Tagalog, official language in the Philippines and used by many Filipinos living in Catalonia; and Soninke, spoken in Senegal, Gambia, Mauritania, Mali, Ivory Coast and Guinea Bissau.

Currently, it seems that a consensus has been achieved between previous positions on the L1 influence on L2 (Corder, 1967, 1981; Lado, 1957), in that it is accepted that the L1 plays an active and important role during the second language acquisition process (Fernández, 1997; Gass, 1996; Larsen-Freeman & Long, 1991; Odlin, 2003). Now the kind of questions that arise concern, for example, what aspects the L1 has an influence on, to what degree it does so and at what point during the learning process, and what principles determine the L1 influence or the transfer of elements from the L1. It is assumed that the L1 can affect the learning process in different ways, and that it is the source of phenomena like avoiding particular structures, omission or overproduction, among others.

In that sense, as already pointed out (Odlin, 2003; Selinker & Lakshmanan, 1993), some controversial issues come up when dealing with the L1 influence on L2 acquisition. One of these issues involves the question of whether or not L1 has any influence during the early years of childhood. It is usually considered that if children are exposed to L2 before they are three years old, L1 does not have any effect on the L2 acquisition process, and that this process is carried out as if it were simultaneous to the acquisition of the L1. If they are exposed to L2 after they are four, it is suggested that a so-called child second language acquisition takes place (Child L2). On the other hand, some researchers hold that the child acquisition of an L2 follows a similar process to that followed by the acquisition of an L1, and that in this case the L1 influence cannot be considered a meaningful aspect (Selinker & Lakshmanan, 1993). Nevertheless, other researchers maintain that L1 does affect children acquiring an L2, and that the pattern of this influence is the same as that found in adults (Bialystok & Hakuta, 1994; Unsworth, 2004).

Another issue that has received attention concerns whether or not the L1 influence on second language acquisition has a similar or different effect on all levels of language, that is, lexicon, syntax, morphology and pragmatics. With regard to what our study is interested in, it has to be stressed that it seems doubtful that the children's native language has any effect as far as morphology is concerned (Schwartz, 2003), although there seems to be an agreement in that L1 syntax does have an effect on L2 acquisition. Bearing in mind that in previous studies we have already observed a morphological influence from L1 (Gràcia & Serrat,

2003), we think a more complete study of this phenomenon would be worthwhile.

We have adapted some methodological aspects from Jarvis' (2000) proposal to the objectives of our investigation. The objective is to find information about which errors are made by speakers of different languages when using the L2, as well as their correct production. This will allow us to observe their frequency and their possible relationship with the structures of their L1. As a starting point, we assume that the learners will show common uses in the acquisition of Catalan as an L2. However, the main issue this study seeks to tackle concerns the differences in production, both with and without errors, among the speakers of diverse L1s. These differences can actually tell us how different L1s affect the acquisition of the same L2.

In short, we want to explore here the influence on morphology that the native language has on the acquisition of Catalan by children who have Tagalog, Chinese or Soninke as their L1. If there is indeed some influence, those speakers are expected to show differences in their production of the L2. Those differences, along with the similarities observed, will let us evaluate the scope of that influence in early ages, as well as establish what direction that influence takes, that is, where it is situated and how strong its morphological influence is.

Description of the L1 Languages Involved

Next we will briefly present how the three L1s of the speakers under examination function with regard to the grammatical aspects we are observing. These are nominal inflection, definiteness and verbal inflection. More information on these languages can be found published in the references provided in this chapter.

Nominal inflection

The nominal inflection in Catalan makes a distinction between two categories: gender (masculine and feminine) and number (singular and plural). None of the three L1 of our speakers possesses gender as a bound morpheme, unlike Catalan. Only Tagalog has some forms containing this distinction in some Spanish loan words.

In terms of number, only Soninke has the morphological singular / plural distinction:

(1) (a) renme   renmu   'child / children'
        mexe   mexo   'hour / hours'

(b) lanpa   lanpanu   'lamp/lamps'
    fo   foo**nu** 'thing/things'
(c) k**e**   k**en** kit**ee**re 'this/that'
    k**u**   k**un** kit**uu**ru 'these/those'

As can be seen in (1), the plural is formed by either changing the last vowel of the singular form, (1a), or adding the suffix -*nu* and lengthening the root vowel if the word is monosyllabic, (1b); the vowels also distinguish the plural and the singular forms in the demonstratives, (1c).

In Chinese, a clearly isolating language, nouns are not inflected in number. Only personal pronouns show number, and, optionally, some nouns referring to a person when they are interpreted as definite nouns.

Nouns are not inflected to form the plural in Tagalog either. Only when it is thought that the number distinction is significant, the free particle *mga* is inserted before the noun, (2a). Qualifying adjectives can also be inflected optionally in their plural form, either by inserting the particle *mga* or by reduplicating the first syllable of the root, (2b):

(2) (a) bata   **mga** bata   'child(ren)–children'
    (b) tamad   **mga** tamad   'lazy.SG./PL–lazy.PL'
        ma-sama   ma-**sa**sama   'bad.SG./PL.–bad.PL'

As opposed to Catalan, where the determiner agrees with the noun, in Tagalog the possible plural marking only appears once in the nominal phrase when a demonstrative shows up. This plural marking is placed preceding the noun, (3a). A noun appearing with a numeral, on the other hand, does not carry the particle *mga* even when that numeral is higher than one, (3b):

(3) (a) itong **mga** aso   this PL. dog   'these dogs'
    (b) dalawang saging   two banana   'two bananas'

Definiteness

None of the three L1s of the speakers under control has an element equivalent to our articles. Only Soninke makes a distinction between definite and indefinite nominal forms. But it does so by means of attaching a suffix to the noun. The so-called definite form is created by inserting the suffix -*n* at the end of the noun. The resulting form is equivalent to the definite or indefinite phrase in Catalan. The non-definite form is the one not containing any determiner in Catalan, sometimes with a partitive value: *sugo/sugo + n* 'goat/the goat, a goat'. The definite form, however, does not show up when a demonstrative is already present (*ke yugo/*ke yugon* 'that man').

Tagalog does not have true articles either. However, it does have the *ang* particle, which precedes the nominal phrases that are considered the theme (old information) of the sentence. Consequently, these phrases are always given a definite interpretation. The rest of the nominal phrases, that is, those that are not theme and do not have the *ang* particle (although they have another one depending on their semantic function) can be interpreted as either definite or indefinite (Schachter & Otanes, 1972: 83):

(4) Nagbigay ng libro sa babae ang lalaki
    give   PART. book PART. woman *ang* man
    'The man gave a/the woman a/the book'

Chinese, which does not possess elements equivalent to the Catalan articles either, uses the sentence word order to indicate definiteness in some nominal phrases (Li & Thompson, 1981: 20–21):

(5) (a) **Rén** lái le   person come ASP.   'The person has come'
    (b) Wǒ **bǎ shū** mǎi le I *bǎ* book buy ASP. 'I bought the book'
    (c) **Shū** wǒ mǎi le   book I buy ASP.   'The book, I bought it'

By and large, the pre-verbal position is that belonging to the theme and, hence, it is always occupied by a definite phrase, (5a). The definite direct objects usually appear preceding the verb carrying the particle *bǎ* before them, (5b). If they are the sentence theme, they show up without the particle at the beginning of the sentence, (5c). If these same phrases (*rén* i *shū*) were placed after the verb, they would receive an indefinite interpretation.

Verbal inflection

In the three L1s taken into account here, the verbal forms are invariable with regard to the subject person and number. In Chinese and Soninke, the verb does not show any mark of agreement with any element of the sentence. In Tagalog, however, the verb agrees with the phrase that is interpreted as the theme of the sentence and it varies depending on the semantic function of the argument (agent, patient, benefactive, and so on), but it does not do so according to person or, usually, number. In this language, there are various affixes showing this type of agreement. They can appear as prefixes (*i* + sulat, *write*-benefactive), infixes (s + um + ulat, *write*-agent) or suffixes (sulat + in, *write*-patient).

In terms of tense, there are no morphemes bound to the verb in any of these three languages, and the differences basically come down to aspect. In Soninke, the verb has a perfective and an imperfective form, (6a). Furthermore, sentences also contain auxiliary-like elements (the so-called predicatives) that represent aspect and modality and vary according to the type of verb (Girier, 1996: 101), (6b). As can be observed, predicatives select one verbal form out of two, the perfective form (*ri*, in the examples in (6b)) or the imperfective one (*riini*), depending on their value:

(6) (a) yige / yigene 'to eat' perfective / imperfective
      katu / katta 'to hit' perfective / imperfective
   (b) A wa riini 'he comes' affirmative imperfective
      A nta riini 'he doesn't come' negative imperfective
      A Ø ri 'he came, he has come' affirmative perfective
      A ma ri 'he didn't come,
              he hasn't come' negative perfective

In Chinese, all aspectual differences are shown through usually independent particles. If necessary, time is expressed by means of elements that define it, such as temporal adverbs. The sentence in (7) clearly shows the invariable nature of the verb and the use of adverbs to express time (Ramsey, 1987: 54):

(7) Wǒ bù zhīdào, tā *zuótiān* **qù**, *jīntiān* **qù**, háishi *míngtiān* **qù**
    I not know he yesterday go today go or tomorrow go
    'I don't know if he went yesterday, is going today, or will go tomorrow'

As far the aspectual particles are concerned, some of them express the perfective aspect, like *le* (8a). Other particles, like *zài*, are used in the imperfective constructions, (8b). A sentence can also lack a special maker when that sentence expresses a habitual action, (8c):

(8) (a) Tā cóng Zhōngguó lái **le** (Li & Thompson, 1981: 24)
       he from China come ASP.
       'He has come from China'
   (b) Zhāngsān **zài** dǎ Lǐsì (Li & Thompson, 1981: 218)
       Zhangsan ASP. hit Lisi
       'Zhangsan is hitting Lisi'
   (c) Mǎ chī cǎo (Po-Ching & Rimmington,
       horse eat grass 1997: 40)
       'Horses eat grass'

In Tagalog, the verb can show up in three different forms depending on whether or not the action has begun and finished (perfective), it has begun but it has not finished (imperfective), or it has neither begun nor finished (the so-called contemplated, which is equivalent to our future). Just like in the forms that show agreement, there are various systems used to mark aspect, and they include both affixation and reduplication. These forms also vary according to the agreement morpheme of the verb. So a verb carrying the agent infix *-um-*, like in *bumasa* 'read', would have the forms in (9a); in (9b) we have the very same verb carrying the benefactive prefix *i-*(*ibasa*); and the patient suffix *-in* (*basahin*), in (9c):

(9) (a) bumasa (perf.) bumabasa(imperf.) babasa(contemplated)
    (b) ibinasa (perf.) ibinabasa (imperf.) ibabasa (contemplated)
    (c) binasa (perf.) binabasa(imperf.) babasahin (contemplated)

Method

Sample

The sample is formed of 12 children distributed in three groups according to their native language. They all were enrolled in elementary schools and were between 6 and 12 years of age when the data were collected. Those children started school in Catalan centres during kindergarten or elementary education. By and large, they have all lived in Catalonia for a similar amount of time. It has to be noted, however, that the Tagalog speakers as L1 are older than the rest of the groups. All speakers had been attending the Catalan education system for at least two years. This was essentially their only source of exposure to Catalan, as this language was not present in those children's family or social environment. The characteristics of the sample are more specifically described in Table 9.1.

Procedure and analysis

The data were obtained through audio recordings of the speakers' speech during a dialogue with an interviewer. There was a spontaneous part in the conversation, when the child talked about issues related to school, family, his or her country of origin, and so on, and food preferences, books, cinema and television or sports. In this part, we were trying to obtain different types of discourse, such as descriptive and explicative. There was also another part in which the narrative discourse was promoted. This was done by having them explain three short stories presented in the form of pictures without text.

The data were transcribed and coded by using the CHAT format from the CHILDES project (MacWhinney, 2000). The categories for the nominal

Table 9.1 Characteristics of the sample

Subject	Sex	Age	Length of stay	Language
MUT	Boy	8	3	Soninke
BAK	Boy	8	8	Soninke
ANK	Girl	8	8	Soninke
MAT	Girl	8	8	Soninke
KIC	Girl	12	2	Tagalog
JOR	Boy	12	8	Tagalog
JAU	Girl	11	7	Tagalog
SEC	Girl	11	6	Tagalog
JAI	Boy	7	6	Chinese
SHA	Girl	6	5	Chinese
YUX	Girl	8	8	Chinese
XIM	Girl	12	4	Chinese

phrase and verbal inflection coding are based on the linguistic description of the grammatical aspects under control. The coding of verb production includes specific codes for tense and mood, as well as for agreement. Specific codes have also been included independently for those cases in which errors in the verbal morphology have been made. In the case of nominal phrases, only the production with errors has been analysed, more specifically errors in the nominal agreement and in the omission of the determiner.

The total data coded (3499 utterances) were analysed by using the CLAN programs. The calculations were done on the proportions/percentages average from each category for each group. The statistical analyses were carried out using the Mann–Whitney non-parametric U-test for independent two-group comparisons. From these analyses, data regarding the use of verbal tenses, both correct and incorrect utterances, as well as errors within the nominal phrase were obtained.

Results

Before presenting specific data on the grammatical questions we are examining here, we will present the speakers' general production, both correct and incorrect, from the general descriptive information

Table 9.2 General descriptive information on the speakers' production

	Soninke	Tagalog	Chinese	Total
Utterances	1212	1054	1233	3499
Nominal phrase	886	582	1020	2488
NP with errors	128	62	166	356
% Errors in NP	15.19	12.87	17.65	
Verbs	1049	616	1388	3053
Verb errors	141	71	202	414
% Verb errors	12.96	13.03	17.08	

The error percentages for the NP and the verb were calculated on the total number of NP and verbs, respectively.

represented in Table 9.2. As can be observed in Table 9.2, the percentages of uses containing errors in the NP and verbal forms are between 12% and 17% of the total number of NPs and verbal forms produced. On the other hand, it should be noted that the error percentages are similar among the speakers of the three languages studied (in fact, the statistical comparison does not give us significant differences).

Noun phrase

In terms of the results related to the nominal phrase, we will first present the data on the type of errors we have found. The data regarding nominal inflection and definiteness will be described in later sections.

Error distribution within the Nominal Phrase

The speakers of the languages involved make the following types of error regarding the nominal phrase: addition of the article when it is not necessary, omission of the article when it is necessary, and errors related to the morphology of the elements within the nominal phrase, that is, errors related to both gender and number. It has to be said that we have also found errors of insertion of elements that do not belong to the nominal phrase. These errors, however, were not taken into account in the study.

Table 9.3 indicates that the speakers of the three languages show a pattern that is quite similar with regard to the frequency of errors involving article omission, and gender and number confusion. Errors related to insertion are much less frequent. From this, one might be led to think that Chinese speakers are more likely to make errors regarding number

First Language Influence on Second Language Acquisition

Table 9.3 Distribution of errors in the NP according to the speakers' language

	Soninke	Tagalog	Chinese
Addition	2.58 (1.51)	6.03 (3.08)	1.38 (0.98)
Omission	30.93 (5.63)	34.74 (7.52)	29.85 (4.61)
Noun	35.58 (5.76)	31.84 (10.94)	38.62 (6.69)
Gender	30.91 (2.75)	27.39 (2.26)	30.14 (6.04)

Percentages of the total number of errors in the nominal phrase. The standard deviation appears in parentheses.

morphology, or that Tagalog speakers make more omissions than the other groups, but there is no statistical significance in any of these tendencies.

Nominal inflection

The error percentages in the nominal inflection can be observed in Table 9.4. Again, there is a common pattern according to which half of the total number of errors involving the nominal phrase morphology relate to the use of singular rather than plural. Furthermore, speakers tend to make more errors by using the masculine form instead of the feminine. Some of those errors can be observed in the following examples:

(10) (a) Tagalog
 *JOR: ... van morir **moltes** **persona**, ...
  go die many FEM.PL person FEM.SG., ...
  '... many people died...'
 (b) Soninke
 *MUT: i **aquell** **dona**...
  and that.MASC.SG. woman.FEM.SG.

Table 9.4 Agreement errors

	Soninke	Tagalog	Chinese
Masculine = feminine	36.13 (6.99)	39.77 (16.25)	27.45 (8.23)
Feminine = masculine	11.13 (4.3)	13.76 (5.68)	16.59 (1.7)
Singular = plural	47.59 (6.18)	46.46 (15.66)	50.06 (4.99)
Plural = singular	5.14 (2.24)*	0 (0)*	5.90 (3.55)

Percentages of the total number of agreement errors. The standard deviation appears in parentheses.
*$p < 0.05$.

(c) Chinese
*XIM: perquè fas **una** **somni**
because do a.FEM.SG. dream.MASC.SG.
molt boniques...
very beautiful.FEM.PL.
'because I have a beautiful dream...'

The differences among the speakers of the three languages considered are not very significant as far as gender is concerned. Nonetheless, it can be observed that the errors involving gender made by Chinese speakers are more balanced than in the other speakers. Thus, they make more errors by using the feminine instead of the masculine and, conversely, fewer errors by using the masculine instead of the feminine when compared to the other speakers. With regard to number inflection, there is a tendency for the Tagalog speakers to not make errors by using the plural rather than the singular. This tendency is shown when they are compared to both Chinese and Soninke speakers, and it is statistically significant when comparing the Tagalog and the Soninke speakers ($p < 0.05$).

Definiteness

Errors related to definiteness effectively concerts the omission of the article (see Table 9.5), because we only found a couple of errors in which an indefinite article was confused for a definite article. We also came across some errors in which a vowel-like sound was used instead of the correct article, but this only occurred in the case of Chinese speakers. The following examples show those errors.

(11) (a) Tagalog
*KIC: el més típic d'allà és **0 carn**.
the most typical from.there is 0 meat
'the most typical thing there is meat'
(b) Soninke
*OBS: quin instrument toques?
'what instrument do you play?
*MUT: **0 triangle**
0 triangle
'the triangle'
(c) Chinese
*OBS: què hi veus a la primera vinyeta?
'what do you see in the first picture?'

```
        *XIM:    0 pilota.
                 0 ball
                 'a ball'
   (d)  Chinese
        *OBS:    la que parles a casa.
                 the one you speak at home
        *YUX:    a xinès, a castellà,    i    a català.
                 a Chinese a Castilian, and a Catalan.
                 'Chinese, Castilian, and Catalan'
```

Table 9.5 shows that errors involving the omission of the article are essentially reduced to the omission of the definite article. Moreover, in this type of error there exists a tendency among Soninke and Chinese speakers to omit more definite articles than the Tagalog speakers. This tendency is statistically significant when comparing Tagalog and Chinese speakers ($p < 0.05$). The data on indefinite article omissions do not show statistically significant differences.

Table 9.5 Distribution of article omissions

	Soninke	Tagalog	Chinese
Definite	81.19 (11.47)	75.71 (14.45)*	82.38 (11.48)*
Indefinite	18.81 (11.47)	24.29 (14.45)	17.62 (11.48)

Percentages of the total number of errors in which the article was omitted. The standard deviation appears in parentheses.
*$p < 0.05$.

Verbal inflection

With regard to the results involving verbal inflection, we will comment first on the correct uses of the verbs. Table 9.6 shows that the verbal form most commonly used is the present indicative, more so in the third person singular. Tagalog speakers use the present in third person singular significantly more than Soninke speakers ($p < 0.05$). Chinese speakers also show this tendency when compared to Soninke speakers, although in this case the tendency is less statistically significant ($p = 0.08$). In short, the Chinese and the Tagalog speakers make more use of the present in the third person singular than the Soninke speakers. On the other hand, the Tagalog speakers use the infinitive form more than the rest of the speakers. This difference becomes significant ($p < 0.05$) when they are compared to the Soninke speakers.

Table 9.6 Correct uses of the verbs

	Soninke	Tagalog	Chinese
Present	66.22 (4.89)*	69.81 (7.84)*	68.62 (6.76)
Infinitive	6.99 (1.32)*	11.63 (2.95)*	8.53 (2.23)
Perfect	6.93 (4.43)	6.81 (8.97)	5.71 (3.02)
Imperfect	8.32 (3.45)	3.77 (3.09)	5.31 (2.22)
Indefinite	5.93 (2.61)	4.74 (5.38)	5.90 (3.39)
Future	1.76 (1.40)	0.81 (0.94)	1.88 (1.44)
Subjunctive	1.68 (0.91)	0.40 (0.48)	0.60 (0.65)
Present third person singular	33.30 (2.85)*	37.76 (0.88)*	39.38 (5.42)

Percentages of the total number of correct verbs. The standard deviation appears in parentheses.
*$p < 0.05$.

Table 9.7 Distribution of errors in the verbal morphology

	Soninke	Tagalog	Chinese
Person and number	27.53 (6.01)*	31.89 (7.21)*	49.92 (2.76)*
TAM	55.06 (7.75)	42.37 (6.92)	36.51 (5.29)
Nonfinite forms	17.41 (11.09)	25.73 (12.3)	13.57 (13.57)

Percentages of the total number of errors in the verbal morphology. The standard deviation appears in parentheses.
*$p < 0.05$.
TAM: tense, aspect and mood.

With regard to the results affecting the errors in verbal inflection, they were grouped by those related to person and number morphology, those affecting the morphological marks of tense, aspect and mood (TAM) and those related to non-finite forms. In terms of person and number errors, in Table 9.7 a quite clear tendency between the Tagalog and the Chinese speakers ($p = 0.05$) and a significant difference between the Soninke and the Chinese speakers ($p < 0.05$) can be observed. The Chinese speakers make more errors in the verbal morphology with regard to person and number than any of the other two groups of speakers, who make more errors related to TAM and the non-finite forms. Some examples of those errors in the verbal morphology are reproduced next. The first three examples show errors involving person and number in the verbal form, whereas the last four are instances of TAM and incorrect use of nonfinite forms:

(12) (a) Soninke
      *MAT: **alguns canta.**
              some.PL sings.SG.
              'some sing.'
   (b) Chinese
      *XIM: **ell volen** ser una noia normal i corrent.
              he want.PL. be a girl normal and regular
              'she wants to be a regular girl'
   (c) Tagalog
      *JAU: **l'any passat he anat a Filipines**
              the.year passed have gone to Philippines
              'last year I went to the Philippines'
   (d) Tagalog
      *LAR: **què fa aquest noi aquí?**
              'what is this boy doing here?'
      *SEC: **esconder.**
              hide.INF.
              'he is hiding'

Table 9.8 shows the distribution of the more frequent errors made by the speakers in person and number morphology and in TAM. A tendency can be observed on the part of the Tagalog and the Chinese speakers to use

Table 9.8 Errors in the verbal morphology

	Soninke	*Tagalog*	*Chinese*
Present third person singular	9.12 (3.13)*	24.42 (6.19)	29.68 (3.9)*
Plural forms	11.97 (5.23)	8.08 (5.65)	10.07 (2.16)
Indefinite	25.9 (7.59)	18.29 (10.72)	8.03 (2.43)
Present	13.11 (1.49)	14.46 (6.92)	15.74 (3.47)
Infinitive	11.41 (8.80)	22.79 (13.69)	10.96 (3.68)
Imperfect	10.61 (6.48)	1.47 (1.47)	3.19 (2.0)
Subjunctive	2.12 (2.11)	0 (0)*	3.21 (0.5)*
Future	0.42 (0.42)	0 (0)	2.48 (1.81)

Percentages of the total number of errors involving the verbal morphology. The standard deviation appears in parentheses.
*$p < 0.05$. The incorrect form is indicated instead of the correct one.

the third person singular more than the Soninke speakers when making an error in the verbal person. This tendency is significant when comparing the Soninke and the Chinese speakers ($p < 0.05$). Therefore, the Chinese speakers do not only make more person and number errors, as shown above, but those errors are concentrated in the use of the third person singular instead of other forms. The Soninke speakers, on the other hand, do not make many errors in person and number morphology, and the ones they make are not concentrated in the incorrect use of the third person singular. It can also be observed in Table 9.8 that all speakers make a certain number of errors involving the use of the person in plural rather than the correct form. It usually has to do with the use of the third person plural, instead of the third person singular. As far as that aspect is concerned, the speakers do not show significant differences.

On the other hand, it can also be appreciated that all speakers frequently and mistakenly use the present and the indefinite instead of other verbal forms, with no significant differences among the three groups. The only significant difference is found when comparing the Chinese and the Tagalog speakers with regard to the errors involving the subjunctive ($p < 0.05$). Although the Tagalog speakers do not make any errors, 3.21% of errors are found in the verbal forms produced by the Chinese speakers. The Tagalog speakers do not make any errors regarding the use of the future tense either.

Discussion

The first important point that has to be discussed involves the number of errors that the children learning Catalan as a second language make. Around 15% of errors have something to do with aspects relating to the main components of the sentence. This means that the communication in Catalan can be greatly affected. Furthermore, this occurs even when some of these children have already been around nine years in the Catalan education system. Moreover, the fact that the number of foreigners reaches 90% or even 100% in some classrooms in Catalonia makes that situation even more complex, particularly in those schools where the linguistic diversity is highest.

With regard to the data that are the main focus of our study and regarding gender and number morphology in the nominal phrase, the preference for forms in singular and in masculine agrees with the results provided in other studies (Finnemann, 1992). On the other hand, we have not found significant differences relating to gender. In fact, that was expected, as there is no morphological distinction in gender in any of the three L1s involved, so the level of difficulty as regards learning this aspect in Catalan should be the same for all of them. There are, however, some differences among speakers regarding the extent of errors in number. It can be observed that the Tagalog speakers make fewer errors in number, whereas the Chinese speakers are more likely to make errors in number inflection. This might be so because there are no plural marks in Chinese (the one there is being very exceptional), so they might have more difficulties connecting the singular/plural semantic distinction with a morphological mark. On the other hand, one could expect the Soninke speakers to make fewer errors in number than the other speakers, because they do possess this morphological distinction in their L1. Nevertheless, the results tell us otherwise. Soninke only has the plural mark in nouns and demonstratives. Therefore, all the errors in the articles or in the adjectives can be attributed to the fact that there is no mark in these cases in their L1. Many plural nouns are not formed by means of a particular suffix (like our -s). Instead, the last root vowel, which is not always the same, is changed, so it might be the case that they actually have difficulties relating the vowel change to the single suffix in Catalan. The significant differences are found in the fact that the Tagalog speakers do not make errors in the use of plural instead of singular. In order to account for this, it has to be kept in mind that the plural mark in Tagalog is the independent particle *mga*. This particle is optional and it is only used when the speaker wants to mark the plurality on the nominal phrase. It therefore seems that, when the speakers make use of the plural mark, they do so because they want to, and they know what they are doing. In other words, the optional nature of the plural mark in their L1 could facilitate the distinction in the use of the plural in the L2.

Another significant difference involves the fewer omission cases of the definite article by the Tagalog speakers. This could probably be attributed to the fact that their particle *ang*, which marks the theme argument in the sentence, apparently carries out a similar function to that of our article, which is also an independent element that shows up in the first position in the phrase. The Chinese speakers, however, cannot count on any particle for them to express definiteness, except for the particle *bǎ*, which is used for some definite direct objects. Definiteness is partly deduced from the syntactic word order. In Soninke, on the other hand, definiteness is marked through a bound morpheme (a suffix) that is attached to the noun. So this probably makes it more difficult for them to relate this suffix to the definite article in Catalan.

Regarding the results on verbal morphology, it has to be said that even when there is no verbal morphology in person and number equivalent to that of Catalan in any of the three languages studied, some errors can be attributed to the speakers' L1. On the one hand, the fact that Chinese is an isolating language, which does not show any morphological feature in almost all types of lexical items, has an effect on the verbal production in Catalan by its speakers. This is the group with the highest percentage of errors in this aspect and the one that has most frequently incorrectly used what has been labeled here as third person singular. This is the most neutral (or less marked) verbal form from a morphological viewpoint, as it is the one that does not include any kind of explicit morpheme indicating person and number. In the present indicative, this form usually coincides with the verbal root or the stem. This is probably the form that the Chinese speakers reproduce given that their L1 has a single verbal form with no inflection at all. The verb is not marked with the subject person and number in Soninke either, but in that language verbs do not have a single form, and nouns are also variable. In other words, its speakers use verbal and nominal inflections. It should therefore be easier for them to acquire the Catalan agreement system. According to the description of Tagalog provided above, one might expect its speakers to make fewer verbal agreement errors, because the verbal forms in their language possess different morphemes, and they know a system that connects the verb with an argument, similar, in part, to our agreement system. The results in Table 9.7, however, do not reflect this expectation, because the error percentage is higher than that in the Soninke speakers. We think that this can be attributed to this type of agreement between the verb and the theme argument of the sentence according to its semantic function, instead of person and number. Although this aspect should be studied in depth in future investigations, we have found some instances that lead us to believe that, in some cases, the supposed morphological errors in inflection are actually errors of a syntactic type. This is so because the agreement is established between the verb and the argument that is interpreted as the theme, rather than between the verb and the subject of the sentence as in Catalan:

(13) *KIC: ella volia anar a l'escola + ...
'she wanted to go to school.'
*KIC: però els seus pares no *la* **deixava**
but the her parents no her let.3ps
'but her parents didn't let her go'

In this example, the Catalan verb *deixava* 'let', here in third person singular (3ps), should have agreed with the nominal phrase *els seus pares* 'her parents', so the correct verbal form in (13) should have been *deixaven*, that is, third person plural (3pp). In this case, the use of the 3ps can be accounted for due to the fact that the discourse theme, represented in the sentence through the clitic *la* 'her', is a 3ps. It seems, then, that some errors that could appear to be just morphological mistakes (verbal inflection) are, in fact, related to the syntactic system of the L1.

Regarding the uses involving tense, aspect and mood in the verbal forms, it can be established that there are essentially no significant differences among the speakers of the three languages. This is expected given that all these languages behave similarly. The difference involving the subjunctive, and to some extend the future, can be accounted for by saying that, even though the Tagalog speakers are those producing fewer forms of this type, it is also true that no errors have been found in these forms; that is, when they produce them, they always appear in the correct context. This can be related to the fact that Tagalog has a verbal form, the so-called contemplated aspect, which is, by and large, equivalent to our future tense. Furthermore, in Tagalog, verbs adopt special forms in some embedded clauses that could be related to the subjunctive use in Catalan. Neither of these two properties is shared by the other two languages.

In summary, these results show us that there is indeed an L1 influence on L2 at a morphological level in young learners. Even though the relationships that we have established would need further investigation in some cases, we believe that the differences that we have found among the speakers are sufficient to support this idea. It is also interesting to point out that the uses that we have come across, involving both the nominal phrase and verbal morphology, would not be equivalent to those of children learning Catalan as an L1. For instance, the percentages of incorrect verb use are equivalent to those typically made by two-year-old children and the error distribution is not exactly the same either (Serrat & Aparici, 2001). In any case, the learners of Catalan as an L1 make these types of error for a short time, whereas the children in this study have been living in Catalonia for more than three years. This also suggests that they are learning Catalan as an L2.

Keeping in mind the difficulties that we have observed in the case of these children, we must underline the importance of this type of study in the field of second language acquisition. Not only does it allow us to understand one of the most controversial aspects in the acquisition of an L2 better, but it can also be particularly useful to the professionals teaching Catalan to people from these communities.

Acknowledgement

This study was partially funded by the *Ministerio de Ciencia y Tecnología* (BFF2003-04043, HUM2006-07217) and a research grant from the *Generalitat de Catalunya* (SGR2005 00634).

References

Bialystok, E. and Hakuta, K. (1994) *In Other Words: The Science and Psychology of Second-Language Acquisition*. New York: Basic Books.
Corder, S.P. (1967) The significance of learner errors. *International Review of Applied Linguistics* 5, 161–170.
Corder, S.P. (1981) *Error Analysis and Interlanguage*. Oxford: Oxford University Press.
Fernández, S. (1997) *Interlengua y análisis de errors en el aprendizaje del español como lengua extranjera*. Madrid: Edelsa.
Finnemann, M.D. (1992) Learning agreement in the noun phrase: The strategies of three first-year Spanish students. *International Review of Applied Linguistics* 30 (2), 121–134.
Gass, S. (1996) Second language acquisition and linguistic theory: the role of language transfer. In A.W. Ritchie and T. Bathia (eds) *Handbook of Second Language Acquisition* (pp. 317–345). New York: Academic Press.
Girier, Ch. (1996) *Parlons Soninké*. París: L'Harmattan.
Gràcia, L. and Serrat, E. (2003) Immigració i adquisició de segones llengües: Una aproximació als errors en la morfologia verbal. *Caplletra* 35, 153–168.
Jarvis, S. (2000) Methodological rigor in the study of transfer: Identifying L1 influence in the interlanguage lexicon. *Language Learning* 50, 245–309.
Jarvis, S. and Odlin, T. (2000) Morphological type, spatial reference, and language transfer. *Studies in Second Language Acquisition* 22, 535–556.
Lado, R. (1957) *Linguistics Across Cultures*. Ann Arbor, MI: University of Michigan Press.
Larsen-Freeman, D. and Long, M. (1991) *An Introduction to Second Language Acquisition Research*. London: Longman.
Li, C. and Thompson, S.A. (1981) *Mandarin Chinese. A Functional Reference Grammar*. Berkeley, CA: Univeristy of California Press.
MacWhinney, B. (2000) *The Childes Project*. Hillsdale, NJ: Erlbaum.
Odlin, T. (1989) *Language Transfer*. Cambridge, UK: Cambridge University Press.
Odlin, T. (2003) Cross-linguistic influence. In C.J. Dougthy and M.H. Long (eds) *The Handbook of Second Language Acquisition* (pp. 436–486). Oxford: Blackwell.
Po-Ching, Y. and Rimmington, D. (1997) *Chinese: An Essential Grammar*. London: Routledge; Sandgak: Norbury Publishers.
Ramsey, R. (1987) *The Languages of China*. Princeton, NJ: Princeton University Press.
Schachter, P. and Otanes, F.T. (1972) *Tagalog Reference Grammar*. Berkeley, CA: University of California.
Schwartz, B.D. (2003) Child L2 acquisition: Paving the way. In B. Beachley, A. Brown and F. Conlin (eds) *Proceedings of the 27th Boston University Conference on Language Development* (pp. 26–50). Somerville, MA: Cascadilla Press.

Selinker, L. and Lakshmanan, U. (1993) Language transfer and fossilization: The Multiple Effects Principle. In S. Gass and L. Selinker (eds) *Language Transfer in Language Learning* (pp. 197–216). Amsterdam: John Benjamins.

Selinker, L. (1972) Interlanguage. *International Review of Applied Linguistics* 10 (3), 209–231.

Selinker, L. (1992) *Rediscovering Interlanguage*. London: Longman.

Serrat, E. and Aparici, M. (2001) Morphological errors in early language acquisition: Evidence from Catalan and Spanish. In M. Algrem, A. Barreña, M.J. Ezeizabarrena, I. Idiazábal and B. MacWhinney (eds) *Research on Child Language Acquisition* (pp. 1260–1277). Somerville, MA: Cascadilla Press.

Unsworth, S. (2004) On the syntax–semantics interface in Dutch: Adult and child L2 acquisition compared. *International Review of Applied Linguistics* 42, 173–187.

Chapter 10
Predicting Enhanced L3 Learning in Bilingual Contexts: The Role of Biliteracy

CRISTINA SANZ

Introduction

Since the 1960s, research on the impact of bilingualism on cognition has associated bilingualism with positive effects on a number of internal variables, including intelligence (Peal & Lambert, 1962), metalinguistic awareness (Ben-Zeev, 1977; Bialystok, 1991), cognitive flexibility and processing mechanisms (McLaughlin & Nayak, 1989; Nation & McLaughlin, 1986; Nayak *et al.*, 1990), and even a more democratic disposition (Pandey, 1991).

It is widely believed that multilinguals learn new languages better than monolinguals, that previous practice provides an edge when it comes to learning other languages. This belief is corroborated by informal observations (Larsen-Freeman, 1983 in Zobl, 1992) and by descriptions of 'the good language learner' (Ramsey, 1980).

Studies comparing bilinguals' and monolinguals' acquisition of a foreign language (Cenoz & Valencia, 1994, with data from the Basque Country; Safont-Jordà 2005, as well as Sanz, 2000, with Catalan data, and Swain *et al.*, 1990 with Canadian data) show that in a sociolinguistic situation that promotes additive bilingualism, like the one described for students in immersion programmes in Canada, the Basque Country and Catalonia, bilingualism appears to exert a positive effect on third language learning, that is, that bilingualism (biliteracy, to be precise) results in more efficient language learning. For example, Sanz's comparison of achievement on tests of English administered to students in Spain instructed in Catalan, the minority language, and in Spanish, the majority language, yielded evidence in favour of bilingualism and bilingual education as positive contributors to foreign language learning. Furthermore, the positive effects of bilingualism were observed regardless of cognitive, sociostructural, sociopsychological, and educational variables. From this study, two new directions for research have emerged: on the one hand, the need to *explain* the positive effects of bilingualism on cognition by designing controlled experimental studies that include psycholinguistic variables such as metalinguistic awareness and cognitive capacity (i.e. working memory) as well as level of bilingualism, and on the other, the need to move away from mono/bilingual comparisons and focus instead on identifying and explaining differences *among* bilinguals.

The present study focuses on a group of high-school junior bilinguals in Catalan and Spanish learning English as a foreign language to identify and explain those factors associated with bilingualism as well as general factors identified in the SLA literature that may predict successful acquisition of a third language (L3) with special attention to the role of oral and written proficiency in both languages in predicting L3 learning. Specifically, the chapter reports on the answers to the following research questions:

(1) What are the individual differences predicting higher L3 development?
(2) Does age of L2 acquisition onset affect L3 development?
(3) Does order of acquisition of the majority and minority languages affect L3 development?
(4) Does the degree of balance between the two languages affect L3 development?

The chapter first reviews previous literature that has incorporated the general factors identified in the SLA literature (Ellis, 1994; Skehan, 1998) and variables associated with bilingualism (Baker, 1993), followed by details on the methodology implemented and a summary of the results, which are discussed in the last section.

Individual Differences and Contextual Factors in the Acquisition of a Non-Primary Language

General factors identified in the SLA literature

Socioeconomic status (SES)

The comparison by Holobow *et al.* (1991) of low and high SES students in an immersion program found no differences among the groups. Cummins (2001), however, proposes that minority students from lower SES homes may be more reliant on the school system to provide not only language instruction, but also background knowledge, as students from middle- to high-SES homes start school with a richer variety of concepts and linguistic structures, putting them at an advantage. Even though previous research in the Iberian Peninsula cited earlier did not identify a relationship between SES and L3 learning, the contradicting evidence requires a closer look at this variable. Also, SES is a classic variable in socioeducational studies.

Gender

The reader should consult Bowden *et al.* (2005) for a detailed discussion of the role of gender/sex on the acquisition of non-primary languages, including a neurocognitive perspective. The scant research that has been conducted on sex differences in the acquisition of non-primary languages has revealed a general trend toward higher achievement for females on most tests (Ellis, 1994; Powell, 1979; Oxford & Ehrman, 1993). These results have been obtained both for children (Burstall, 1975; Lynn & Wilson, 1992, 1993) and adults (Boyle, 1987). In addition to this research on L2 performance, differences in learning strategies show that females employ more learning strategies than males, and they also use them more often (Oxford *et al.*, 1988). Ellis (1994) reported on research that indicated that females may, in general, be more motivated to learn a second language and may have more positive attitudes toward speakers of the L2. Further research that includes gender as a variable is therefore needed.

IQ

The relationship between bilingualism and intelligence used to focus on whether bilinguals were more or less intelligent than monolinguals almost always showing a negative correlation (see Sanz, 1998, for a detailed critique). After Peal and Lambert's classic study (1962), however, the discussion brought in a key variable, that of balance. In their study, they included only balanced bilinguals and found that they were superior to monolinguals in different measurements, including non-verbal and some types of verbal intelligence. However, a substantial number of studies followed that yielded contradictory results on the cognitive advantages of bilingualism. The need for an explanation prompted Cummins to propose the Threshold Hypothesis (1976), which establishes a relationship between cognition and language proficiency.

Exposure

Although the effects of this variable have been established, exposure had to be included in the design in order to observe any possible correlations between exposure and other variables.

Motivation

Undoubtedly, Gardner and colleagues have dominated the field of SLA on the topic of motivation (see the discussion in *Modern Language Journal*, 1995, between Gardner, Oxford, Dornyei and Schmidt). In a nutshell, orientation (which contributes to the overarching construct of motivation) can be classified into two types, integrative and instrumental. Although the latter cannot be disregarded, in fact the power of integrative orientation showed up again and again as predictor of higher success in studies carried out mostly in Canada. Questionnaires have been tested and adapted to other contexts, both second and foreign language contexts, with different degrees of success.

Variables associated with bilingualism

Age

A great deal of research (see Birdsong, 1999, for an excellent review) has investigated the issue of age as it relates to acquisition of non-primary languages. Studies that compare groups that differ on age of initial exposure to the L3 can be found in García Mayo and García Lecumberri (2003). However, the present study investigates the relationship between the age at which the L2 was acquired and success in the acquisition of the L3. All participants started learning the L3 at age 9. It could be hypothesised that earlier bilinguals, that is, simultaneous bilinguals and those who acquired the L2 before age 7, have benefited from more extended practice with two languages and show greater ability in learning the L3. For a greater period, they have used the switching mechanism that enables them to move from one language to another and which results in heightened language awareness and analysis and explains cognitive advantages, especially those related to verbal intelligence (see Bowden *et al.*, 2005, for references).

Order

This variable does not affect simultaneous bilinguals, half the sample in our case. But, for the other half of the sample, it would be interesting to see whether significant differences can be observed in L3 success between those who learned the majority language (Spanish) first and then learned the minority language (Catalan) vs. the group that learned Catalan first. The difference between the two lies in the relationship between mother tongue and language of education. It is important to remember that Catalan and Spanish are typologically close and that most middle-class children have been exposed to Catalan before they enter school through the media.

Language use (frequency and context) of Catalan and Spanish

Baker (1993) points out the importance of incorporating language use and not just language knowledge into any study dealing with bilingualism. The difference between knowledge of the two languages and actual use of the two languages can be especially acute in Barcelona, where the unequal status of Catalan vs. Spanish is more greatly felt. It is commonplace in Catalan sociolinguistics to refer to the difference between the language of the classroom (Catalan) and the language of recess (Spanish).

Biliteracy and bilingualism (balance)

Some scholars attribute the cognitive benefits of bilingualism to literacy in two languages (Bialystok, 1986–2004; Cook, 1997; Cummins, 1981; Swain *et al.*, 1990). Swain and colleagues investigated the effect of L1 (a number of Romance and non-Romance languages) literacy on L3 (French) learning among 319 eighth-graders for whom English was the L2 in Toronto. Results of this study suggest that the crucial factor in successful L3 acquisition is development of heritage language literacy skills, rather than exclusively oral skills. Their conclusion supports Cummins' (1981) linguistic interdependence hypothesis, according to which children learn to use language as a symbolic system in the process of acquiring literacy skills in their first language, and that results in ability to classify, abstract, and generalise linguistic information in a way that can be transferred to subsequent language learning contexts. Earlier, Cummins had elaborated the Threshold Hypothesis (1976) in order to explain contradictory results found in studies on cognitive advantages (and disadvantages) of bilingualism. Cummins does not claim that only balanced bilinguals benefit from the bilingual experience, but that an upper threshold must be reached to observe cognitive benefits. Cummins defines the upper threshold as 'age appropriate skills in both languages'. The Threshold Hypothesis is a working hypothesis that needs to be developed; precisely one of the goals of the present study is to further specify the definition of 'age appropriate skills' within the context of high- school juniors in a Catalan immersion programme whose goal is to produce fully biliterate bilinguals with superior level of control over both languages and who frequently use both as required by the sociolinguistic situation that surrounds them.

Ongoing research by Ellen Bialystok and her team at York University also shows a strong relationship between literacy and bilingualism. It tests previous hypotheses positing greater processing control, superior working memory, and enhanced metalinguistic awareness as factors positively affected by biliteracy and resulting in enhanced acquisition of an L3 (Ben-Zeev, 1977; Bialystok, 1986–2004; Cummins, 1976; Díaz, 1985; Galambos and Goldin-Meadow, 1990; Ricciardelli, 1992a, 1992b; Yelland *et al.*, 1993). But why is it important that bilinguals use processing strategies more efficiently? Possibly because of cognitive limitations. Working memory is a flexible workspace with limited capacity (Daneman & Carpenter, 1980). Available capacity is seen as a trade-off between storage and processing demands. Controlled processes require more processing space than automatic processes. If controlled processes are automatised faster, there is more space available and thus more information can be extracted, segmented, and transformed into intake that will be incorporated later into the L3 system.

I have argued (Sanz, 2000) that bilingualism has a double face, that is, societal and individual, and that individual bilingualism is determined in most cases by societal bilingualism. Thus, in the end, it is the social aspect of bilingualism, and especially the availability of bilingual education, which determines the development of cognitive benefits deriving from experience with two languages, including benefits involved in the acquisition of an L3.

Methodology

Participants completed a release form, and all tests and questionnaires were completed in two 50-minute sessions in their own classrooms. During the first session, participants signed the release form, completed the questionnaire and section 8 of the Raven's Progressive Matrices Test, rather than the full version, due to time constraints. During the second session, participants completed the vocabulary and structure sections of the CELT English proficiency test. Both sections followed a multiple-choice format and each included 75 items. Participants also completed a questionnaire presented in its full version in the appendix. For space reasons, details on the questionnaire and scoring procedures are presented together with details on the sample in the next subsection.

Sample

120 bilinguals participated in the study.[1] The participants were male and female high-school juniors from a private religious school in

downtown Barcelona that caters for middle-class families and implements strict rules in areas such as student failure, thus narrowing the range on variables such as SES and age in the sample.

Answers to the questionnaire completed by all bilingual participants confirm that they use both Catalan and Spanish on a daily basis in and out of school, for activities as different as shopping, watching TV, playing sports, and taking notes. Almost 50% of them were born in bilingual homes, where one of the parents speaks Catalan and the other Spanish. As high-school juniors, they are working towards preparation for the State Entrance Exam (*Selectivitat*), which grants access to college. The exam requires academic written ability in both Spanish and Catalan. Participants from multilingual households (with languages other than Spanish or Catalan) were eliminated from the final sample.

Socioeconomic status (SES)[2]

The questionnaire asks for approximate income and profession for both parents. Each parent is then assigned into one category where 1 stands for working class, 2 stands for middle class and 3 stands for upper-middle class (Cenoz, 1991). By combining both parents in each household, five different categories are obtained, 2 to 6. Previous research has based SES solely on the father's data. In urban areas of Spain, however, a significant percentage of women work and contribute to household income. Of the households, 7% belonged to category 2, 20% to category 3, 38% to category 4, 21% to category 5, and 14% to category 6.

Two variables, *IQ*, as measured by the Raven's Progressive Matrices Test (mean = 10.91; SD = 1.19; max = 12), and *Age at time of testing* (mean = 16.53; SD = 0.59; max = 17) were not included in the analyses due to lack of variation linked to testing conditions and school characteristics.

Gender

In total, 61 females and 59 males participated.

Exposure to the foreign language

This included number of English courses and hours per course at the school as well as after school, and summer courses in Spain and abroad. Special attention was paid to eliciting detailed information on informal exposure to English: music, television, pen pals, and so on. The score was calculated by adding the number of hours of English instruction at the school, in after-school programmes and tutoring, and in summer programmes in Spain or abroad. Also added was the frequency of informal contact with English. For example, subject A commented that she listened to music in English and watched CNN, for which she was given a score of 2, while subject B said he had an American pen pal, watched MTV, and read graded readings, for which he was given a 3.[3] The total scores were submitted as raw scores to the analyses. The mean was 966.80 and the standard deviation was 343.56.

Degree of motivation

A Likert-format questionnaire (adapted from Gardner, 1985, and Cenoz, 1991) included ten statements to which the participant reacted by choosing among five possible answers. The questionnaire included positive and negative statements such as 'I will use English after graduation' and 'Learning English is difficult'. A score was calculated for each participant by adding the scores from the ten items in the questionnaire. Raw scores were used in the analyses. The mean obtained was 5.48, SD = 4.71 (max = 18).

Attitudes

Information on this and the following variables was elicited by means of a questionnaire that followed Osgood's semantic differentials format. It consisted of five pairs of antonyms[4] that were applied to each population group, and two other antonyms, to their linguistic variety. The adjectives chosen had been successfully tested in Sanz (1992), a study with a similar population, and were presented following this example: 'What do you think people in the United States are like? "cultivated _ _ _ _ _ ignorant"' The subjects were expected to choose one among the five spaces provided. For the variable *Attitudes towards the British*, the score for each subject was calculated by adding the scores from the 5-semantic differential items section of the questionnaire. Raw scores were used. The mean obtained was 1.84, SD = 3.88 (max = 10). *Attitudes towards the US population* were calculated following the same procedure. The mean obtained was 0.25, SD = 3.33 (max = 9). *Language attitudes towards the 'British' variety* were calculated by adding the scores from the 2-semantic differential items. Raw scores were used. The mean obtained was 0.64 (max = 4). *Language attitudes towards the 'American' variety*. The same procedure as above was used to calculate the raw scores for this factor. The mean obtained was 0.22 (max = 4). The rest of the variables capture the relationship between Catalan and Spanish. These variables can be classified into three groups: variables related to use, knowledge, and acquisition of either language.

Language use

This variable can be further subdivided into two classes: (1) information on interlocutors (7 total) and language choice, and (2) information on activities (12 total) and the language in which they were performed. The participants had to indicate the frequency of use of Spanish or Catalan for each category. The interlocutors are father, mother, siblings, friends (at school), friends (other), teachers and neighbours. The activities are watching TV, reading for pleasure, reading the newspaper, listening to music, listening to the radio, shopping, playing sports, talking on the phone, note taking, writing, thinking, and dreaming. Raw scores were introduced for each variable. Exploratory analyses and observation of participants while completing the questionnaire suggested eliminating the following variables from the final analyses: language spoken with the neighbours, reading the newspaper, listening to music, listening to the radio, dreaming. What follows is Table 10.1 summarises descriptive statistics for the remaining variables.

Table 10.1 Contexts of use and interlocutors. (Simple Statistics)

Variable	Mean	SD	Min	Max	N
Father	−0.39	1.83	−2	2	120
Mother	−0.4	1.86	−2	2	
School	−0.67	0.97	−2	2	
Friends	−0.26	1.27	−2	2	
Teachers	−1.53	0.73	−2	2	
TV	−0.13	0.85	−2	2	
Reading	−0.05	1.17	−2	2	
Shopping	−0.43	1.10	−2	2	
Notetaking	−1.65	0.68	−2	2	
Writing	−0.68	1.35	−2	2	
Thinking	−0.70	1.58	−2	2	

Order of acquisition

Participants could choose among three options: simultaneous acquisition, [Spanish L1–Catalan L2] and [Catalan L1–Spanish L2]. When choosing either the second or the third option, the participant had to specify the age of acquisition of the L2. Participants were divided into two groups, labelled simultaneous vs. non-simultaneous according to order of acquisition. These second group was further divided into two groups, those who had learned the L2 before age 8 and those who had learned it at age 8 or after. Group 1 acquired the L2 simultaneously (both L1 & L2 before 4th birthday; $n = 68$ or 53% of sample); Group 2 learned L2 between their 4th and 7th birthday) ($n = 42$ or 37.9%), finally, Group 3 learned the L2 after literacy in L1 had been acquired (after 7th birthday $n = 10$ or 8.9%). Of the non-simultaneous bilinguals, $n = 23$ learned Spanish first, and $n = 29$ learned Catalan first.

Knowledge of Catalan and Spanish

For each language skill, participants had three choices: I can speak/understand/read/write Catalan and Spanish equally well/Catalan better than Spanish/Spanish better than Catalan. For the purposes of this study, participants were given a score of 2 for each skill for which they chose the option 'equally well' and a score of one for any other answer. Therefore, the balance index for oral skills ranges between 2 $(1+1)$ and 4 $(2+2)$. A 'balance index' was elaborated based on their responses, one for oral skills and one for written skills. To be more precise and focusing on literacy, a key variable in the study, a scale going from 2 to 4 was elaborated based on participants' self-ratings of their reading and writing proficiency in Catalan and Spanish. A score of 2 means that a participant feels more comfortable in one of the two languages, Catalan and Spanish, for both reading and writing. A score of 3 means that s/he feels equally comfortable in both languages when either reading or writing, but prefers one of the two languages for one of the two skills. A score of 4 means that the participant feels equally comfortable in both languages when reading *and* when writing. Tables 10.2 and 10.3 summarise the descriptive statistics.

Table 10.2 Sample distribution by skills in both languages

Language skill	Both, N	Catalan > Spanish, N	Spanish > Catalan, N
Understand	87	27	6
Speak	35	53	32
Read	69	32	19
Write	40	49	31

Table 10.3 Descriptive statistics for self-assessed oral and written ability

Variable	Mean	SD	Min	Max	N
Oral ability	3.008	0.75	2	4	120
Written ability	2.906	0.79	2	4	

Analysis

Correlations, hierarchical multiple regressions and a number of ANOVAs were applied to raw scores in order to assess the relationship between cognitive (IQ), sociostructural (SES, language use), sociopsychological (attitudes, motivation), and educational variables (age, order, balance, exposure) associated with bilingualism and the acquisition of English as a foreign language (correlation and regressions), as well as the effects on L3 achievement of age of L2 acquisition, order of acquisition, and balance of skills in the L1 and L2 (ANOVAs). The dependent variable was English achievement, calculated as the sum of the scores from the vocabulary and the structure tests. The mean obtained was 46.79 and the standard deviation was 8.5.

Results

RQ 1. What are the individual differences predicting higher L3 development?

The first analysis consisted of a set of correlation analyses. A number of independent variables correlated with achievement, including Exposure, Motivation, Attitudes towards the UK and US varieties of English, a number of variables linked to Language Use (Language Spoken to the Mother, to Friends, Shopping). Importantly, Language Proficiency (i.e.

Table 10.4 Significant correlations between the independent factors and grammar, vocabulary, and achievement scores

Variables	Exposure	Motivation	UK lang	US lang	Mother
Achievement	0.37**	0.47**	0.24*	0.23*	0.28**
	Friends	Shopping	Balance: Oral	Balance: Written	
Achievement	0.21*	0.18*	0.19	0.22*	

$^*p < 0.05.$
$^{**}p < 0.01.$

Table 10.5 Multiple regression of all variables on English achievement

Variable	Parameter estimate	t	r^2
Exposure	0.006	0.0016*	
Motivation	0.681	0.0001*	
UK language	0.086	0.813	
US language	0.444	0.216	
Mother	0.601	0.255	
Friends	0.631	0.376	
Shopping	0.374	0.552	
Balance: Literacy	1.421	0.173	
			0.40

*$p < 0.01$.

Balance) also correlated significantly with achievement, but only for written skills. Significant results are reported in Table 10.4.

Subsequently, a regression analysis was performed with the key eight variables identified by the correlation analysis and the literature. The analysis was significant overall, but only Exposure and Motivation were significant predictors of L3 development. Table 10.5 summarises the results.

The very powerful nature of the relationship between Motivation and Exposure and the dependent variable could possibly hide other relationships. For this reason, a second regression analysis was performed with the same independent variables excluding Motivation and Exposure.

Table 10.6 Multiple regression of all variables on English achievement

Variable	Parameter estimate	t	r^2
UK language	0.849	0.031*	
US language	0.651	0.110	
Mother	0.354	0.593	
Friends	0.925	0.247	
Shopping	0.353	0.457	
Balance: Oral	0.237	0.849	
Balance: Literacy	2.075	0.079	0.25

*$p < 0.05$.

Attitudes towards the British variety of English surfaces as a significant predictor, as shown in Table 10.6. Although the percentage of variance explained was somewhat lower (25% rather than 40%), the results were still significant overall. Note that neither Oral nor Written proficiency in Spanish and Catalan significantly predicts overall achievement.

RQ 2. Does age of L2 acquisition onset affect L3 development?

Subjects were classified into three groups: simultaneous bilinguals, those who had learned the L2 between age 4 and age 7, and those who had learned it after age 7. The ANOVA ($F_{2,197} = 0.72, p < 0.49$) on achievement scores failed to yield any significant results.

RQ 3. Does order of acquisition of the majority and minority languages affect L3 development?

Subjects were classified into three groups: simultaneous bilinguals, those who had learned Spanish before Catalan, and those who had learned Catalan before Spanish. The ANOVA ($F_{2,197} = 0.56, p < 0.57$) on achievement scores failed to yield any significant results.

RQ 4. Does the degree of balance between the languages affect L3 development?

A 'balance index' was elaborated based on participants' responses, one for oral skills and one for written skills, with a range between $2(1+1)$ and $4(2+2)$. The subjects were then classified into three groups, from least to most balanced: subjects scoring 2, scoring 3 and scoring 4. This was done twice, once for oral and one for written skills. Because a significant correlation was identified between the independent variable 'Written Skills' and the dependent variable 'Achievement', a second analysis was run to identify whether one of the sections of the test, either the structure section of the vocabulary section or both, was responsible for the correlation. As shown in Table 10.7, it was actually the scores on the structure section of the test that correlate with written skills. No significant

Table 10.7 Pearson correlation analysis. Dependent variables: Grammar, Vocabulary and Achievement and Catalan/Spanish oral and written skills

Variables	Grammar	Vocabulary	Achievement
Oral skills	0.13	0.13	0.19
Written skills	0.17*	0.05	0.22*

*$p < 0.05$.

Table 10.8 Means and standard deviations for Literacy balance

Level	N	Mean	SD
2	21	22	6.2
3	41	25.109	5.29
4	58	35.375	6.16

correlations were identified for balance of oral skills nor for scores on the vocabulary test. These results show a positive relationship between the ability to read and write in both languages and the more efficient development of structural knowledge of a third language.

Given these encouraging results, scores on the structure section were submitted to an ANOVA in order to identify any causal effects rather than just relationships. An added advantage of ANOVAs, provided results are significant, is that they allow for *post hoc* multiple comparisons and identify contrasts between levels. Table 10.8 summarises the descriptives for this variable. The ANOVA ($F_{2,197} = 4.20$, $p < 0.01$) yielded significant results for level, and the Student–Newman–Keuls shows significant contrasts between the lowest and the other two levels. The two higher levels (levels 3 and 4) did not contrast significantly. Table 10.8 summarises means and standard deviations for each group.

Discussion, Implications and Further Research

Results from the present study identified motivation, exposure, language attitudes, language use, and language knowledge of the L1 and L2 as independent variables significantly related to overall L3 achievement. After controlling the overpowering effects of motivation and exposure in predicting English proficiency, analyses further identified language attitudes and balance of written skills as significant predictors of L3 proficiency. Finer-grained analyses showed that in fact balance is a predictor of L3 *grammar* development, but not of development of *lexical* knowledge. Furthermore, no effects for age of L2 acquisition or order of L2 acquisition were identified, but the ANOVA shows that balance affects L3 development, and that these effects are felt at level three or beyond, suggesting the existence of a threshold.

As expected, no gender differences were identified due to the nature of the dependent variable, achievement. Achievement informs about the product of learning, and according to the literature, it is in the processing of the language for acquisition and the strategies employed where male/female differences are identified. SES was not a significant predictor either, probably due to the small range. Although the numbers seem to indicate otherwise, in fact the highest and the lowest category are not extremely different in terms of class; the sample was made up of mostly middle-class students. Motivation, however, turned out to be a significant predictor, one that had to be controlled in the stepwise regression in order to identify other factors. The statistical power of motivation lies not only in its relationship with the dependent variable achievement, but in its correlations with multiple other variables, a finding worth investigating in future research. Finally, related to motivation, language attitudes, and specifically a positive attitude towards what is known in Spain as 'British English', was observed to predict L3 achievement. This paragraph has centred on general variables. The rest of the section looks at variables related to bilingualism, namely age, order of acquisition, and L1/L2 proficiency.

Neither age nor order of acquisition was identified as having predictive value over the dependent variable achievement. When finer-grained tests were conducted comparing three groups that differed in age or in order alternatively, no differences were identified either. In other words, simultaneous bilinguals did not show an advantage when compared with those who had learned the L2 at age 7, after exposed to literacy in their L1. Also, having learned the minority or the majority language first did not enhance or hinder L3 learning. This may be explained by the high level of control over both the L1 and L2 by all participants and the similarity between the languages, both belonging to the Romance family. An effort was made to control for order and age of acquisition. The five resulting groups were compared (simultaneous, early Catalan, early Spanish, late Catalan, late Spanish) with no significant differences elicited, surely due to the enormous size of the simultaneous bilinguals cell in comparison with the other four cells. These results run parallel to those in Muñoz (2000), who found a relationship in degrees of proficiency in the L1, L2, and L3, but no relationship between proficiency in any of their three languages and order of acquisition (operationalised as 'home language') of the L1 and the L2.

Although neither order of acquisition nor age of L2 acquisition did contribute to explaining L3 achievement in the present study, use of the minority language was a predictor of L3 achievement. Specifically, using Catalan with mothers and friends is positively related to success in learning the L3. This finding suggests that more attention should be paid to language use, rather than focus exclusively in proficiency, in sociolinguistic situations where a minority and a majority language coexist.

No effects were found for balance in oral skills, but degree of bilingual literacy is key to success in L3 acquisition. These results agree with those in Muñoz (2000), Lasagabaster (2000), and Sagasta (2003), and take them further by showing that it is not overall L1 and L2 proficiency but biliteracy that contributes to cognitive benefits resulting in enhanced ability to learn languages. Our study concludes, like Thomas' classic study (1988), that the key variable is the ability to read and write in two languages. Her comparison of 26 monolingual, bilingual, and biliterate subjects (English (L1)/Spanish (L2)) learning French (L3) shows that bilinguals outperform monolinguals, but more importantly, just like in our case, it shows that biliterates outperformed bilinguals on grammar, but not on vocabulary tests.

Just as important as identifying biliteracy as the key variable predicting L3 success is the ability to narrow down the threshold. The Threshold Hypothesis is a working hypothesis that needs to be developed; precisely one of the goals of the present study is to further specify the definition of 'age-appropriate skills' within the context of high-school juniors in a Catalan immersion programme whose goal is to produce fully biliterate bilinguals with superior level of control over both languages and who frequently use both as required by the sociolinguistic situation that surrounds them. As detailed in the methods section, based on participants' self-ratings of their reading and writing proficiency in Catalan and Spanish, a scale going from 2 to 4 was elaborated. A score of 2 means that a participant feels more comfortable in one of the two languages, Catalan and Spanish, for both reading and writing. A score of 3 means that s/he feels equally comfortable in both languages when either reading or writing, but prefers one of the two languages for one of the two skills. A score of 4 means that the participant feels equally comfortable in both languages when reading *and* when writing. The *post hocs* identified the threshold as standing between levels 2 and 3. Therefore, we must conclude that equal ability in one of the two skills defines 'age-appropriate skills' and is sufficient for cognitive benefits, operationalised as enhanced ability to learn a non-primary language, to emerge.

Conclusions

Prior research conducted in the Basque Country by Cenoz and colleagues (REAL, http://www.vc.ehu.es/depfi/real) as well as in Catalonia by Muñoz, Pérez, and colleagues in the BCNSLA group (http://www.ub.es/filoan/BCN-SLA/BCN-SLA.html) and by Sanz, shows that experience with language learning in socioeducational situations that promote additive bilingualism gives bilinguals an edge. The latest published comparison of bilinguals and monolinguals learning an L3 (Safont Jordà, 2005) shows the main effect for experience was prevalent, constant, and uncomplicated by possible interactions. Instruction did not level the field: bilinguals retained their advantage even after instruction focused on specific pragmatic functions.

Careful inspection of data from the studies above show clear differences among participants in the bilingual groups. Neither did all bilinguals perform equally well, nor were they comparable in terms of cognitive, psychosocial, and linguistic variables related to command and use of the L1 and L2. Also, the cognitive benefits identified for bilingualism have been attributed to literacy in two languages. This study was prompted by a need to explore the role of individual variables in L3 learning and especially the role of biliteracy in enhancing L3 learning.

The results obtained lead us to conclude that motivation and exposure are the most important factors in predicting success in L3 acquisition by bilinguals. Once these variables are controlled, however, a higher level of biliteracy – the ability to read and write in Catalan and Spanish – is associated with a higher level of English proficiency. We interpret these results as confirming the existence of cognitive benefits of bilingualism for cognition as it pertains to subsequent language learning, and specifically of the existence of a Threshold Level associated with equal ability to either read or write in both Catalan and Spanish.

In considering these arguments, the reader should bear in mind the typological relationship between the languages involved. Both Catalan and Spanish are Romance languages; therefore further research is necessary that incorporates the same variables in a comparable socio-educational context that involves typologically different languages. Furthermore, the study reported here does not operationalise those factors, such as enhanced working memory capacity or metalinguistic knowledge, that could explain the advantage of bilinguals over monolinguals on L3 acquisition. Research that is explanatory in nature is very much needed. Also, our data allow linking balance and L3 learning success as well as motivation and L3 learning success (plus other variables), and some of these variables were also shown to be interrelated (based on correlations). However, directionality is not always clear. For example, does L1/L2 balance predict L3 success? Absolutely. But does success feed motivation, or do more motivated learners become more successful learners? These and many other questions remain to be answered in a field that promises to grow as the number of multilinguals worldwide keeps growing.

Notes

1. $N = 120$ instead of 124, the original sample, because four outliers were identified and eliminated from the final sample.
2. The scores from each parent were introduced separately in the first round of analyses. However, neither the scores of the mothers nor those of the fathers reached significance.
3. Calculating the scores consisted in adding the number of items mentioned. The task was facilitated by the participants, who followed the instructions carefully.
4. The questionnaire includes 6 and 3 items, respectively. However, an important number of participants (over 80%) scored 3 on each of them, that is, chose the middle position. This and a number of complaints from the participants in relation to those two items while completing the questionnaire suggested they had to be eliminated from the final count. The items were 'trustworthy/non-trustworthy' and 'simple/complex'.

References

Baker, C. (1993) *Foundations of Bilingual Education and Bilingualism*. Clevedon: Multilingual Matters.
Ben-Zeev, S. (1977) Mechanisms by which childhood bilingualism affects understanding of language and cognitive structures. In P.A. Hornby (ed.) *Bilingualism: Psychological, Social, and Educational Implications* (pp. 29–55). New York: Academic.
Bialystok, E. (1986) Factors in the growth of linguistic awareness. *Child Development* 57, 498–510.
Bialystok, E. (1987) Words as things: Development of word concept by bilingual children. *Studies in Second Language Learning* 9, 133–140.
Bialystok, E. (1991) *Language Processing in Bilingual Children*. Cambridge: Cambridge University Press.
Bialystok, E. (2004) Language and literacy development. In W.C. Bhatia and T.K. Ritchie (eds) *Handbook of Bilingualism*. Malden, MA: Blackwell.
Birdsong, D. (1999) *Second Language Acquisition and the Critical Period Hypothesis*. Mahwah: Lawrence Erlbaum Associates.
Bowden, H.W., Sanz, C. and Stafford, C. (2005) Individual differences: Age, gender, working memory, and prior knowledge. In C. Sanz (ed.) *Mind and Context in Adult Second Language Acquisition*. Washington, DC: Georgetown University Press.
Boyle, J. (1987) Sex differences in listening vocabulary. *Language Learning* 37, 273–284.
Burstall, C. (1975) Factors affecting foreign-language learning: A consideration of some relevant research findings. *Language Teaching and Linguistics Abstracts* 8, 105–125.
Cenoz, J. (1991) *Enseñanza-aprendizaje del Inglés como L2 o L3*. Donostia, Spain: Universidad del País Vasco.
Cenoz, J. and Valencia, J.F. (1994) Additive trilingualism: Evidence from the Basque Country. *Applied Psycholinguistics* 15, 195–207.

Cook, V. (1997) The consequences of bilingualism for cognitive processing. In J. de Groot and J.F. Kroll (eds) *Tutorials in Bilingualism: Psycholinguistic Perspectives* (pp. 279–300). Mahwah: Lawrence Erlbaum.

Cummins, J. (1976) The influence of bilingualism on cognitive growth: A synthesis of research findings and explanatory hypotheses. *Working Papers on Bilingualism* 9, 1–43.

Cummins, J. (1981) The role of primary language development in promoting educational success for language minority students. In California Statement of Education (ed.) *Schooling and Language Minority Students: A Theoretical Framework* (pp. 3–49). Los Angeles: Evaluation, Dissemination and Assessment Center, California State University.

Cummins, J. (2001) Instructional conditions for trilingual development. *International Journal of Bilingual Education and Bilingualism* 4 (1), 61–75.

Daneman, M. and Carpenter, P. (1980) Individual differences in working memory and reading. *Journal of Verbal Learning and Verbal Behavior* 19, 450–466.

Diaz, R.M. (1985) Bilingual cognitive development: Addressing three gaps in current research. *Child Development* 56, 1356–1378.

Ellis, R. (1994) *The Study of Second Language Acquisition*. Oxford: Oxford University Press.

Galambos, S.J. and Goldin-Meadow, S. (1990) The effects of learning two languages on levels of metalinguistic awareness. *Cognition* 34 (1), 1–56.

Garciá Mayo, M.P. and Garciá Lecumberri, M.L. (eds) (2003) *Age and the Acquisition of English as a Foreign Language*. Clevedon: Multilingual Matters

Gardner, R.C. (1985) *Social Psychology and Second Language Learning*. London, UK: Arnold.

Holobow, N.E., Genesee, F. and Lambert, W.E. (1991) The effectiveness of a foreign language immersion program for children from different ethnic and social class backgrounds: Report 2. *Applied Psycholinguistics* 12 (2), 179–198.

Klein, E.C. (1995) Second versus third language acquisition: Is there a difference? *language Learning* 45, 419–465.

Lasagabaster, D. (1998) *Creatividad y Conciencia Metalingüística: Incidencia en el Aprendizaje del Inglés como L3*. Leoia: University of the Basque Country.

Lasagabaster, D. (2000) Three languages and three linguistic models in the Basque educational system. In J. Cenoz, U. Jessner and B. Hufeisen (ed.) *English in Europe: The Acquisition of a Third Language* (pp. 179–197). Clevedon: Multilingual Matters.

Lynn, R. and Wilson, R.G. (1992) Foreign language ability and its relation to general intelligence. *Research in Education* 47, 40–53.

Lynn, R. and Wilson, R.G. (1993) Sex differences in second-language ability: An Irish study. *School Psychology International* 14 (3), 275–279.

McLaughlin, B. and Nayak, N. (1989) Processing a new language: Does knowing other languages make a difference? In H.W. Dechert and M. Raupach (eds) *Interlingual Processes* (pp. 5–16). Tübingen: Gunter Narr.

Muñoz, C. (2000) Bilingualism and trilingualism in school students in Catalonia. In J. Cenoz and U. Jessner (eds) *English in Europe. The Acquisition of a Third Language* (pp. 157–178). Clevedon: Multilingual Matters.

Nation, R. and McLaughlin, B. (1986) Novices and experts: An information processing approach to the good language learner problem. *Applied Psycholinguistics* 7, 41–56.

Nayak, N., Hansen, N., Krueger, N. and McLaughlin, B. (1990) Language-learning strategies in monolingual and multilingual adults. *Language Learning* 40 (2), 221–244.
Oxford, R.L. and Ehrman, M. (1993) Second language research on individual differences. *Annual Review of Applied Linguistics* 13, 188–205.
Oxford, R.L., Nyikos, M. and Ehrman, M. (1988) Vive la Difference? Reflections on sex differences in use of language learning strategies. *Foreign Language Annals* 21 (4), 321–329.
Pandey, P. (1991) A psycholinguistic study of democratic values in relation to mono-, bi- and trilingualism. *Psycho-Lingua* 21 (2), 111–113.
Peal, E. and Lambert, W.E. (1962) The relation of bilingualism to intelligence. *Psychological Monographs: General and Applied* 76 (27), 1–23.
Pons, E. and Vila, F.X. (2005) *Informe sobre la Situació de la Llengua Catalana.* Barcelona: Observatori de la llengua catalana.
Powell, R.C. (1979) Sex differences and language learning: A review of the evidence. *Audio Visual Language Journal* 17 (1), 19–24.
Ramsey, R.M.G. (1980) Language-learning approach styles of adult multilinguals and successful language learners. *Annals of the New York Academy of Sciences* 345, 73–96.
Raven, J.C. (1998) *Raven's Progressive Matrices and Vocabulary Scales.* San Antonio, TX: Harcourt Assessment.
Ricciardelli, L.A. (1992a) Bilingualism and cognitive development in relation to threshold theory. *Journal of Psycholinguistic Research* 21 (4), 301–316.
Ricciardelli, L.A. (1992b) Creativity and bilingualism. *Journal of Creative Behavior* 26 (4), 242–254.
Safont-Jordà, M.P. (2005) *Third Language Learners: Pragmatic Production and Awareness.* Clevedon: Multilingual Matters.
Sagasta, M. (2003) Acquiring writing skills in a third language: Positive effects of bilingualism. *International Journal of Bilingualism* 7 (1), 27–42.
Sanz, C. (1992) Actituds envers les varietats bilingüe i monolingüe del castellà a Barcelona. *Catalan Review* 2, 121–136.
Sanz, C. (1998) El papel del bilingüismo en el aprendizaje de una lengua extranjera: Contextos sociales/contextos mentales *LynX 21.* València, Spain: Universitat de València.
Sanz, C. (2000) Bilingual education enhances third language acquisition: Evidence from Catalonia. *Applied Psycholinguistics* 21, 23–44.
Skehan, P. (1998) *A Cognitive Approach to Language Learning.* Oxford: Oxford University Press.
Swain, M., Lapkin, S., Rowen, N. and Hart, D. (1990) The role of mother tongue literacy in third language learning. *Language, Culture and Curriculum* 3 (1), 65–81.
Thomas, J. (1988) The role played by metalinguistic awareness in second and third language learning. *Journal of Multilingual and Multicultural Development* 9, 235–246.
Torres, J. (2005) *Estadística sobre els Usos Lingüístics a Catalunya 2003. Llengua i Societat a Catalunya en els Inicis del Segle XXI.* Barcelona: Generalitat de Catalunya.

Wagner, D.A., Spratt, J.E. and Ezzaki, A. (1989) Does learning to read in a second language always put the child at a disadvantage? Some counterevidence from Morocco. *Applied Psycholinguistics* 10, 31–48.

Yelland, G., Pollard, J. and Mercury, A. (1993) The metalinguistic benefits of limited contact with a second language. *Applied Psycholinguistics* 14, 423–444.

Zobl, H. (1992) Prior linguistic knowledge and the conservation of the learning procedure: Grammaticality judgements of unilingual and multilingual learners. In S. Gass and L. Selinker (eds) *Language Transfer in Language Learning* (pp. 176–196). Amsterdam: John Benjamins.

Chapter 11
Learning Context Effects on the Acquisition of a Second Language Phonology

JOAN C. MORA

Introduction

A remarkable body of research in second language acquisition over the past 25 years has been concerned with the potential differential effects of learning contexts on learners' ability to communicate fluently and accurately in a foreign language (L2). The essential motivation for this research interest lies in the need to find empirical support for the long-held assumption that learners obtain greater benefits in linguistic competence through study-abroad (SA) periods than through instruction taking place in other language learning settings, such as regular formal instruction taking place in an 'at home' (AH) institution (Collentine & Freed, 2004). Rooted in this assumption is the common-sense expectation that linguistic immersion in the L2 native speech community will provide learners with intensive (and often extensive) exposure to the target language, thus enhancing L2 input quantity and quality through unlimited opportunities for out-of-class communicative interaction with native speakers in real everyday situations.

In the European Union (EU) context, mobility of university students (and European citizens), and multilingualism, of which foreign language learning is an essential component, has always been a major concern and is at the heart of the EU policy towards the integration of its country members. The promotion of multilingualism and student mobility in the EU has had a huge impact in recent years in Spain, which has now become, together with France and Germany, one of the countries with more students going abroad on an ERASMUS programme (a student mobility scheme involving more than 1800 European universities in 30 countries). However, whereas a period of residence abroad is compulsory for most students of modern language degrees in countries like the United Kingdom (Coleman, 1998), a stay-abroad period is generally optional for Spanish university students studying modern languages. For the university students who participated in the present study, the stay-abroad term (3 months) was a compulsory part of their degree, and is therefore not representative of the typical residence abroad experience of modern language students in Spain.

The present chapter seeks to contribute to the general European context of enhancing multilingualism and, more specifically, multilingualism in Spain by focusing on the acquisition of English as a foreign language by bilingual Catalan-Spanish speakers. In particular, the study we report on here investigates the differential effects of two learning contexts, a formal instruction period in the home university (AH) and a stay-abroad term (SA) in an English-speaking country (UK), on learners' perceptual and productive phonological competence. The varying gains in competence observed highlight the prevailing role of the amount and quality of the input received in L2 speech learning, which has a bearing on critical methodological issues underlying the design of oral competence measures for younger L2 learners (e.g. Mora, 2006) and may provide an explanation as to why early bilinguals typically outperform late bilinguals in speech perception and production. As one of the fundamental tenets of the Speech Learning Model (Flege, 1995; henceforth SLM) claims, the interaction between a bilingual's first language (L1) and L2 phonetic subsystems within a single phonological space and the nature of the resulting merged phonetic categories is a reflection of the L1 and L2 input received (Flege, in press). The present study, therefore, also represents a contribution to understanding how second language acquisition (SLA) may be affected by the context where language learning takes place and to evaluating the extent to which a relatively short SA experience may have positive effects on bilingual learners' phonological competence, an area of inquiry that remains largely under-researched in SLA.

Learning-Context Effects on the Perceptual and Productive Phonological Competence of Advanced Learners of English

Despite the growing interest in context of learning as one of the variables that may account for differences in L2 learners' linguistic ability, research to date has focused mainly on measuring overall oral proficiency, grammatical development and sociolinguistic competence. The differential effects of AH and SA learning contexts have been investigated for a wide variety of L2 skills, but the main body of research has focused on oral communication skills and related cognitive processes. Thus, many studies have examined overall oral proficiency (e.g. Segalowitz & Freed, 2004), oral fluency (Freed, 1995, 2000; Towell, 2002), and oral cognitive processing ability (e.g. Segalowitz & Freed, 2004). A considerable amount of research has also been devoted to the analysis of the sociolinguistic dimension of learning a foreign language abroad, including the analysis of communication strategies (Lafford, 2004), learning strategies (Huebner, 1995), psychological factors (Pellegrino Aveni, 2005) and the development of sociolinguistic skills (e.g. Regan, 1995). The overall picture that emerges from this research suggests that the SA experience has positive effects on the learners' linguistic competence leading to substantial linguistic gains, particularly in the domain of oral skills. However, SA studies investigating more specific dimensions of linguistic competence such as grammatical development (Collentine, 2004; DeKeyser, 1991), lexical growth (Milton & Meara, 1995) or phonology (Díaz-Campos, 2004; Højen, 2003) are scarce and have often produced conflicting results.

The present study further explores this line of research by examining perceptual and productive accuracy in the speech of adult Catalan-Spanish bilingual advanced learners of English before and after (1) a period of formal instruction in their home university in Barcelona (AH), (2) a three-month stay in an English-speaking environment (SA) and (3) a one-year period during which learners did not receive formal instruction in English for six months.

Method

The present study is part of two larger projects with a longitudinal design investigating SA effects on the process of acquisition of English as a foreign language at an advanced stage by measuring learners' gains in linguistic competence over time (see Pérez-Vidal et al., 2006; Turell et al., 2005). The participants were selected from a larger pool of European exchange undergraduate students at Universitat Pompeu Fabra (UPF) in Barcelona reading for a degree in Translation and Interpreting. All of them were advanced EFL students and bilingual speakers of Catalan and Spanish. Data were collected at four times (see Figure 11.1): upon students' enrolment at UPF (T1), after two terms of formal instruction (FI; about 80 hours) at UPF (T2), after a SA term (T3) in an English-speaking country (this included about 40 hours of FI), and 15 months

Academic year	2002/2003			2003/2004			2004/2005		
Term	1	2	3	1	2	3	1	2	3
Instruction/exposure to English	FI (40 h)	FI (40 h)	–	SA	FI (40 h)	FI (40 h)	–	–	–
	↑T1	↑T2		↑T3			↑T4		

Figure 11.1 Data collection times

later after a two-term period without instruction/exposure to English. The criterion for selection was their participation in the speech perception or the speech production tasks at T3 and T4. In order to compensate for the low number of valid subjects at T4, the scores the larger pool of valid subjects at T3 ($N = 25$) obtained for the perception and production tasks across data collection times were also independently analysed. This allowed us to obtain more robust measures of the scores obtained at T2 and T3 and to carry out a more reliable comparison of the gains in perceptual and productive ability obtained in the FI and the SA learning contexts. Data collection at T4 was originally planned to explore the extent to which hypothesised linguistic gains obtained through a SA term would be maintained or would be lost in the medium term, particularly in the absence of FI or exposure to the L2. Improvement, or even maintenance, of linguistic gains at T4 would therefore be suggestive of positive mid-term effects of SA on the learners' perceptual and productive phonological competence in English.

The categorial AX discrimination test

The effect of context of learning on the perception of English phonemic contrasts was assessed through a categorial AX auditory discrimination test containing 135 English word pairs expressing nine phonemic contrasts through minimal pairs. The words constituting the aural stimuli for the perception test were read on a falling tone from the screen of a laptop computer by a native speaker of British English as they appeared on Microsoft PowerPoint slides at regular intervals and were digitally recorded in a soundproof booth. The test contained 108 minimal pairs (15 per contrast) and 27 same-word pairs (distractors). The target contrasting phonemes in the minimal pairs were presented in a variety of phonetic environments and in alternating order at an inter-stimulus interval of 1 second and an inter-trial interval of 3 seconds. The word pairs were presented in two blocks (vowels vs. consonants) in randomised order and distributed in six sections of 20–25 trials each.

Table 11.1 Distribution of item types according to phonemic contrast

Phonemic Contrasts (PhCs)			Examples	Word pairs		
				Minimal pairs	Distractors	Total
PhC1	/iː/-/ɪ/	Tense vs. lax	Feet–fit	12	3	15
PhC2	/æ/-/ʌ/	Front vs. central	Began–begun	12	3	15
PhC3	/æ/-/ɑː/	Front vs. back	Back–bark	12	3	15
PhC4	/ɪ/-/ə/	Close front vs. central	Illusion–allusion	12	3	15
PhC5	/e/-/eə/	Front mid vs. centring diphthong	Belly–barely	12	3	15
PhC6	/t/-/d/	Voicing	Card–surd cart	12	3	15
PhC7	/s/-/z/	Voicing	Loose–lose	12	3	15
PhC8	/tʃ/-/dʒ/	Voicing	Choke–joke	12	3	15
PhC9	/d/-/ð/	Alveolar plosive vs. dental fricative	Breathing–breeding	12	3	15
Total				108	27	135

The phonemic contrasts (see Table 11.1) were selected on the basis of their relative difficulty for Catalan-Spanish speakers (Cebrián, 2006; Mora, 2005a). These contrasts are predicted to cause perceptual difficulties to Catalan-Spanish learners of English by current L2 speech-learning models, such as Flege's (1995) SLM or Best's (1995) Perceptual Assimilation model (PAM). On the one hand, the vowels in the contrasts /iː/-/ɪ/, /æ/-/ʌ/-/ɑː/ and /e/-/eə/ fall within the perceptual space of a single vowel category in Catalan and Spanish: /i/, /a/ and /e/, respectively (see Figure 11.2). On the other hand, the voicing contrasts examined (/t/-/d/, /s/-/z/, /tʃ/-/dʒ/) exist in Catalan at the phonemic level (only /t/-/d/ exists in Spanish), but do not occur in the positions in which

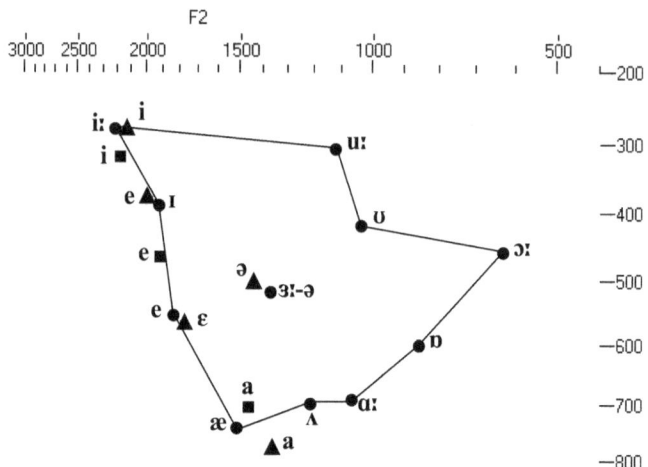

Figure 11.2 Vowel format plot for British English vowels (●), Spanish (■) /i/, /e/ and /a/, and Catalan (▲) /i/, /e/, /ɛ/, /a/ and /ə/. The F1 and F2 values (male voice in citation forms) from Deterding (1997) for English, Recasens (1991) for Catalan and Martínez-Celdrán *et al.* (2003) for Castilian Spanish

they appear in the English minimal pairs in the discrimination task and are therefore likely to perceptually assimilate to the corresponding voiceless Catalan and Spanish categories /t/, /s/ and /tʃ/.

The AX test was administered in a language lab and the stimuli were presented aurally over headphones. The instructions for the test and six preliminary examples for practice were presented to the subjects in written form as well as aurally, whereas the test word pairs were provided aurally only; the subjects were asked to put a tick in a box marked 'S' for 'same' or 'D' for 'different' according to whether they had heard the two items in the word pair as the 'same' word or as two 'different' words.

VOT in voiceless oral stop production

The effect of context of learning on the production of English oral stops was assessed through the analysis of VOT durations. Cross-linguistic research has shown that English and Catalan-Spanish speakers consistently differ with respect to VOT duration in the production of voiceless oral stops, which present a long-lag (aspirated) realisation in English vs. a short-lag (non-aspirated) realisation in Catalan and Spanish. The time between closure release and the onset of vocal cord vibration in the production of English word initial /p t k/ ranges from 40 ms to 80 ms approximately, whereas in Romance languages the characteristic VOT range for voiceless stops is 0–30 ms. Early learners of English living in the L2 community whose L1 has short-lag stops manage to increase VOT significantly when producing English long-lag stops, but fail to realise English stops authentically, producing VOT values that fall between the long-lag VOT range of English stops and the short-lag VOT range of their native language (Flege et al., 1998). The present study, however, focuses on Catalan-Spanish speakers who first started learning English as adults (i.e. late learners) in a formal instruction context, rather than in an immersion context where they are massively exposed to English. In accordance with the SLM, it was assumed that the English learners in this study would produce English stops inaccurately because the degree of perceived phonetic dissimilarity between English and Spanish /p t k/ is relatively small and essentially based on VOT duration differences. English /p t k/ will be perceptually linked to the corresponding Catalan-Spanish oral stop categories /p t k/ to which they will be assigned, thus preventing L2 sound category formation and creating a merged L2–L1 sound category for /p t k/. Consequently, Catalan-Spanish learners are expected to produce English /p t k/ with compromise VOT values. It was hypothesised that exposure to English, particularly during the three-month SA period, would have some effect on the learners' production of English stops: learners were expected to obtain greater gains in VOT values at T3 than at T2. If modification of glottal–supraglottal timing is directly affected by exposure to English and amount of language use, then we would expect VOT values at T4 to decrease after a six-month period without formal instruction or exposure to English.

The production data analysed were obtained from a reading aloud task. The task was performed individually in sound-proof booths and the speech samples were recorded on tape, digitised (22.05 kHz, 16 bit) and computer-edited for subsequent acoustic analysis. Only the stops in the reading passage that were phonologically voiceless (i.e. /p t k/), word-initial and followed by a stressed vowel were included in the VOT analysis. There were seven bilabial stops (*people* ×4, *period, passports, put*), six alveolar stops (*time, take, tickets, tight, tour, talk*) and two velar stops (*catching, currency*), i.e., 15 word-initial voiceless stops ×16 valid subjects at T4 × 4 data collection times, which resulted in a total of 960 VOT measurements. The VOT values were obtained by measuring the distance in milliseconds from sound waveforms and wide-band spectrograms between the onset of the release burst and the first vertical striations corresponding to the first positive peak of periodic energy in the waveform representing the onset of vocal cord vibration.

Data analysis and results

AX discrimination test

The subjects' scores on the AX discrimination test ($N = 15$ at T4) were submitted to a one-way repeated measures ANOVA (see the means [M] and standard deviations [SD] in Table 11.2), with *time* as the within-subject factor (i.e. the independent variable) and the four data collection times (T1, T2, T3, T4) as the within-subjects variables. The results revealed an overall significant effect for *time* ($F[3,12] = 15.91$, $p < 0.0005$) with a very large effect size (multivariate partial eta squared $= 0.8$) on the subjects' performance, showing a steady improvement in subjects' ability to perceive phonological contrasts in English (see Figure 11.3). The subjects' responses to the 27 same-word pairs functioning as distractors in the AX test (3 per contrast) were not included in the statistical analysis. However, despite this trend towards a general improvement, further paired comparisons revealed that only the differences between the subjects' scores at T1 and T2 (after the formal instruction period) were significant ($p = 0.001$). The gains the subjects obtained at T3 with respect to T2 (i.e. after the SA period) and at T4 with respect to T3 (i.e. after 80 hours of formal instruction and a six-month period without exposure to English) did not reach statistical significance ($p = 0.071$ for T2–T3 and $p = 0.251$ for T3–T4). A T2–T4 paired comparison, however, did show a significant difference ($p = 0.003$). Due to the low number of valid subjects at T4 ($N = 15$) and in order to confirm the general improvement in perceptual ability observed between T1 and T2 and between T2 and T3, the scores of a larger pool of subjects ($N = 25$), those measured at T1, T2 and T3, were submitted to a one-way repeated measures ANOVA. The results confirmed an overall significant effect for *time* ($F[2,23] = 26.48$, $p < 0.0005$) and further paired comparisons revealed again significant differences between T1 and T2 ($p < 0.0005$), but not between T2 and T3 ($p = 0.114$).

The same pattern of results is obtained when the mean percent correct discrimination scores are examined according to phonemic contrast type: vowels (Vs = PhC1–5), consonant voicing (Con.Voice = PhC6–8) and /d/-/ð/, with all contrast type differences being significant between T1 and T2 both at T3 ($N = 25$; $F[2,23] = 25.48$, $p < 0.0005$ for vowels; $F[2,23] = 13.21$, $p = 0.001$ for consonant voicing; and $F[2,23] = 7.78$, $p = 0.009$ for /d/-/ð/) and at T4 ($N = 15$; $F[3,12] = 7.93$, $p = 0.004$ for vowels; $F[3,12] = 11.11$, $p = 0.007$ for consonant voicing; and $F[2,23] = 7.78$, $p = 0.009$ for /d/-/ð/), but not between T2 and T3

Table 11.2 Mean correct percentage discrimination (Standard deviations in parentheses) in the AX discrimination test for valid subjects at T4 ($N = 15$) and valid subjects at T3 ($N = 25$)

Mean %		PhC1 /i:/-/ɪ/	PhC2 /æ/-/ʌ/	PhC3 /æ/-/ɑː/	PhC4 /ɪ/-/ə/	PhC5 /e/-/eə/	PhC6 /t/-/d/	PhC7 /s/-/z/	PhC8 /tʃ/-/dʒ/	PhC9 /d/-/ð/	Vs	CVoice	PhCs
Valid subjects at T4 ($N = 15$)	T1	80.55 (18.00)	86.67 (19.36)	95.56 (8.83)	96.67 (6.9)	61.67 (15.69)	80 (17.48)	55.56 (24.53)	86.11 (8.72)	65 (15.17)	84.22 (11.46)	73.89 (13.96)	78.64 (10.92)
	T2	87.22 (17.78)	91.11 (11.56)	98.33 (4.67)	97.22 (5.14)	73.89 (11.73)	86.11 (12.47)	64.44 (25.68)	91.11 (8.01)	71.11 (15.06)	89.56 (7.9)	80.55 (11.64)	84.51 (8.07)
	T3	86.67 (24.35)	92.78 (15.39)	98.33 (6.45)	96.11 (9.38)	80.56 (9.27)	91.67 (9.45)	70 (22.89)	92.22 (8.01)	77.78 (18.28)	90.89 (11.77)	84.63 (11.35)	87.35 (11.03)
	T4	91.67 (17.82)	94.44 (13.24)	97.22 (10.76)	98.33 (6.45)	85 (11.44)	90.56 (13.31)	73.33 (22.32)	91.67 (7.72)	77.22 (17.95)	93.33 (11.07)	85.19 (12.97)	88.82 (10.46)
Valid subjects at T3 ($N = 25$)	T1	72.67 (20.35)	77.33 (26.19)	94 (10.63)	92.33 (9.6)	60.33 (15.27)	72.67 (20.06)	48.33 (23.56)	81.67 (10.49)	57.33 (17.23)	79.33 (13.06)	67.56 (15.33)	72.96 (12.83)
	T2	81.67 (21.25)	83 (20.76)	93.67 (13.67)	96.33 (6.4)	70 (12.27)	79.67 (15.61)	57.33 (25.95)	85.33 (11.1)	66.67 (15.77)	84.93 (12.03)	74.11 (14.07)	79.30 (11.32)
	T3	81.67 (23.81)	83.67 (23.75)	95 (12.5)	95.67 (7.65)	76 (11.86)	83.67 (18.4)	59.67 (25.65)	87.33 (11.81)	69.67 (19.97)	86.4 (13.23)	76.89 (16.41)	81.37 (13.71)

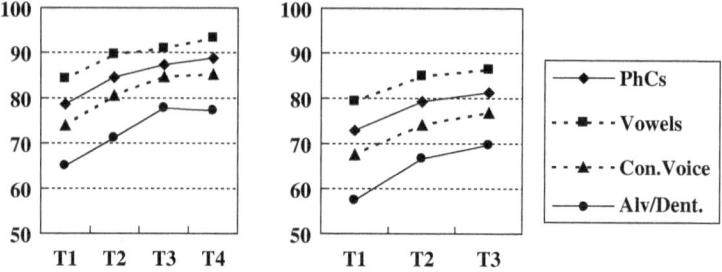

Figure 11.3 Mean percentage correct responses in the AX discrimination test at T4 ($N = 15$) and at T3 ($N = 25$)

(except for consonant voicing at T4: $F[3,12] = 11.11$, $p = 0.008$) and between T3 and T4 (see Figure 11.3).

As expected, scores were found to vary substantially across phonemic contrasts, with mean percent discrimination ranging from chance level (50% correct discrimination) for the consonant voicing contrast /s/-/z/ at T1 ($M = 48.33$, $SD = 23.56$) to near 100% correct discrimination for the vowel quality contrast /æ/-/ɑː/ at T3 ($M = 98.33$, $SD = 6.45$). This variability in perceptual ability across vowel contrasts may be accounted for by predictions of SLM and PAM. For example, the higher mean percentage of correct discrimination obtained for /æ/-/ɑː/ ($M = 81.33\%$ across T1–T2–T3, $N = 25$) with respect to /æ/-/ʌ/ (94.22%) is to be attributed to the fact that English /æ/ and /ʌ/ constitute better exemplars of Catalan and Spanish /a/ than English /ɑː/ (see Figure 11.2). Thus, as predicted by SLM and PAM, discrimination was poorer for the /iː/-/ɪ/ and /æ/-/ɑː/ contrasts than for the other vowel contrasts in the AX task.

Variability in perceptual ability across voicing contrasts in obstruents, however, cannot directly be accounted for only by reference to cross-linguistic differences with respect to allophonic or phonemic distribution or the way the voicing distinction is implemented. For example, in word-final position the voicing contrasts in /s/-/z/ and /t/-/d/ are implemented similarly (i.e. through duration differences) and they do not differ with respect to how they are mapped onto their corresponding Catalan-Spanish categories in this particular context, and yet discrimination results are much poorer for the /s/-/z/ contrast ($M = 55.11\%$ across T1–T2–T3, $N = 25$) than for the /t/-/d/ contrast (78.67%). Differences in the inherent or cross-linguistic perceptual salience of sounds, or in the functional load of phonemic contrasts in the subjects' L1 and L2, might be responsible for the differences in perceptual ability observed across the voicing contrasts. The mean percent correct discrimination scores are on average 8.43% (range 6.26–10.33%) higher for vowel contrasts than for the consonant voicing contrasts at T4 ($N = 15$) and 10.7% (range 9.51–11.77%) higher at T3 ($N = 25$).

This relatively large difference in the mean scores between vowel quality and consonant voicing contrasts is maintained across data collection times and suggests that the subjects' performance on the perception test is substantially poorer on consonant voicing contrasts (and even poorer on the /d/-/ð/ contrast) than on vowel quality contrasts. Vowel contrasts are known to present less perceptual difficulty in a discrimination task than certain consonant contrasts (e.g. voicing) and may even yield near-ceiling discrimination scores for non-native vowels classified as instances of a single native category (Højen & Flege, 2006). The lack of significant improvement in the discrimination of vowel contrasts at T3 and at T4 could therefore be attributed to ceiling effects. Examination of frequency data revealed that for two of the vowel contrasts, PhC3 (/æ/-/ɑː/) and PhC4 (/ɪ/-/ə/) this was indeed the case, with more than 70% of the subjects obtaining mean correct discrimination scores above 90% already at T1. The performance of a group of native speakers of British English ($N = 6$) on a similar AX discrimination test (Mora, 2005b) was used here as baseline data. Consequently, there was very little possibility of subjects improving their scores across subsequent data collection times. For the other vowel and consonant contrasts ceiling effects were much less severe, with only some subjects (2–4) obtaining 100% correct responses for some of the contrasts. Statistically significant differences between mean percent correct discrimination scores across data collection times were found for seven phonemic contrasts out of nine at T2.

Despite the overall improvement, however, only two of the seven phonemic contrasts for which a statistically significant gain was observed at T2 present significant gains at T3 (PhC5 and PhC6), and such gains are relatively small with respect to gains at T2. At T4 ($N = 15$) none of the phonemic contrasts examined presented significant gains in correct discrimination with respect to T3, and four of the contrasts (PhC3, PhC6, PhC8 and PhC9) presented slight non-significant loss of discrimination ability.

These results suggest that the FI period had a greater effect on the subjects' ability to perceive non-native phonemic contrasts than a three-month SA period. Despite the lack of significant differences between T3 and T4, the fact that subjects' scores on the AX test do not drop significantly after a period without FI/exposure to the L2 might suggest that the learners managed to keep the gains in perceptual ability obtained over time. In order to obtain an estimate of the differential effect of the AH and the SA learning contexts on the subjects' perceptual ability, the size of the effect of the independent variable (*time: data collection times*), as measured by *eta squared* values (0.01 = small effect; 0.06 = moderate effect; 0.14 = large effect) was calculated on the basis of a series of paired-samples *t*-tests comparing the AX test mean percent correct discrimination scores (T1 vs. T2, T2 vs. T3, and T3 vs. T4).

The mean percentage difference between data collection times and the *eta squared* values showed that significant differences (i.e. $p < 0.05$) in mean percent correct discrimination across data collection times always represent an improvement in perceptual ability. The graphs in Figure 11.4 and Figure 11.5 represent the size of the gains in mean percent correct discrimination across data collection times. When the difference in mean percent correct discrimination across data collection times (T1 vs. T2, T2 vs. T3, and T3 vs. T4) was analysed according to phonological contrast type (Vowels, Con.Voice), gains were always found to be greater between T1 and T2 (range +0.33% to +9.67%) than between T2 and T3 (range 0.00% to +6.00%) or between T3 and T4 (range −1.11% to +5.00%), suggesting that the FI period had a greater effect on the subjects' perceptual phonological competence than the SA term (see Figure 11.4). This pattern of results is also obtained (with the exception of PhC3) when gains in vowel quality and consonant voicing contrasts are independently analysed for the nine phonemic contrasts in the AX test (see Figure 11.5).

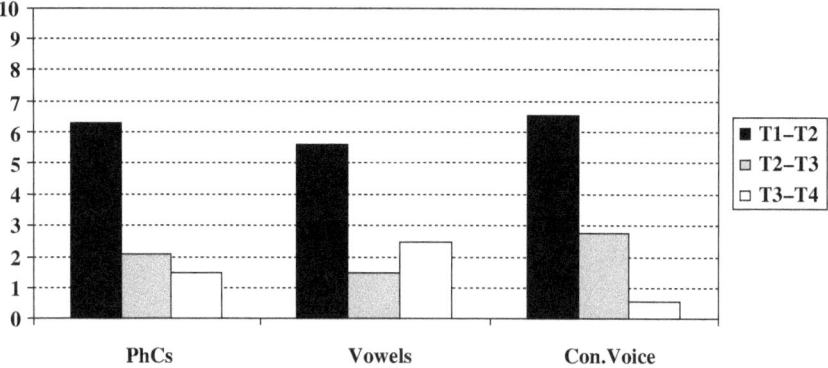

Figure 11.4 Mean percent correct discrimination gains according to phonemic contrast type

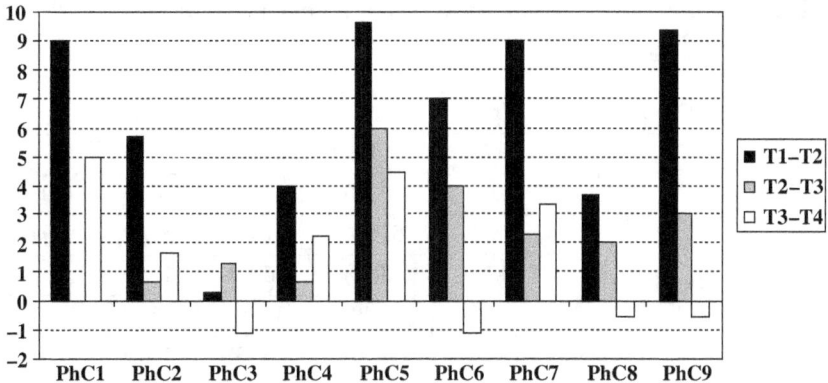

Figure 11.5 Mean percent correct discrimination gains according to phonemic contrast

The subjects' performance on the perception test, therefore, revealed a steady improvement across data collection times characterised by statistically significant gains occurring during the FI period (T1–T2) and much smaller non-significant gains occurring during the SA term (T2–T3) and the period without FI/exposure (T3–T4). The FI period in the home university, but not the SA term, exerts a significant positive influence in the subjects' ability to discriminate phonemic contrasts.

VOT analysis

The VOT durations were submitted to a one-way repeated measures ANOVA (see the M and SD values in Table 11.3) with *time* as the within-subject factor and the four data collection times (T1, T2, T3, T4) as the within-subjects variables. The results show an overall effect for *time* ($F[3,13] = 5.41$, $p = 0.012$) with a large effect size (multivariate eta squared $= 0.56$). However, as may be inferred from the mean VOT values plotted in Figure 11.6, further paired comparisons revealed that the difference between the means was significant only at T4 ($p = 0.006$). Except for /k/, of which only two VOT measures were obtained, the same pattern of results is obtained when the mean VOT durations are examined for each oral stop individually.

As expected, the measures obtained show that Catalan-Spanish learners of English produce VOT values (mean 36.60–40.11 ms) that are longer than the typical VOT values reported for voiceless oral stops in Catalan and Spanish (0–30 ms) but shorter than the typical English

Table 11.3 Mean VOT duration (Standard deviations in parentheses) in word-initial oral stops for valid subjects at T4 ($N = 16$) and valid subjects at T3 ($N = 25$)

Mean VOT (ms)		/p/	/t/	/k/	/p t/	/p t k/
Valid subjects at T4 ($N = 16$)	T1	26.70	54.49	38.97	53.95	39.46
		(8.02)	(19.78)	(13.36)	(14.20)	(10.55)
	T2	27.32	53.40	41.75	54.02	39.68
		(9.13)	(13.54)	(16.41)	(13.20)	(9.57)
	T3	28.26	54.40	38.79	55.45	40.12
		(7.22)	(14.30)	(10.33)	(11.74)	(8.01)
	T4	25.41	50.11	35.29	50.46	36.60
		(7.37)	(13.47)	(9.28)	(12.08)	(8.34)
Valid subjects at T3 ($N = 25$)	T1	28.43	54.03	40.39	41.23	40.95
		(7.99)	(19.78)	(15.23)	(11.08)	(11.22)
	T2	29.09	53.06	42.80	41.08	41.65
		(8.41)	(13.54)	(14.50)	(9.45)	(10.03)
	T3	31.37	56.68	42.01	44.02	43.35
		(9.06)	(14.30)	(14.02)	(11.19)	(10.76)

VOT durations for such stops (the mean VOT values obtained from the production of the target oral stops by two English native speakers was 68.83 ms). The results at T4 ($N = 16$) suggest that neither the FI nor the SA periods have an effect on the learners' production of English stops: T1 and T2 means are almost identical, and the slight increase in VOT values at T3 is not significant (a T1–T3 paired comparison did not reveal a significant increase in VOT duration either), suggesting that neither the FI nor the SA periods had a positive effect on the subject's VOT. The much shorter VOT values obtained at T4, however, indicate that the one-year period without FI/exposure to English did have a negative effect on the subjects' degree of accuracy in the production of English stops. When all valid subjects at T3 ($N = 25$) were included in the analysis, no overall significant effect of *time* on VOT duration was observed either ($F[2,23] = 0.79$, $p = 0.467$). Further paired tests confirmed the lack of significant gains in VOT duration between T1 and T2 and revealed a tendency for VOT values to increase slightly at T3 (see Figure 11.6), but

Acquisition of a Second Language Phonology

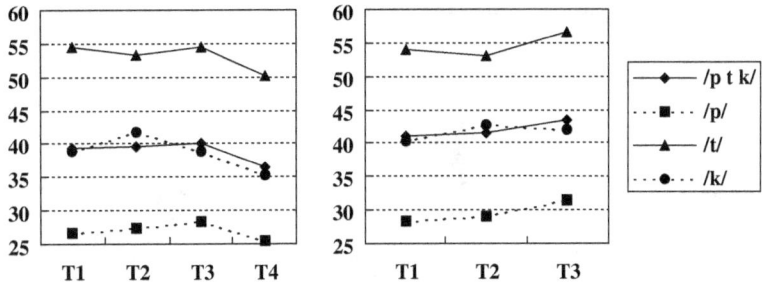

Figure 11.6 Mean VOT values in milliseconds at T4 ($N = 16$) and at T3 ($N = 25$)

the difference between the means at T2 and T3 did not reach statistical significance ($p = 0.382$).

The standard deviations in Table 11.3 indicate huge variability in the range of VOT durations obtained according to oral stop. Given the relative small number of stop consonants measured (15), the uneven distribution of stop consonants according to place of articulation (7 labials, 6 alveolars and 2 velars), and the difference in the mean VOT durations obtained between /p/, /t/ and /k/, it seemed appropriate to analyse the data for each stop independently. The fact that the mean VOT values obtained for /k/ were based on the measurement of only two /k/ tokens could have seriously affected the reliability of overall means obtained by averaging the results obtained for each oral stop (except for /k/, mean VOT was always longer at T3 than at T2), so the results are also reported for /p t/ excluding /k/.

The differential effect of the AH and the SA learning contexts on the subjects' ability to produce oral stops with longer VOT values was explored by comparing mean VOT gains in milliseconds across data collection times. Effect sizes (*eta squared*) were calculated on the basis of a series of paired-samples *t*-tests comparing the mean VOT values (T1 vs. T2, T2 vs. T3, and T3 vs. T4). These data showed that at T2 the subjects' production of /p t k/ did not present any noticeable pattern of VOT duration gain or loss with respect to the measures obtained at T1, except for /k/, for which a non-significant noticeable gain in VOT duration (2.41 ms) is observed. At T3 a slight increase in VOT duration is observed for /p/ and /t/, but it did not reach statistical significance. At T4, however, VOT values show a consistent decrease in duration for all oral stops, suggesting that the one-year period without FI/exposure to English had

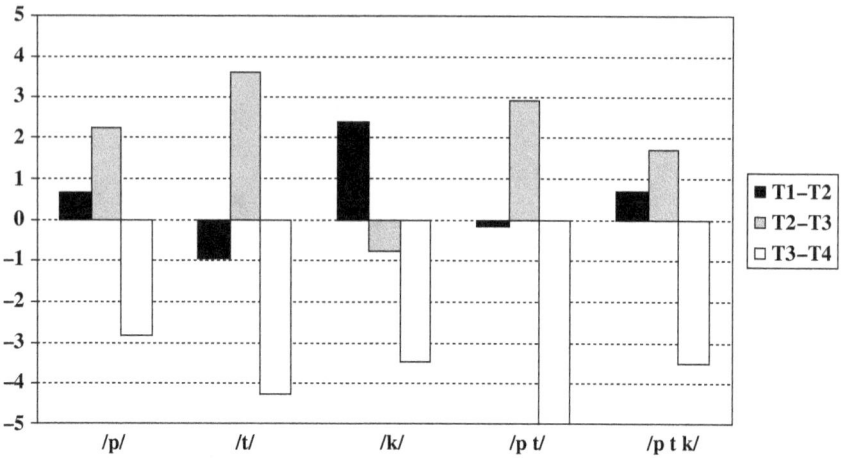

Figure 11.7 Mean VOT gains according to oral stop

a negative effect on the subjects' ability to produce /p t k/ with longer VOT durations (see Figure 11.7). Paired comparisons revealed that the shorter VOT values obtained at T4 with respect to T3 were statistically significant for /p t k/ ($p = 0.006$), for /p t/ ($p = 0.011$) (i.e. when /k/ was excluded), and for /p/ ($p = 0.023$) (the size of the effect was very large in these cases: *eta squared* = 0.41, 0.36, 0.30, respectively).

Independent evidence for the robustness of the slight increase in VOT between T2 and T3 may be provided by speech rate. The speech rate measure used was *Speech Rate in Syllables* (SRS), which was obtained by measuring (from sound waveforms) the time the subjects took to read the 152-word passage and then calculating the number of syllables uttered per second, including pause time (Riggenbach, 1991). The results reveal a considerable increase in speech rate in syllables (SRS) at T3, that is, a decrease in the total amount of time (TT) needed to read aloud the 152 words in the text and a general T1–T3 increase in speech rate (see Figure 11.8).

The speech rate measures obtained were submitted to a one-way repeated measures ANOVA (see the M and SD in Table 11.4) with *time* as the within-subject factor and the four data collection times ($N = 16$) as the within-subjects variables. The results show an overall effect for *time* ($F[3,13] = 5.87$, $p = 0.009$) with a large effect size (multivariate *eta squared* = 0.57). Further paired comparisons revealed that the difference between the means was only significant at T3 ($p = 0.048$). The results of

Acquisition of a Second Language Phonology

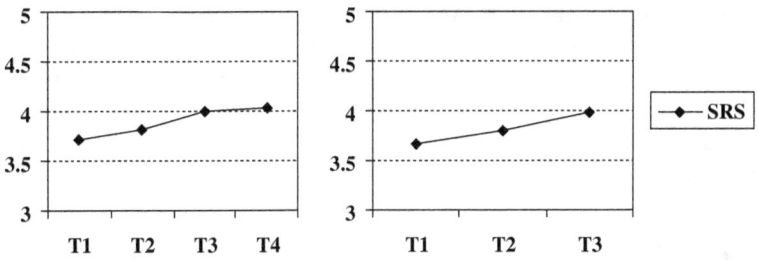

Figure 11.8 Mean speech rate in syllables per second (SRS) at T4 ($N = 16$) and T3 ($N = 25$)

the statistical analysis (ANOVA) for valid subjects at T3 (T1–T2–T3; $N = 25$) further confirm the increase of speech rate across data collection times ($F[2,23] = 12.92$, $p < 0.0005$; partial *eta squared* = 0.53) and the significant gains in speech rate between T2 and T3 ($p = 0.008$). The fact that a longer mean VOT at T3 with respect to T2 was maintained

Table 11.4 Mean speech rate (Standard deviations in parentheses) in total time taken to read the 152-word text (TT) and in syllables per second (SRS) for valid subjects at T4 ($N = 16$) and valid subjects at T3 ($N = 25$)

Speech Rate (SRS)		TT (s)	SRS (syllables/s)
Valid subjects at T4 ($N = 16$)	T1	57.14	3.71
		(5.54)	(0.37)
	T2	55.62	3.81
		(5.92)	(0.42)
	T3	52.80	4.00
		(3.93)	(0.38)
	T4	52.46	4.03
		(4.70)	(0.37)
Valid subjects at T3 ($N = 25$)	T1	57.93	3.66
		(6.58)	(0.39)
	T2	55.74	3.80
		(4.90)	(0.34)
	T3	53.10	3.99
		(4.38)	(0.31)

despite the significant increase in speech rate supports the view that the SA period had some effect on the subjects' VOT. Thus, contrary to what one might expect if a faster speech rate caused shortening of the VOT in the production of the English stops (e.g. Schmidt & Flege, 1996), mean VOT was longer at T3 with respect to T2 despite the significant increase in speech rate.

Discussion

The results of the AX discrimination task and the VOT analysis suggest that the learning contexts examined (an 80-hour FI period, a three-month SA term and a period without FI/exposure to English) do not have the same effects on the subjects' perceptual ability as on their productive ability with respect to the degree of gain obtained across data collection times. Thus, at least for the phonetic/phonological dimensions analysed in the present study, the differential effect of FI and SA on phonological competence manifests itself differently in the perceptual and productive domains; whereas segmental perceptual ability, as assessed through a categorial discrimination task, improves steadily over time and significant gains are mainly obtained after a period of FI (i.e. between T1 and T2), segmental productive ability, as assessed through VOT duration in voiceless oral stops, improves little over time but substantial gains were obtained after the SA term (T2 vs. T3 gains). Moreover, whereas at T4, after a period without FI/exposure to English, gains in perceptual ability were maintained, there was a significant loss in productive ability (i.e. a sharp decline in VOT duration).

These results, if confirmed by research conducted with a larger pool of learners and using improved testing instruments capable of avoiding ceiling effects (e.g. Pérez-Vidal *et al.*, 2006), have important implications for future research on the effects of learning contexts on L2 phonological acquisition. For example, certain aspects of L2 speech segmental accuracy, such as the laryngeal timing patterns responsible for VOT duration in voiceless oral stops investigated in the present study, may be more sensitive to short-term immersion periods than other productive or perceptual characteristics of L2 speech and may prove more successful in detecting modest gains in L2 phonological competence than more holistic measures of pronunciation improvement such as foreign accent ratings by L2 native speakers. Similarly, the learners' performance on a categorial AX discrimination task is highly dependent on the stage of development of their L2 perceptual system and the interactions between their L1 and L2 phonetic sub-systems. Consequently, short-term immersion is unlikely to produce the type of dramatic gains in perceptual ability that might be achieved through long-term immersion and a categorial discrimination task may be unsuitable for capturing the type of gains in perceptual ability that might result from short-term immersion. Some of the methodological aspects discussed in this chapter concerning the design of testing instruments, the choice of the phonetic/phonological dimension under investigation, or the learners' level of competence in the L2, were not fully successful in avoiding ceiling effects, which represents a serious shortcoming when assessing the benefits of an SA experience on a group of advanced learners of English in terms of gains in perceptual and productive phonetic/phonological ability. Research investigating the benefits of short-term SA periods on phonological acquisition should carefully consider the reasons for investigating a particular phonetic/phonological dimension and should approach the design of testing instruments accordingly.

Conclusions

In the present study, advanced learners' ability to auditorily discriminate between English contrastive sound units was found to improve over time as a result of the two different contexts of learning in which formal instruction took place: a two-term period in the home university and a one-term SA period. However, it is only at T2 (after a formal instruction period in the home university) that statistically significant gains were obtained. The SA term, therefore, had relatively little effect on the overall improvement of learners' perceptual phonetic/phonological ability when compared to the at-home FI period. At T4, after a period without FI/exposure to English, no significant loss in perceptual ability was observed, suggesting that the overall improvement trend in the discrimination of non-native phonemic contrasts was maintained even in the absence of FI/exposure to English. These results are consistent with the results for some of the fluency, complexity and accuracy measures obtained by Pérez-Vidal and Juan-Garau (2006) with respect to writing in a study conducted with the same group of subjects. It was expected, however, that due to an intensive period of exposure to the spoken language in a linguistic immersion context, the SA term would have a much greater effect on the subject's perceptual phonological competence than on the subjects' writing skills. Although significant gains in perceptual ability were also expected to be greater after a SA term than after a FI period, the findings of the present study, as in previous research (e.g. Díaz-Campos, 2004), point in the opposite direction. One possible explanation is to be sought in the type of SA experience the learners took part in: a three-month term may not be a long enough immersion period to produce significant gains in advanced learners' perceptual ability. However, it may also be argued that the experimental design used was not sensitive enough to be able to reveal significant gains in perceptual ability due to ceiling effects, at least for some of the phonemic contrasts examined.

The same group of learners were tested on their ability to produce English voiceless oral stops authentically (i.e. with long-lag VOT) in a reading-aloud task. VOT did not consistently improve over time as a function of learning context; the two-term FI period in the home university seemed to exert very little influence on the learners' laryngeal timing patterns. A greater influence of learning context was observed after a three-month SA period, which led to a slight (non-significant) but consistent increase in VOT duration. This is interpreted as the SA period having a positive effect on the subjects' articulatory timing patterns. Measurements at T4, however, revealed a significant decrease in VOT duration, which is interpreted as a significant loss in the learners' ability to produce oral stops accurately, suggesting that exposure to English is essential if learners' productive ability in terms of L2 laryngeal timing is to be maintained. Unlike the results obtained in the categorial discrimination task for the learners' perceptual ability, the results obtained in the VOT analysis suggest that the learners' ability to produce more English-like VOT in voiceless stops is more sensitive to the type of massive L2 exposure in SA contexts than to the more limited L2 exposure in an FI context.

For the advanced L2 learners in the present study, language-specific articulatory features such as the laryngeal timing patterns we measured through VOT duration were more sensitive to learning context, and therefore to type and amount of L2 exposure, than the type of speech perception ability we assessed through a categorial AX discrimination task. Despite the fact that the relative weight of FI and SA varied according to the phonetic/phonological contrast examined, both learning contexts had a positive effect on the subjects' perceptual and productive ability in English.

Acknowledgements

This research was supported by research grants BBF2001-0820 and HUM2004-05442-C02-01/FILO from the Spanish Ministry of Science and Education. I would like to thank Brian Mott for reading aloud the stimuli for the AX test, Marianna Nadeu for digitising the speech samples and taking most of the VOT measures, and all the UPF students who kindly volunteered to do the perception and production tests analysed in the present study. Special thanks are due to Carmen Pérez and Maria Juan for their patience and useful comments on earlier versions of this chapter.

References

Best, C. (1995) A direct realist view of cross-language speech perception. In W. Strange (ed.) *Speech Perception and Linguistic Experience: Theoretical and Methodological Issues* (pp. 171–204). Timonium, MD: York Press.

Cebrián, J. (2006) Experience and the use of non-native duration in L2 vowel categorization. *Journal of Phonetics* 34, 372–387.

Coleman, J.A. (1998) Language learning and study abroad: The European perspective. *Frontiers* 4, 167–203.

Collentine, J. (2004) The effects of learning contexts of morphosyntactic and lexical development. *Studies in Second Language Acquisition* 26, 277–248.

Collentine, J. and Freed, B.F. (2004) Learning contexts and its effects on second language acquisition: Introduction. *Studies in Second Language Acquisition* 26, 153–171.

DeKeyser (1991) Foreign language development during a semester abroad. In B. Freed (ed.) *Foreign Language Acquisition: Research and the Classroom* (pp. 104–119). Lexington, MA: D.C. Heath.

Deterding, D. (1997) The formants of monophthong vowels in Standard Southern British English pronunciation. *Journal of the International Phonetic Association* 27, 47–55.

Díaz-Campos, M. (2004) Context of learning in the acquisition of Spanish second language phonology. *Studies in Second Language Acquisition* 26, 249–273.

Flege, J.E. (1995) Second-language speech learning: Theory, findings and problems. In W. Strange (ed.) *Speech Perception and Linguistic Experience: Theoretical and Methodological Issues* (pp. 229–273). Timonium, MD: York Press.

Flege, J.E. (in press) Language contact in bilingualism: phonetic system interactions. In J. Cole and J. Hualde (eds) *Laboratory Phonology 9*. Berlin: Mouton de Gruyter.

Flege, J.E., Frieda, E.M., Walley, A.C. and Randazza, L.A. (1998) Lexical factors and segmental accuracy in second language speech production. *Studies in Second Language Acquisition* 20, 155–187.

Freed, B.F. (1995) What makes us think that students who study abroad become fluent? In B.F. Freed (ed.) *Second Language Acquisition in a Study Abroad Context* (pp. 123–148). Amsterdam: Benjamins.

Freed, B.F. (2000) Is fluency, like beauty, in the eyes (and ears) of the beholder? In H. Riggenbach (ed.) *Perspectives on Fluency* (pp. 243–265). Ann Arbor: The University of Michigan Press.

Højen, A. (2003) Second language speech perception and production in adult learners before and after short-term immersion. PhD thesis, University of Aarhus.

Højen, A. and Flege, J.E. (2006) Early learners' discrimination of second-language vowels. *Journal of the Acoustical Society of America* 119, 3072–3084.

Huebner, T. (1995) The effects of overseas language programs: Report on a case study of an intensive Japanese course. In B.F. Freed (ed.) *Second Language Acquisition in a Study Abroad Context* (pp. 171–193). Amsterdam: Benjamins.

Lafford, B. (2004) The effect of the context of learning on the use of communication strategies by learners of Spanish as a second language. *Studies in Second Language Acquisition* 26, 201–225.

Martínez-Celdrán, E., Fernández-Planas, A.M. and Carrera-Sabaté, J. (2003) Castilian Spanish. *Journal of the International Phonetic Association* 33 (2), 255–259.

Milton, J. and Meara, P. (1995) How periods abroad affect vocabulary growth in a foreign language. *Review of Applied Linguistics* 107–108, 17–34.

Mora, J.C. (2005a) Discrimination of vowel and voicing contrasts by Catalan/Spanish learners of English. Paper presented at the 29th AEDEAN Congress, Jaén, Spain: 15–17th December 2005.

Mora, J.C. (2005b) Lexical knowledge effects on the discrimination of non-native phonemic contrasts in words and nonwords by Catalan/Spanish bilingual learners of English. *Proceedings of the ISCA Workshop on Plasticity in Speech Perception* (pp. 43–46). London: Department of Phonetics and Linguistics, University College London.

Mora, J.C. (2006) Age effects on oral fluency development. In C. Muñoz (ed.) *Age and the Rate of Foreign Language Learning* (pp. 65–88). Clevedon: Multilingual Matters.

Pellegrino Aveni, V.A. (2005) *Study Abroad and Second Language Use: Constructing the Self*. Cambridge: Cambridge University Press.

Pérez-Vidal, C. and Juan-Garau, M. (2006) Oral and written competence in English after a 'Stay Abroad' period: Contrasting gains and contact effects. Paper presented at the 16th EuroSLA Conference, 13–16 September 2006, Antalya, Turkey.

Pérez-Vidal, C., Trenchs, M., Beattie, J., Figueras, N., Juan, M., McCullough, J., Mora, J.C., Prieto, J.I., Salazar, J. and Varela, J.R. (2006) El factor 'Estancia en el país de lengua meta' en la adquisición de una lengua extranjera (inglés) a corto y medio plazo: Objetivos y metodología del proyecto. *Stay Abroad and Language Acquisition (SALA) Project*. Paper presented at the 24th AESLA Conference, March 30–April 1 2006, Madrid, Spain.

Recasens, D. (1991) *Fonètica descriptiva del català*. Barcelona: Institut d'Estudis Catalans.

Regan, V. (1995) The acquisition of sociolinguistics native speech norms. Effects of a year abroad on second language learners of French. In B. Freed (ed.) *Second Language Acquisition in a Study Abroad Context* (pp. 245–267). Amsterdam: John Benjamins.

Riggenbach, H. (1991) Toward an understanding of fluency: A microanalysis of nonnative speaker conversations. *Discourse Processes* 14, 423–441.

Schmidt, A.M. and Flege, J.E. (1996) Speaking rate effects on stops produced by Spanish and English monolinguals and Spanish/English bilinguals. *Phonetica* 53, 162–179.

Segalowitz, N. and Freed, B. (2004) Context, contact, and cognition in oral fluency acquistion: Learning Spanish in at home and study abroad contexts. *Studies in Second Language Acquistion* 26, 173–199.

Towell, R. (2002) Relative degrees of fluency: A comparative case study of advanced learners of French. *International Review of Applied Linguistics* 40, 117–150.

Trenchs, M., Juan-Garau, M., Mora, J.C. and Pérez-Vidal, C. (2006) El factor 'estancia en el país de la lengua meta' en la adquisición de una lengua extrnjera (inglés) a corto y medio plazo: Objectivos y metodología de un estudio en proceso. Paper presented at the 24th AESLA Applied Linguistics Congress, Madrid, Spain: March 30–April 1 2006.

Turell, M., Beattie, J., Fontana, J.M., Forcadell, M., González, M., Juan, M., McNally, L., Mora, J.C., Pérez-Vidal, C., Vallduví, E. and Varela, J.R. (2005) La estandarización de las pruebas en un estudio sobre los efectos de la movilidad (estancia en el país de lengua meta) en la competencia oral y escrita de los estudiantes de inglés universitarios. In J.M. Oro, J. Varela Zapata and J. Anderson (eds) *La Enseñanza de las Lenguas en una Europa Multicultural* (pp. 117–134). Santiago de Compostela: Servizo de Publicacións e Intercambio Científico.

Chapter 12
Non-Adult Long-Distance wh- Questions in the Non-Native Acquisition of English

JUNKAL GUTIERREZ MANGADO and
MARÍA DEL PILAR GARCÍA MAYO

Introduction

One of the most long-standing discussions in the generative literature on second language (L2) acquisition revolves around whether older subjects acquire an L2 in the same way as children acquire their first language (L1). L1 acquisition is assumed to be guided by innate principles made available by Universal Grammar (UG), which constrains the hypothesis space for formulating the grammars underlying the language children are acquiring. The question that arises in L2 acquisition is whether it is also constrained by the same UG principles that guide L1 acquisition or whether L2 subjects resort to general learning mechanisms.

Traditionally, two main hypotheses have been proposed in the literature regarding the presence of UG in L2 acquisition. One of the hypotheses, the *No Access* Hypothesis, states that L2 learners cannot access the same linguistic mechanisms as L1 learners. Researchers such as Bley-Vroman (1990), Clahsen and Muysken (1986) and Schachter (1988) claim that what guides the L2 learner is not UG, as understood in L1 acquisition, and that any access to UG would be through the L1 grammar. Under this view, the process of acquiring an L2 is guided by other mechanisms such as general learning strategies.

The second hypothesis related to the role of UG in L2 acquisition contends that L2 learners have *Access* to UG in that UG in its entirety constrains L2 acquisition (Epstein *et al.*, 1996; Flynn, 1987).

A variant of the Access Hypothesis, the Full Transfer/Full Access Hypothesis (FT/FA) (Schwartz & Sprouse, 1996) claims that both UG and the L1 are responsible for L2 acquisition. More specifically, Schwartz and Sprouse (1996) and White (2003) argue that the L2 subjects' initial state corresponds to the entire L1 grammar (all abstract properties but excluding specific lexical items). When the L2 input data cannot be accommodated by the L1 grammar, then UG may guide resetting the parameter in question from the L1 to the L2 value. In other words, when the L1 and the L2 grammars differ in certain aspects, the L2 learner can access the options allowed by UG and choose the option found in the L2.

In this chapter we explore the different predictions made by the Access/No Access hypotheses referred to above on the role of UG and the L1 in L2 acquisition in the light of data obtained from an oral production task eliciting L2 English long-distance (LD) wh- questions of the type in (1)[1]:

(1) Who do you think John loves?

The next section briefly surveys the different options for LD wh- question formation cross-linguistically in order to show some possibilities attested in natural languages and made available by UG. Special emphasis will be placed on the languages directly related to this investigation: English, our learners' target language, Basque and Spanish, their L1s. We then report on the findings in the acquisition literature on LD wh- questions, in particular on the L1 English study carried out by Thornton (1990) and L2 acquisition data by L1 Japanese learners (Wakabayashi & Okawara, 2003; Yamane, 2003), and specific predictions are put forward. The participants and elicitation procedure are next described, and finally results, discussion and conclusions.

Long-Distance wh- Questions Cross-Linguistically

A cross-linguistic examination of LD wh- movement questions reveals at least four different options.[2] Among wh- *in situ* languages, we have languages such as Japanese where the wh- phrase (*dare*) remains *in situ*, as shown in (2):

(2) (anata-wa) [kare-ga **dare**-o aisiteita to] omoimasu ka
    (you-TOP) he-NOM who-ACC loved COMP think Q
    'Who do you think he loved?'

                         (Wakabayashi & Okawara, 2003: 223)

Hindi, also a wh- *in situ* language, uses another strategy for LD wh- question formation: the wh- phrase in the embedded clause stays *in situ* and matrix scope is established by a wh- phrase in the form of 'what', as shown in (3):

(3) Raam-ne   **kyaa** kahaa thaa ki **kis-ne kis-ko** maaraa?
    Raam-erg.   WH   said   who   whom   hit
    'Who did Ram say hit whom?'

(Lutz *et al.*, 2000: 7)

Among wh- movement languages such as English (4), Basque (5) or Spanish[3] (6) we find that the wh- phrase in the embedded clause is pronounced in the left periphery[4] of the matrix clause, as illustrated below:

(4) Who do you think he kissed?
(5) Zer   uste duzu   ikusi   duela   Mirenek?
    what-ABS think aux   see   aux-comp   Miren-ERG
    'What do you think Mary saw?'
(6) Qué   crees   que ha visto María?
    what think-you that has seen Maria
    'What do you think that Mary has seen?'

Finally, among wh- movement languages we have languages such as German and Frisian, which make use of the so-called partial wh- movement structure. Frisian, as in (7), illustrates this option where one wh- phrase is pronounced in the left periphery of the embedded clause (*wa*) and another wh- phrase in the left periphery of the matrix clause (*wat*):

(7) **Wat** tinke   jo   **wa't**   ik sjoen haw?
    what think   you who-cl.   I seen have
    'Who do you think I have seen?'

(Hiemstra, 1986: 97)

As we have seen above, both the native (Spanish, Basque) and target languages (English) of our learners form LD wh- questions by moving the questioned wh- phrase to the left periphery of the matrix clause. Crucially, none of these languages makes use of the partial movement strategy, as (8) below illustrates for English:

(8) *What do you think who is coming today?

L1 and L2 Acquisition of LD wh- Questions

A look at previous research on the acquisition of LD wh- questions shows that L1 and L2 learners of English go through a stage where they produce partial wh- movement and wh- copying questions, structures that, as we have seen above, are allowed in natural languages but are completely absent from adult English. This section reviews L1 and L2 research eliciting LD wh- questions; in the study of the acquisition of L1 English LD wh- questions, Thornton (1990) shows that the non-adult questions produced by children are a reflection of UG, since they are an option completely absent in the adult language. The research on the acquisition of L2 English LD wh- questions by L1 Japanese learners concludes that non-adult questions arise due to the different parameter settings in the two languages involved. Specific predictions for the present study are then provided.

L1 acquisition of LD wh- questions

Pioneering work by Thornton (1990) on the acquisition of LD wh- questions showed that some children acquiring L1 English produced partial wh- movement and wh- copying questions.

In an oral experimental task Thornton (1990) and Thornton and Crain (1994) found that some of their children, ranging in age from 2;11 to 5;5 (mean 4;3), produced non-adult LD wh- questions. Example (9) features partial wh- movement and (10) wh- copying:

(9) What do you think *who* jumped over the can? (Thornton, 1990: 213)

(10) Who do you think *who* is in the box? (Thornton, 1990: 212)

The elicitation experiment used by Thornton engaged the children in a guessing game. They had to ask questions to a puppet called 'Ratty' manipulated by a researcher. Using this technique, Thornton elicited subject, object and adjunct questions. A careful examination of the non-adult questions led Thornton to conclude that they bore none of the hallmarks of performance errors. She showed that these non-adult questions were not the result of warm-up effects or tiredness and that they were not affected by length effects, as they appear both in shorter and longer questions. She also found that these non-adult questions were produced not only by younger children, who may be prone to make performance errors, but also by older children. Thornton also noticed that performance errors typically involve deletion of material rather than insertion as in the present case.

The non-adult questions produced by the children in Thornton's studies had the following characteristics:

- They never appeared in questions extracting from infinitival embedded clauses, that is, questions such as (11) below were never produced:

    (11) *Who* do you want *who* to eat the pizza?

- A copy of a discourse-linked (D-linked)[5] wh- phrase (Pesetsky, 1987) cannot appear in the embedded CP. That is, when a D-linked wh- phrase moves to the embedded CP, the wh- phrase in the matrix has to be a bare wh- phrase such as 'what' in German or Frisian. Questions (12) and (13) below show the strategies used by the children to avoid producing wh- copying questions with D-linked wh- phrases:

    (12) *What* do you think *which Smurf* really has roller skates?
    (13) *Which Smurf* do you think *who* has roller skates on?

Question (12) is a partial wh- movement question with the D-linked wh- phrase in the embedded CP and 'what' as a scope marker in the matrix. In question (13), on the other hand, the D-linked wh- phrase is in the matrix CP and a reduced wh- phrase, agreeing with the one in the matrix in person features, is overtly realised in the embedded CP position. Note that these options are also possible in natural languages.

To sum up, Thornton found that some of the children in her study produced non-adult wh- questions involving partial wh- movement and wh- copying questions. She concluded that these questions could only arise from UG directly as they are found in languages such as German (Fanselow & Cavar, 2001), Romani, Russian and Hindi (Lutz *et al.*, 2000), among others. What is more, these types of questions are absent in adult English, hence in the input these L1 English children are exposed to.

Recent L1 studies eliciting LD wh- questions in other languages have lent additional support to Thornton's claim that these non-adult questions stem from UG (see Van Kampen, 1997 for L1 Dutch, Oiry, 2000, for L1 French). As for our participants' L1s, longitudinal investigations of L1 Basque (Gutierrez 2003, 2004) and L1 Spanish (Gutierrez, 2006) have also revealed the presence of partial wh- movement and wh- copying questions as shown in (14) for L1 Basque and (15) for L1 Spanish:

(14) *Nor* uste duzu *nor* bizi dela etxe horretan? (A. 5;10)
who think aux who lives aux-comp house that-in
Who do you think lives in that house?

(15) *Dónde* crees *dónde* ha ido el niño? (M. 5;7)
where think-2sg where has gone the child
Where do you think the child has gone?

Note once more that these types of questions are completely absent in adult Dutch, French, Basque and Spanish.

The L2 acquisition of LD wh- questions

In the L2 acquisition of English LD wh- questions, Wakabayashi and Okawara (2003) and Yamane (2003) have reported the presence of partial wh- movement questions in the L2 English of L1 Japanese learners. The examples in (16) and (17) have been adapted from Wakabayashi and Okawara (2003: 231–232) and example (18) from Yamane (2003: 96):

(16) *What* do you think *who* loved Mr. Yellow?
(17) Do you think *what* is in the bag?
(18) *What* do you think *whose present* he likes best?

As we saw above (cf. (2)), Japanese is a wh- *in situ* language and therefore this type of non adult questions is absent from adult Japanese as well as from the target language, English. The production of these questions has been interpreted as an attempt by the L1 Japanese learners of L2 English to produce L2 target-like structures. As their L1 grammar cannot accommodate LD wh- movement, they resort to an option allowed by UG: the partial wh- movement option. In the next section, however, we will see that failure by the L1 to accommodate the target language structure is not necessarily the trigger for these non-adult questions, because the L1s of our learners, Basque and Spanish, form LD wh- questions moving the wh- phrase long distance, just as in the target language, English.

Hypotheses

We have seen above that partial wh- movement and wh- copying are completely absent in our participants' native languages (Basque and Spanish) but are part of the L1 and L2 acquisition process. Bearing in mind the different positions on the role of UG in L2 acquisition, we entertain the following hypotheses:

- On the basis of the No Access hypothesis, our L2 participants will have no difficulty in producing target-like questions, because the three languages use the same mechanism (LD movement). Furthermore, no partial wh- movement nor wh- copying phenomena are predicted, as these are absent from both the participants' L1s and their L2.
- On the basis of the Access-to-UG hypothesis, partial wh- movement and wh- copying would be expected, because they are both options sanctioned by UG.

We believe there is no room for hypotheses based on the FT/FA position, because our elicited data do not cover the participants' initial contact with the foreign language.

The Present Study

The cross-sectional experiment reported in this paper is based on that of Thornton's (1990) oral elicitation task and was designed to investigate the acquisition of LD wh- questions in L2 English learners in a school context.

Participants

The participants were 260 bilingual Basque-Spanish learners ranging in age from 8 to 18. The bilingual status of the participants stems from the fact that all of them speak Basque, the minority language, either because it is the language spoken in the family and/or because they have been instructed in Basque from preschool. All the learners were enrolled in Model D (one of the three models of language schooling in the Basque Country), where Basque is the language of instruction, and Spanish, the majority language, is taught as a subject for three to five hours a week. Spanish is the language spoken by all the community in a context that has been defined as one of additive trilingualism (Cenoz & Valencia, 1994): Basque is the minority language, which is nowadays used increasingly and valued in the community; Spanish is the majority language, and English is taught as a foreign language. The participants can also be considered balanced bilinguals; that is, they possess age-appropiate competence in their two L1s. Table 12.1 features information on the

Table 12.1 Information about subjects and data collection

Dates	Groups	Age (years)	No. of subjects	Oral production task
February–March 2000	A	8/9	11	Task 1: Subject, object and adjunct questions extracting from finite embedded clauses
		11/12	18	
		15/16	10	
		17/18	12	
October–December 2000	B	9/10	3	Task 1 plus elicitation of D-linked wh- questions and of questions extracting from infinitival complements.
		10/11	4	
		11/12	3	
		12/13	14	
		13/14	19	
		14/15	18	
		15/16	16	
		16/17	23	
		17/18	22	
March 2003	C	15/16	49	Task 1 plus D-linked wh- questions
		17/18	38	

participants in this study and also includes relevant information that will be referred to later on.

All the participants were learning English as a foreign language in a school context and none of them participated in any content-based programme. Their level of proficiency in the language was established by a written and listening Oxford Placement Test (OPT) (Allan, 1992), which was administered only to the oldest learners.[6] Figure 12.1 shows the results of the OPT for the oldest learners; the test places them in a low–intermediate proficiency level.

The learners younger than 15 had a beginner proficiency level, as attested by the teachers responsible for the different groups. Regarding the type of classroom instruction the learners received, this obviously varied depending on the age group they belonged to. Thus, the younger learners (8–12 years) followed a communicative approach (Nunan, 1989) based on oral activities, whereas the older groups also

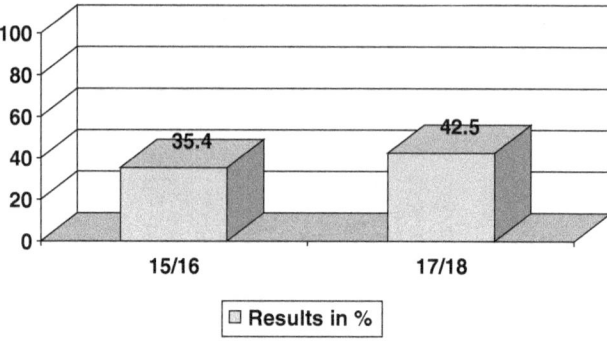

Figure 12.1 Results of the Oxford Placement Test for the oldest participants

followed that approach but attention to formal aspects of the language was clearly emphasised.

Method

The oral production task

An oral production task, adapted from Thornton (1990), was used, as LD wh- questions are scarce in spontaneous speech.[7] The original task used by Thornton had to be adapted to the age of our participants (from 8 to 18). In our experiment, the participants had to choose a photograph from two alternatives. If the researcher guessed which photograph had been chosen by the participant she received one point. If the investigator did not guess correctly, the participant obtained the point. The one with more points at the end of the session would win the guessing game. See the Appendix for a sample of the materials used.

Procedure

One of the researchers explained to the participant how the game worked (this was done in Basque for all the participants, even the older ones). The materials for all the questions were placed in front of the participant, who chose them one by one in random order. Each piece of material consisted of a see-through envelope containing a colour cardboard with a photograph on it. Below the photograph a square was drawn with a question mark in the middle. The main picture in the cardboard represented the scenario for a particular question. Then, the researcher presented two additional smaller pictures and described the scenario and the small photographs. The participant had to choose which small picture he thought would fit the scenario and place the small photograph face down on the square with the question mark. While the participant chose the photograph, the researcher kept her eyes closed. When the participant was ready, the researcher, with her eyes still closed, asked the participant to produce the question.

Excerpt (19) below features the protocol used to elicit object questions:

(19) *Protocol for eliciting object extraction questions:*
  Researcher: Here we have a man (showing the main photograph to the subject) and a blue car and a yellow car (showing the two small photographs to the subject). OK? You choose which car the man bought. OK? (experimenter places folder between herself and the subject so as not to see what the subject chooses).
  Researcher: Ready?
  Participant: Yes
  Researcher: Now ask me which car I think he bought
  Participant: Which car do you think he bought?
  Researcher: (with her eyes still closed) The blue one.
  Participant: No.
  Researcher: OK well done, you beat me so you get the point. Now let's do the next one.

Note also that the lead-in used in our experiment differed from the one used in Thornton (1990), which included an elided wh- question. We felt that many of the L2 learners would not be able to figure out how to complete the question. We decided to run the risk of including the elided part of the question introduced by a null complementiser. We were aware that by doing so we were giving the participant an important clue as to how to form LD wh- questions. However, we reasoned that if the participants ignored the lead in and nevertheless produced the non-adult questions, then their productions would give strong evidence of being part of UG rather than a performance error.

This technique was used for eliciting subject, object and adjunct LD wh- questions with bare wh- phrases such as *what* or *where* and D-linked wh- phrases such as *which boy*. Questions were elicited featuring extraction out of tensed as well as infinitival complements. The types of target questions elicited are shown in (20) below:

(20) (a) Who do you think lived in this house? (tensed, subject, bare wh- phrase).
(b) What do you think they watched? (tensed, object, bare wh- phrase).
(c) How do you think she ate her food? (tensed, adjunct, bare wh- phrase).
(d) Which girl do you think bought this plant? (tensed, subject, D-linked wh- phrase).
(e) Which car do you think he bought? (tensed, object, D-linked wh-).
(f) What time do you think they went surfing? (tensed, adjunct, D-linked wh-).
(g) Who wants to eat the ice-cream? (infinitive, subject).
(h) What does he want to eat? (infinitive, object, bare wh-).
(i) Where does he want to drive? (infinitive, adjunct, bare wh-).

As indicated in Table 12.1, the elicitation task was collected at three different points in time and the participants were divided accordingly into three groups (A, B and C). The participants in Groups A and C were from Urretxu and those in Group B from Bergara, both middle-sized towns in the heart of the Basque Country. Due to time constraints, the participants in Group A were administered only bare wh- phrases, and those in Group B bare and D-linked wh- phrase questions (one token per type) and wh- questions extracting from an infinitival embedded clause (one token per type). Finally, those in Group C were given bare and D-linked wh- questions.

Results

The results show that most participants, 228/260 (87.6%), produced adult-like LD wh- questions. However, from the 260 participants tested, 32 (12.3%) produced 106 non-adult questions of the type reported in Thornton (1990).[8] The different non-adult question types produced by these 32 participants featuring two related wh- phrases are given below with a sample question for each type:

(A) (a) WHAT ... wh- (partial movement)
(21) *What* do you think *who* lived in that house? (participant 92)
(b) WHAT ... D-linked wh- phrase
(22) *What* do you think *which baby* had eaten the cake? (participant 180)

(c) HOW ... wh- phrase (partial wh- movement + other scope marker)
    (23) *How* do you think *who* is going to eat the cake? (participant 36)
(B) (a) Wh- copy ... wh- copy (wh- copying)
    (24) *Who* do you think *who* lives in the house? (participant 56)
   (b) Reduced wh- phrase ... D-linked wh- phrase
    (25) *Who* do you think *which girl did* buy that plant? (subject 254)
   (c) D-linked wh- phrase ... reduced wh- phrase
    (26) *What time* do you think *when what* they surfing? (participant 135)
(C) (a) WHAT that wh- phrase
    (27) *What* do you think *that what film* they see? (participant 183)
   (b) Wh- phrase ... that wh- phrase
    (28) *Who* do you think *that who* lived in the house? (participant 183)

Question (21) features a partial wh- movement subject question with extraction of a bare wh- phrase. Question (22) shows the same construction but this time the extracted element is a D-linked wh- phrase. Question (23) features a partial wh- movement question where the wh- scope marker is 'how' instead of 'what'. Question (24) is a wh- copying question. When the questioned wh- phrase is D-linked, one of the alternatives produced by the participants to avoid wh- copying is (25), where a reduced wh- phrase agreeing in person features with the D-linked wh- phrase in the embedded CP appears in the matrix CP. Another strategy found in our data for avoiding wh- copying is (26), where the reduced copy appears in the embedded CP and the true wh- phrase occupies the matrix CP position. Questions (27) and (28) show partial wh- movement and wh- copying versions where the embedded wh- phrase is preceded by the overt complementiser 'that'. Figure 12.2 features the frequency of each type of non-adult question.

From the 106 non-adult questions produced by the 32 participants 58 (53.7%) were partial wh- movement questions of the types (Aa), (Ab) and 0.9% of type (Ac). Wh- copying on the other hand was used 10.3% of the time. Let us recall, however, that when the questioned wh- phrase is D-linked wh- copying is avoided. In these cases, wh- copying versions featuring a reduced copy in the matrix (Bb) or in the embedded clause (Bc) were produced 8.5% of the times. Finally, partial wh- movement and wh- copying preceded by the complementiser 'that' were

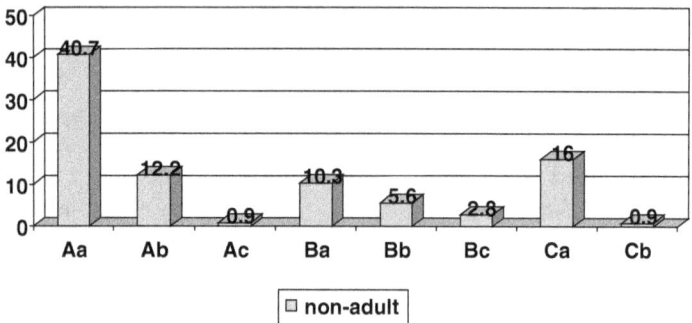

Figure 12.2 Percentages of the different types of non-adult questions involving two related wh- phrases

produced with a frequency of 16% and 0.9%, respectively. Object extraction questions where the questioned wh- phrase was 'what' as in (29) below have been excluded from this classification as they could both be analysed as partial wh- movement questions or as wh- copying questions. These types of questions constituted 9.4% of the non-adult questions:

(29) *What* do you think *what* is in the car? (subject 28, 11/12 age range)

Note, however, that all the participants who produce these types of non-adult questions know how to form matrix wh- questions. That is, they know from matrix questions in English that the wh- phrase must move to the matrix CP. The examples below illustrate some matrix questions produced spontaneously during the experiment:

(30) Who made the cake? (subject 183)
(31) What girl bought the plant? (subject 195)

Looking at the production of non-adult questions across question types, we found that the total number of partial wh- movement and wh- copying was significantly higher for subject extraction questions than for object and adjunct questions, as Figure 12.3 shows.

A two-sided two-sample binomial test showed that this difference in subject extraction questions was statistically significant when compared with object extraction questions ($p = 0.0364$) at a significance level of $\alpha = 0.05$ and adjunct extraction questions ($p = 0.0039$), while the difference between object and adjunct questions was not significant ($p = 0.4194$).

All the non-adult questions involving partial wh- movement and/or wh- copying featured an overt wh- scope marker. That is, none of our

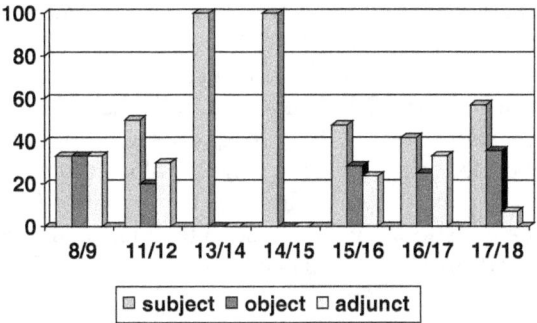

Figure 12.3 Distribution of WHAT ... WH- and wh- copying questions across different types of questions in all age groups

subjects produced non-adult questions of the type reported in the L2 English of L1 Japanese speakers, L1 French or L1 Spanish, as a (32):

(32) Do you think *what* is in the bag?

Regarding questions involving extraction from infinitival embedded clauses, none of the subjects who produced these non-adult structures in questions extracting from finite embedded clauses did so when extracting from an infinitival complement. Finally, when the questioned wh- phrase was D-linked, we found no wh- copying cases.

Discussion

The most interesting piece of data that has emerged from the present experiment is clearly the production of non-adult questions involving partial wh- movement and wh- copying questions of types A and B. These types were the most frequent types of non-adult question produced by the participants and were of the same type as those reported by Thornton (1990) for L1 English.

Two non-adult question types produced by our participants were not reported in Thornton's study. These are questions as in (25), on the one hand, and (27) and (28), on the other. Questions as in (25) involving an auxiliary in the embedded clause were also reported in the data from Japanese learners of English in Wakabayashi and Okawara (2003) and Yamane (2003). One of Thornton's arguments for analysing wh- copying questions as one single question rather than two consecutive matrix questions of the type 'who do you think, who came' was that these non-adult questions lacked inversion in the embedded clause, as would be expected if they involved two matrix questions. So the presence of inversion in the embedded clause in some of our participants' non-adult questions could be taken as indication that they involved two single questions rather than one question involving extraction from the embedded clause. However, we also found questions with auxiliary inversion in the embedded clause produced by participants who moved the questioned wh- phrase to the matrix, that is, participants who produced adult-like long-distance wh- questions. This is illustrated in question (33):

(33) Where do you think *does* she use this hat? (subject 129, 16/17 age group)

Thus, participant 254, who produced inversion in the embedded clause, did so both when the question involved partial wh- movement but also when the wh- phrase moved to the matrix [Spec CP], as shown in (34):

(34) How do you think did she eat the food? (participant 254, 17/18 age group)

LD wh- questions involving inversion in the embedded clause were also produced by subjects who never produced partial wh- movement or wh- copying questions. From the 22 subjects who produced questions with inversion in the embedded clause, 12 (54.5%) never produced partial wh- movement or wh- copying questions. Note that one of the well-known characteristics of the L1 acquisition of English is that children go through a stage where they invert in the embedded clause (Ellis, 1985; Plunkett, 1991), as illustrated in (35):

(35) I know where are you going

This leads us to conclude that inversion in the embedded clause in non-adult questions cannot be taken as evidence that these involve two independent questions rather than a single LD one.

Turning now to questions (27) and (28), involving partial wh- movement and wh- copying preceded by the complementiser 'that', to our knowledge these have not been reported in the L2 acquisition literature so far. These types of questions were produced by participant 183 consistently and by participants 195 and 256 sporadically:

(36) Who do you think that who lived in the house? (participant 183)
(37) What do you think that how she eat? (participant 183)

We should emphasise that these types of questions have been found in a longitudinal investigation of the acquisition of LD wh- questions in L1 Spanish (Gutierrez, 2006; cf. (38)) and L1 Basque (Gutierrez, 2003; cf. (39)):

(38) *Dónde crees   que dónde ha ido   el señor?* (M. 5;7)
    where think-2sg that where has gone the man
    Where do you think the man went?
(39) *Zer uste   duzu   ze   ikusi zutela?* (A. 5;2)
    what think aux-2sg what see aux-comp
    What do you think they saw?

As the glosses show, in the non-adult Basque question in (39) the subordinating suffix *–ela* is attached to the embedded auxiliary as in adult Basque. Note also that in Spanish the sequence of the complementiser followed by a wh- phrase is also found:

(40) *Me preguntó que a   quién había visto en el   bar.*
    to me asked that to whom I had seen in the bar.
    He asked me who I had seen in the bar.

Considering all the types of non-adult questions produced by our L2 learners, we could say that most of them are of the same type as those reported by Thornton (1990) for L1 English. As for those non-adult questions involving partial wh- movement and wh- copying preceded by the overt complementiser 'that', although absent in the English child data, they have been reported in the L1 Spanish data.

Several characteristics of these non-adult questions led Thornton (1990) to conclude that they stem from UG. These characteristics are also found in our L2 questions. Thus, the non-adult questions produced by our participants:

- are absent from our subjects' L1 (Basque and Spanish) and also from the target language, English;
- constitute an option found in several natural languages such as Bavarian German or Frisian;
- obey two of the constraints of partial wh- movement and wh- copying questions in Bavarian and Frisian. On the one hand, learners who produce these non-adult questions in questions extracting from a finite embedded clause never produce them when extraction is from an infinitive embedded clause. On the other hand, wh- copying questions are avoided when the questioned wh- phrase is D-linked.

Turning now to the predictions made by the Access to UG theories discussed above, the No Access hypothesis does not predict these non-adult questions in the interlanguage of the participants. It could be argued that in partial wh- movement questions the relationship between the matrix clause and the embedded clause is not a subordinating dependency but, rather, it could involve a paratactic relationship of the type illustrated in (41):

(41) What do you think? Who lives in that house?

However, two observations from our learners' data lead us to reject this analysis. First, if these questions had involved a paratactic dependency, no complementiser 'that' would be expected to appear in the embedded clause. But, one of the non-adult structures produced by our subjects makes productive use of questions where the embedded CP is preceded by the complementiser 'that', as seen in (42):

(42) What do you think that how she eat? (participant 183)

The presence of the complementiser clearly establishes that the relationship between the two clauses is a subordinating relationship. Secondly, a paratactic analysis of these non-adult questions would not be able to account for wh- copying questions, because wh- copying questions do not involve a paratactic dependency:

(43) *Who do you think? Who lives in that house?
(44) *Where do you think? Where has the child gone?

Note also that instruction could not be the source of these non-adult questions, because they are absent from adult English, and also LD wh- questions of the type discussed here are not taught explicitly at school. Thus, the presence of non-adult questions is not expected under the No Access hypothesis.

As noted, our subjects' L1s form LD wh- questions in the same way as the target language, moving the questioned wh- phrase to the matrix. Under the Access hypothesis then, it is predicted that our learners should produce target-like English LD wh- questions, as far as movement of the questioned wh- phrase is concerned. Thus, the finding of the non-adult options leads us to conclude that they may stem from UG. In this regard, our investigation shows that L2 acquisition data of a language that shares the same parametric option as the L1 can provide interesting insights into the interplay between UG and the L1s, as the emergence of structures absent in both languages cannot be attributed to restructuring in response to an L1 option.

An alternative that adequately accounts for the non-adult productions in our data is that put forward by White (2003). According to her proposal, both UG and the subjects' L1s interact in the process of L2 acquisition. Non-adult questions involving the spelling out of the wh- phrase in the intermediate position constitute a stage prior to full movement of the wh- phrase in the English type LD wh- questions, at least for some L1 learners. This is reflected in the more general strategy available in the L1 acquisition of languages such as English, Dutch, French, Basque and Spanish, where partial wh- movement and wh- copying have been reported. However, besides the more standard partial wh- movement and wh- copying strategies described by Thornton (1990), L1 French (45) and Spanish (46) seem to allow variants where the wh- scope marker is null:

(45) Tu crois quoi qui   est caché dans le sac ?
     you think what that/which is hidden in   the bag?
     What do you think is hidden in the bag?

(46) Tú crees dónde fue el niño? (M. 4;10)
     you think-2sg where went the child
     'Where do you think the child went?'

A second variant is found in L1 Spanish and Basque partial wh- movement and wh- copying questions, where the embedded clause is introduced by the overt complementiser 'que'/'-ela' as we have seen above in (38) and (39).

In the L2 acquisition of English, some learners have been found to use the same alternative reported by Thornton (1990) for L1 English. These options can only stem from UG, because they are absent in both the target and the L1s of the learners (both the L1 Japanese and the L1 Basque-Spanish learners). This would constitute direct evidence that UG can be accessed in older L2 acquisition. However, the role of the subjects' L1 also seems to play a role, as different variants have been found to be produced by the L1 Japanese and the L1 Basque-Spanish absent from the L1 English data (but not from the L1 acquisition of other languages such as French or Spanish). Thus, in the acquisition of L2 English by L1 Japanese speakers, questions with a null wh- scope marker have been reported. Watanabe (1992a, 1992b) claims that a null wh- scope marker is present in adult Japanese wh- questions, so the production of these types of questions in the acquisition of L2 English may be influenced by the possibility of this option in adult Japanese. As for the acquisition of L2 English by L1 Basque and Spanish learners, partial wh- movement and wh- copying preceded by the overt complementiser 'that' have been reported in the L1 acquisition of Spanish.

What these facts seem to indicate is that the spelling out of the wh- phrase in the intermediate position is an option allowed by UG to form LD wh- dependencies cross-linguistically. However, the production of variants of these non-adult questions by learners with different L1s (the L1 Japanese and the L1 Basque-Spanish) indicates that the subjects' L1s do indeed interact in complex ways with the options allowed by UG.

Therefore, we are led to conclude that UG is indeed accessible in L2 acquisition, which, as White (2003) pointed out, cannot be interpreted in exclusion of L1 influence. The conditions offered by our participants' L1s and the target language meet the requirements of underdetermination mentioned above and needed to tease apart whether the non-adult options stem from UG through the L1 or solely from UG. Note that UG is invoked because of the presence of these types of non-adult questions. Had these non-adult questions not been produced, the acquisition of LD wh- questions by the participants would not have led to the conclusion that UG cannot be accessed in L2 acquisition. The data would simply have been irrelevant to the issue, because the L2 participants could have been resorting to the strategy found in their L1s for LD wh- questions formation.

Conclusions

The data we have presented have shown that L2 learners of English produce partial wh- movement and wh- copying questions in the process of acquiring LD wh- questions. These questions have been reported in the L1 acquisition of LD wh- questions of several languages, including English. We have concluded from the characteristics of these non-adult questions that they seem to stem from UG, which would show that UG is indeed accessible in L2 acquisition. However, we have also reported that these non-adult partial wh- movement and wh- copying questions show variants that have not been reported in the L1 acquisition of English. Nevertheless, these variants have been reported in the L1 acquisition of LD wh- questions in Spanish and Basque, our learners' L1s, which has led us to conclude that the learners' L1s are indeed interacting with the options allowed by UG. This finding supports the claims made by White (2003), where it is proposed that both UG and the L1 are indeed involved in L2 acquisition.

The data reported in this chapter also show that access to UG can be better observed when the L1s and the target language share the same parametric option. It is the case that the two native languages of our participants and their target language share the same strategy for LD wh- question formation. Nevertheless, some of our L2 learners produce non-adult structures that are absent from the languages involved, and thus constitute a case of underdetermination.

Many questions arise in the light of the data presented in this article that can only be answered by further research. It remains to be seen whether older adults learning English show productions of these same non-adult structures and data need to be collected from a wider range of questions involving other types of main verbs as well as different matrix subjects (Gutierrez, 2005). Nevertheless, the picture that emerges from the production of these non-adult questions, both in L1 and L2 acquisition, supports Thornton's original proposal that they are not performance errors but, rather, real options allowed by UG and accessible in L2 acquisition.

Acknowledgements

Junkal Gutierrez Mangado wishes to acknowledge a research grant awarded by the Basque Government/The University of the Basque Country (00103.130-13578/2001). Special thanks are also due to Ricardo Etxepare, Mari Jose Ezeizabarrena, Itziar Laka, Vicente Núñez Antón, Javi Ormazabal, Juan Uriagereka, Myriam Uribe-Etxeberria and Vidal Valmala.

Notes

1. In long distance wh- movement the questioned element, the wh- phrase (*who* in the example), is understood as the object of the embedded clause in (1), namely the person John loves. The wh- phrase corresponding to the object is pronounced in the left edge of the matrix clause, that is, it has moved from the object position of the embedded clause to the left edge of the matrix clause. In matrix questions such as (i) below, on the other hand, we see that the object of 'love' that originates in the object position indicated by 't', is pronounced at the left edge of its own clause.

    (i) Who does John love t ?

    This type of movement that occurs within the same clause gives rise to matrix questions. When the questioned wh- phrase originates in one clause but is pronounced in the matrix as we saw in (1), then we have a long-distance wh-question.

2. See Gutierrez (2005) for a review of the different movement options cross-linguistically.

3. Questions in Spanish begin with the symbol ¿ but it has been omitted in the Spanish examples in order not to confuse it with a grammaticality judgement.
4. By left periphery we mean the left edge of the clause.
5. A D-linked wh- phrase refers to wh- phrases of the type *which boy, which car,* which contrast with bare wh- phrases such as *who* and *what.*
6. This test was administered to subjects in Groups A and C, who were taking part in a larger study that investigated the age factor in the acquisition of English as a foreign language (see García Mayo & García Lecumberri, 2003). The larger study was undertaken by the research group REAL (Research in English Applied Linguistics; www.vc.ehu.es/depfi/real), currently with 12 members led by Dr María del Pilar García Mayo, and has been funded by the Spanish Ministry of Education with different projects (PS95-0025, PB97-0611, BFF2000-0101 and BFF2003-0409-C02-01) since 1996. REAL analyses the acquisition of English as a foreign language in formal contexts from different research perspectives.
7. See, however, Van Kampen's (1997) investigation. The participants in her study produced these types of questions in spontaneous speech.
8. The reason why the percentage of subjects producing these non-adult questions is not as high as in experiments in L1 acquisition lies in the choice of participants. In L1, the age ranges of the children vary less (from the one-word stage to around 5–6 years of age in most experiments). The wide age range in our study (from 8 to 18) may account for the large number of correct LD -wh- questions. The rationale for collecting the data from such a wide range was precisely to try to find at which ages and under what circumstances these non-adult questions were produced. See Gutierrez (2005) for a detailed discussion of these issues.

References

Allan, D. (1992) *Oxford Placement Tests.* Oxford: Oxford University Press.
Bley-Vroman, R. (1990) The logical problem of foreign language learning. *Linguistic Analysis,* 20, 3–49.
Cenoz, J. and Valencia, J. (1994) Additive trilingualism: Evidence from the Basque Country. *Applied Psycholinguistics* 15, 195–207.
Clahsen, H. and Muysken, P. (1986) The availability of Universal Grammar to adult and child learners: a study of the acquisition of German word order. *Second Language Research* 5, 93–119.
Ellis, R. (1985) *Understanding Second Language Acquisition.* Oxford: Oxford University Press.
Epstein, S., Flynn, S. and Martohardjono, G. (1996) Second language acquisition: Theoretical and experimental issues in contemporary research. *Brain and Behavioral Sciences* 19, 677–758.
Fanselow, G. and Cavar, D. (2001) Remarks on the economy of pronunciation. In G. Müller and W. Sternefeld (eds) *Competition in Syntax* (pp. 107–150). Berlin: Mouton de Gruyter.
Flynn, S. (1987) *A Parameter Setting Model of L2 Acquisition: Experimental Studies in Anaphora.* Dordrecht: Reidel.

García Mayo, M.P. and García Lecumberri, M.L. (eds) (2003) *Age and the Acquisition of English as a Foreign Language*. Clevedon: Multilingual Matters.
Gutierrez, M.J. (2003) Extra medial wh- questions in long-distance wh- questions in L1 Basque acquisition. Paper presented at the 1st EHU- U.Nantes-CSL Workshop on Syntax and Semantics, Vitoria-Gasteiz, Spain, 19–21 June.
Gutierrez, M.J. (2004) The acquisition of L1 Basque long distance wh- questions: a longitudinal investigation. Paper presented at the first Bilbao-Deusto Student Conference in Linguistics, Bilbao, Spain 8–10 July.
Gutierrez, M.J. (2005) The acquisition of English LD wh-questions by Basque/ Spanish bilingual subjects in a school context. PhD dissertation, University of the Basque Country.
Gutierrez, M.J. (2006) Non-adult questions in the acquisition of L1 Spanish long-distance wh- questions: A longitudinal investigation. In V. Torrens and L. Escobar (eds) *The Acquisition of Syntax in Romance Languages* (pp. 251–287). Amsterdam: John Benjamins.
Hiemstra, I. (1986) Some aspects of wh-questions in Frisian. *Nowele* 8, 97–110.
Lutz, U., Müller, G. and von Stechow, A. (2000) *Wh- scope Marking*. Amsterdam: John Benjamins.
McDaniel, D. (1989) Partial and multiple wh- movement. *Natural Language and Linguistic Theory*, 7, 565–604.
Nunan, D. (1989) *Designing Tasks for the Communicative Classroom*. Cambridge: Cambridge University Press.
Oiry, M. (2002) *Acquisition des questions à longue distance (On the acquisition of long-distance questions)*. Mémoire de Maîtrise, Université de Nantes, France.
Pesetsky, D. (1987) Wh- in situ: movement and unselective binding. In E. Reuland and A. ter Meulen (eds) *The Representation of (In)definiteness* (pp. 98–129). Cambridge, MA: MIT Press.
Plunkett, B. (1991) Inversion and early wh- questions. In T.L. Maxfield and B. Plunkett (eds) *UMOP Special Edition: Papers in the Acquisition of Wh* (pp. 125–154). Amherst, MA: GLSA Publications.
Schachter, J. (1988) Second language acquisition and its relationship to Universal Grammar. *Applied Linguistics*, 9, 219–235.
Schwartz, B.D. and Sprouse, R. (1996) L2 cognitive states and the full transfer/full access model. *Second Language Research*, 12, 40–72.
Thornton, R. (1990) *Adventures in long-distance moving: The acquisition of complex wh-questions*. PhD dissertation, University of Connecticut, Storrs.
Thornton, R. and Crain, S. (1994). Successful cyclic movement. In T. Hoekstra and B. Schwartz (eds) *Language Acquisition Studies in Generative Grammar* (pp. 215–252). Amsterdam: John Benjamins.
Van Kampen, J. (1997) *First Steps in Wh-movement*. Wageningen: Ponsen & Looijen.
Wakabayashi, S. and Okawara, I. (2003) Japanese learners' errors on long-distance wh-questions. In S. Wakabayashi (ed.) *Generative Approaches to the Acquisition of English by Native Speakers of Japanese* (pp. 215–245). Berlin: Mouton de Gruyter.
Watanabe, A. (1992a) Wh- in-situ, subjacency, and chain formation. *MIT Occasional Papers in Linguistics* 2.

Watanabe, A. (1992b) Subjacency and S-structure movement of wh- in-situ. *Journal of East Asian Linguistics* 1, 255–291.

White, L. (2003) *Second Language Acquisition and Universal Grammar*. Cambridge: Cambridge University Press.

Yamane, M. (2003) On the interaction of first-language transfer and universal grammar in adult second language acquisition: Wh- movement in L1-Japanese and L2-English interlanguage. PhD Dissertation, University of Connecticut.

Appendix: Oral Production Task, Sample Material

Index

Accent 258
Affective category 68, 69
Age 19, 22, 24, 30, 31, 40, 41, 45-47, 50, 51, 54, 57-59, 63, 65, 66-67, 78, 80-83, 86-90, 92-106, 120-122, 137, 139, 141-153, 155, 160, 164-169, 171-174, 176, 183, 185-187, 196, 202, 206, 207, 221, 223-224, 226, 229-230, 232-235, 267, 270-272, 276-278, 284
ANOVA 230, 232, 233, 248, 253, 256, 257
Attitude 1, 23, 222, 227, 230, 232-234
Awareness 82, 220, 221, 223, 225
AX test 244, 246, 248-252, 258, 260

Bilingualism 19-21, 23-24, 26, 28, 30, 39, 44-45, 54-56, 86, 88, 107, 112, 120, 135, 139, 40-141, 143, 156, 159, 185, 220-225, 230, 234, 236
– bilingual 18-22, 24, 26-31, 39-46, 50-60, 63-64, 69, 80, 86-99, 101, 103, 105-107, 111-114, 118-120, 123, 127, 131, 135-136, 140-144, 147, 152-155, 159, 163, 172, 175-176, 185, 189-190, 220-221, 223-226, 229, 232, 234-236, 242, 270
– bilingual acquisition 18-19, 21, 26, 28-32, 39, 87, 88, 135-136, 159
– bilingual community 63
– bilingual context 39, 136, 147, 155, 190, 220
– bilingual education 24-25, 185, 225
Borrowing 27, 142

Clarification category 68, 69, 71-75, 79, 81
Code-switching 22, 26, 27, 141-142, 144, 147
Cognition 188, 220-222, 236
Cognitive 220-225, 230, 235-236, 243
– cognitive development 20, 40, 80
– cognitive maturity 187
Communication 65, 139, 143, 188, 214, 243
Communicative competence 63-66, 69, 72, 81-83
Communicative Development Inventories (CDI) 40, 42-43, 46, 49-50, 58, 60, 89-90, 92, 98
Communicative strategies 72, 243

Comprehension 28, 41, 44, 47-49, 51, 57, 59, 136, 187
Confirmation 68-69, 72-74, 78, 81
Context 18, 19, 21-30, 39, 47, 64-65, 83, 94-95, 120, 123, 136, 139, 141, 142, 144, 145, 147, 148, 153, 155, 165, 166, 185-190, 195-197, 217, 220, 221, 223-224, 228, 235, 236, 241-244, 246-247, 250, 252, 255, 258-260, 270-271, 284
Conversation 42, 70, 71, 79-82, 143, 147, 148, 206
Critical mass 43, 87, 106
Cross-linguistic influence 22, 26, 29-30, 70, 87, 130, 159

Directive function 66, 81
Discourse 26, 30-31, 68, 69, 72, 74, 76, 79, 118, 160-163, 165-166, 173, 186, 187-191, 197, 206, 217, 268
Discrimination test 244, 248-251
Dominant language 41, 140, 155

Early bilingualism 107, 143
– early bilingual acquisition 88
– early bilingual education 185
– early bilinguals 31, 64, 80, 242
Early starters 187
Early trilingualism 63
Elicitation 265, 267, 270, 271, 274
English as a foreign language 221, 230, 242, 243, 271, 284
Exchange 25, 68-70, 72, 74-76, 78-79, 81, 243
Exposure 241, 244, 247-248, 251, 253-255, 258-260
– limited exposure 63, 186
Expressed guess 69

Feedback 69
Fluency 259
– oral fluency 187, 243
Foreground 161, 166-167, 173-174
Foreign accent 258
Form and meaning 63
Formal context 284

Formal instruction 19, 25, 27, 241-243, 247-248, 259
Fossilisation 20
Frequency 90, 94, 105, 106, 141, 153, 176, 192, 195, 202, 208, 224, 227, 228, 251, 276
Function words 27, 138, 139
Functional category 66, 68-70, 72, 81-83, 112, 156

Grammar 4, 22, 30, 42, 43, 48-50, 54, 56, 58, 59-60, 64, 86, 87, 90, 112-114, 116-119, 122-123, 130, 141, 144, 159, 160, 163, 187, 230, 232-233, 235, 264-265, 269
– grammar development 42, 43, 59
Grammatical complexity 43
Grammatical words 27

Illocutionary act 64
Imitation 47, 49, 51, 187
Immersion 24-25, 163, 185, 188, 190, 196-197, 220, 221, 224, 235, 241, 247, 258-260
Implicit process of learning 155
Initial exposure 223
Instruction 24-26, 186, 222, 226, 236, 241, 244, 270, 271, 280
– formal instruction 25, 27, 241-243, 247-249
Integrative orientation 223
Interaction 22, 25-27, 66, 68, 71, 74-75, 80, 82, 89, 160, 186, 187, 241, 242
Interactive category/function 68-69, 71-74, 79, 81
Interference 20, 22, 26, 113-114, 118, 123, 172
Interlanguage 280
Interrogative 29, 44, 68
– Interrogative in English 31, 63
Interview 187
Intonation 75, 80

Knowledge 19, 24, 27, 28, 30, 44, 48, 51, 57, 63-65, 79, 83, 88-89, 91-93, 97, 98, 101-104, 173, 190, 222, 224, 227, 229, 233, 236
Known information 68-70, 72-74, 76, 79-81

L1 acquisition 112, 264, 265, 267, 278, 281-284
L1 influence 201, 217, 282
L2 acquisition 25, 112, 201, 221, 230, 232-234, 264-265, 267, 269-270, 278, 280-283
L2 status 27
L3 achievement 230, 233, 234
L3 acquisition 25, 27, 28, 221, 223-225, 235-236

L3 competence 28
L3 development 221, 230-233
L3 learning 220-224, 234, 236
Language competence 20, 57
Language deficit 117
Language delay 137
Language mixing 26
Language of instruction 14, 16, 270
Language processing 117, 140
Language transfer 26, 30, 59
Late learners 274
Learning situations 196
Learning strategies 222, 243, 264
Lexical acquisition 28
Lexical development 28, 40, 54, 57, 87, 92, 97, 98, 101-102, 105, 106, 137
Lexical production 98, 106
Lexicalisation patterns 29, 162, 168, 172, 175
Lexicon 22, 28, 86, 87, 98, 101, 117, 125, 137, 151, 201
Loan words 202
Locutionary act 64
Long-distance (LD) wh-questions 30, 264-270, 272-274, 278-284
Longitudinal data/study/investigation 24, 63, 87, 89-90, 92-94, 96-97, 105-106, 142, 176, 243, 268, 279

Majority language 23, 27, 28, 68, 148, 220, 223-224, 232, 270
MANOVA 50
Mean length of utterance (MLU) 42, 48, 49, 51, 52, 54-58, 67, 74, 82, 90, 92-94, 96, 98-100, 102-103, 105, 106, 120-121
Methodology 89, 119, 142, 190, 221, 225
Minimal grasp 69
Minority language 25, 28, 43, 66, 68, 220, 221, 223, 232, 234, 270
Monolingual 19-22, 24, 29-30, 39-43, 45-46, 50-60, 64-65, 67, 80-82, 87-97, 100, 101, 105-106, 113, 120, 123, 127, 135, 140-142, 144, 152-154, 159, 160, 166, 168, 172-173, 175, 235
Morphemes 26, 48, 57, 92, 98, 99, 102, 105, 114, 125, 138-140, 205, 216
Motivation 187, 223, 227, 230-231, 233-234, 236, 241
Move 68
Multicompetence/multicompetent 19, 65
Multilingualism 18-20, 23, 241-242
– multilingual 18-21, 24, 28, 31, 65, 226

Native 185, 241, 251, 266
– native children 188

Index

- native language acquisition 135
- native language/tongues 29, 67, 162, 163, 200-202, 206, 247, 269, 283
- native speakers 19, 20, 25, 29, 89, 91, 119, 163, 188, 190, 241, 244, 251, 254, 258
- non-native acquisition 264
- non-native phonemic contrasts 251, 259
Natural context 25, 185-190, 196
Natural functional production 31, 189, 190
Natural language 31, 265, 267, 268, 279

Obligatory context 144

Perception test 244, 251, 253, 261
Perceptual Assimilation Model (PAM) 245, 250
Performance 21, 29, 46, 58, 112, 114, 118, 119, 122, 125, 187, 196, 222, 248, 251, 253, 258
- performance account 112, 114, 119, 122,
- performance error 125, 267, 273, 283
Perlocutionary act 64
Phonetic 27, 242, 244, 247, 258-260
Phonological acquisition 258, 259
Phonological competence 29, 242, 244, 252, 258, 259
Phonological development 29
Phonology 27-30, 60, 137, 148-149, 241, 243
Pragmatic 30-31, 65, 66, 69, 75, 82, 112-115, 118, 122, 141, 188, 191, 197, 201, 236
- pragmatic competence 30, 31, 63, 64, 65
- pragmatic flexibility 82
Processing 140, 220, 225, 233, 243
Production 21, 28, 31, 41, 47, 49, 57, 69, 86-88, 93, 94, 98-101, 103-107, 112, 119-120, 125, 127, 137, 138, 141, 144-145, 148, 152-155, 172, 186-191, 195, 196, 202, 207-208, 216, 242, 244, 246-247, 254-255, 258, 261, 276, 277, 281, 282-283
- oral production 265, 271, 272, 286
- vocabulary/word production 41, 44, 47, 48, 50-60
Productive ability 244, 258, 260
Proficiency 20, 27, 67, 187, 196, 221, 222, 225, 229, 230, 232-236, 243, 271

Pronunciation 29, 258

Questionnaire 89-91, 105, 223, 225-228, 237
Question function 66, 69, 71, 72, 74, 80-82

Rate 12, 103, 117, 127, 164, 256
Real information 68-70, 72-75, 77-81
Recency 27
Reformulation 69, 76, 81
Repetition 69, 71, 76, 81, 121, 165
Role play 196

Second language acquisition 19, 140, 200-201, 217, 241, 242
Self-repairs 121
Short-term immersion 258-259
Sociolinguistic 23, 26, 64, 220, 224, 234, 235, 243
Speech acts 64-66,
Speech learning 242
Speech Learning Model (SLM) 242, 245, 247, 250
Speech perception 88, 242, 244, 260
Speech rate 256-258

Target language 22, 185, 186, 197, 241, 265, 266, 269, 279, 280, 282-283
Text 30, 31, 160, 162, 163, 166, 206, 256, 257
Timing patterns 258, 260
Transfer 26-27, 30, 59, 114, 127, 131, 163, 201, 265
T-test 50, 192-193, 252, 255
TTR 67
Typology 137
- typological 27, 111, 138, 141, 155, 162, 168, 224, 236

Verbal interaction 68
Vocabulary 30, 40-44, 48, 50, 54, 56-60, 92, 98, 102, 105-106, 125, 154, 187, 225, 230, 232-233, 235
Vocabulary acquisition/development 28, 40, 45, 105, 175
Vowel contrasts 245, 250-252

Young learners 186-188, 196, 217

For Product Safety Concerns and Information please contact our EU Authorised Representative:

Easy Access System Europe

Mustamäe tee 50

10621 Tallinn

Estonia

gpsr.requests@easproject.com

www.ingramcontent.com/pod-product-compliance
Lightning Source LLC
Chambersburg PA
CBHW071157300426
44113CB00009B/1233